modern
israeli
drama

in translation

modern
israeli
drama

in translation

THE SORROWS OF JOB by Hanoch Levin
JEWISH SOUL by Joshua Sobol
THE AMERICAN PRINCESS by Nissim Aloni
POSSESSIONS by A. B. Yehoshua
DIFFICULT PEOPLE by Yosef Bar-Yosef
BUBA by Hillel Mitelpunkt

Edited by Michael Taub

HEINEMANN   *Portsmouth, NH*

Heinemann Educational Books, Inc.
361 Hanover Street
Portsmouth, NH 03801−3959
Offices and agents throughout the world

© 1993 by Michael Taub.
 The Sorrows of Job © 1981 by Hanoch Levin; © 1993 by The Hebrew Book Club. Translated by Barbara Harshav. Reprinted by permission of Tel Aviv Books.
 Jewish Soul © 1982, 1989 by Joshua Sobol; © 1989 by Modern International Drama. Translated by Michael Taub. Reprinted by permission of International Creative Management, Inc.
 The American Princess © 1963 by Nissim Aloni; © 1980 by the Institute for the Translation of Hebrew Literature Ltd., and the W.Z.O. Translated by Richard Flantz. Reprinted by permission of the Institute for the Translation of Hebrew Literature.
 Possessions © 1986 by A. B. Yehoshua; © 1989 by Formations.
Translated by Michael Carasik. Reprinted by permission of the author.
 Difficult People © 1973 by Yosef Bar-Yosef; © and Translation © 1993 by Yosef Bar-Yosef. Translated by Barbara Harshav. Reprinted by permission of the author.
 Buba © 1982 by Hillel Mitelpunkt; © 1987 by Modern International Drama. Translated by Michael Taub. Reprinted by permission of the author.

 The Sorrows of Job: Dani Tracz, Tel Aviv Books, 78A Shenkin Street, P.O. Box 14235, Tel Aviv 61142, Israel.
 Jewish Soul: Bridget Aschenberg, International Creative Management, Inc., 40 West 57th Street, New York, NY 10019.
 The American Princess: Nissim Aloni, c/o The Institute for the Translation of Hebrew Literature, P.O. Box 10051, Ramat Gan 52001, Israel.
 Possessions: A. B. Yehoshua, Department of Hebrew and Comparative Literature, University of Haifa, Haifa, Israel.
 Difficult People: Yosef Bar-Yosef, 22A Bialik Street, Tel Aviv 63324, Israel.
 Buba: Hillel Mitelpunkt, 16 Bar Ilan Street, Tel Aviv, Israel.

Library of Congress Cataloging-in-Publication Data is on page 329.

Designed by Wladislaw Finne
Printed in the United States of America
93 94 95 96 97 5 4 3 2 1

To my teacher
Professor Eugene H. Falk
of the University of North Carolina
at Chapel Hill,
a man of integrity, humanity,
and professionalism.

contents

acknowledgments

I would like to recognize the efforts expended by Nilly Cohen of the Institute for Translation of Hebrew Literature in Israel in obtaining some of the copyrights.

My thanks also to Professor George E. Wellwarth, of SUNY Binghamton, for his valuable suggestions and guidance; Glenda Abramson, of Oxford University, author of *Modern Hebrew Drama*, the only historical-critical work in English on the subject; Shimon Lev-Ari, director of the Israeli Theatre Archives at Tel Aviv University; and Leonard Rogoff and Alan Huisman, for correcting my English.

I am deeply grateful to Lisa Barnett of Heinemann Educational Books, a true professional, for her warmth and understanding.

The support of my wife, Pat, and my brother, Martin, is greatly appreciated.

israeli drama: an introduction

Although Israeli prose writing had received attention earlier, Israeli drama did not attract serious notice until the seventies, with the advent of Hanoch Levin and Joshua Sobol, still the dominant figures on the Israeli stage. This relatively late recognition also marked a shift from earlier preoccupations with social realism to styles ranging from poetic realism to the absurd. Dramatic writing in Israel reflects the evolution of the state as well as typical Jewish concerns with the past, both recent and ancient.

Not surprisingly, Israeli drama from the early years deals primarily with problems facing the new state: absorbing the immigrants, settling the land, building an independent Jewish society in a troubled part of the world. The heroes of these socially realistic plays of the fifties and sixties are East European Zionists, Holocaust survivors, kibbutzniks, and North African Jews. Thus, some of the recurring themes in plays by Moshe Shamir, Aharon Megged, Yosef Bar-Yosef, Ygal Mossinzon, and Hanoch Bar-Tov are the conflict of values among various generations of immigrants, the cultural differences between the old and new worlds, and the search for a national identity. Shamir's *Hedva and I* (1954), Bar-Tov's *Each with Six Wings* (1958), and Bar-Yosef's *Tura* (1963) are typical examples of this kind of drama.

The main theme of a relatively small number of plays, like Leah Goldberg's *Lady of the Castle* (1955), Megged's *Hanna Senesh* (1958), Shamir's *The Heir* (1963), and Ben-Zion Tomer's *Children of the Shadows* (1963), is the Holocaust. While styles and plots may vary, these works have in common the bearing witness to a past that many new Israelis of that time would rather have forgotten.

Also departing from the predominant social realism of this period are several historical and biblical plays: Nissim Aloni's *The King Is Most Cruel* (1953), Megged's *The First Sin* (1962), and Yehuda Amichai's *Journey to Nineveh* (1964).

Though these plays re-create well known historical and biblical events, their tone, language, and psychology are modern, all designed to draw attention to a variety of current sociopolitical issues. In *The King Is Most Cruel*, Aloni is obviously less interested in the conflict between two ancient kings — Yerovam, a pacifist, and Rechavam, a militarist — than in the increasing danger presented by right-wing ideologies advocating radical nationalism and aggression toward the Arabs.

The two decades following the Six Day War of 1967 finds a handful of dramatists consistently at the forefront of Israel's theatrical scene: they are Hanoch Levin, Joshua Sobol, Hillel Mitelpunkt, Yosef Mundy, Yosef Bar-Yosef, and Nissim Aloni. (Although Aloni, it should be noted, has not written a new play in over ten years.) Though much less prolific, A. B. Yehoshua, Daniel Horowitz, and Motty Lerner have also contributed significantly. The works of Sobol, early Levin, and Mundy are primarily political, although they stem from different aesthetics. While political messages are always lurking, the main focus of Bar-Yosef, Mitelpunkt, and A. B. Yehoshua is a domestic conflict perhaps best described as a mixture of Chekhov and Pinter. Aloni, however, defies this sort of clear-cut categorization. A typical Aloni play — *Eddy King*, for example — contains elements of expressionism, surrealism, and Brechtian epic theatre. An Aloni production features elaborate costumes, scenery, lighting, and electronic gadgetry, in sharp contrast to the plain realistic settings of Yehoshua, Mitelpunkt, and Bar-Yosef. Also, unlike his counterparts, Aloni does not necessarily choose "Jewish" or even Israeli themes. In fact, his classical plays are "universal," incorporating European or American settings and characters. Aloni's plots are drawn from stories particular to European culture: the Oedipal myth, medieval pageant, and Hans Christian Andersen among others.

For these playwrights and the literary trends they herald, 1967's Six Day War constitutes a turning point as to subject matter. Though one would expect Sobol, Mundy, and Levin to have written political drama anyway, they would likely not have been as passionate and controversial. In any case, immediately after the war, Levin, a drama student at Tel Aviv University, wrote a number of satirical works that are highly critical of the government and the military establishment.

His *You and I and the Next War* (1968) and *Queen of the Bathtub* (1970) are two outstanding works from the postwar period. These cabaret-style plays openly attack just about everything hitherto considered sacrosanct in most Hebrew drama — the early settlers, the army, the Zionist ideals, even grandmotherly figures like Golda Meir, the country's leader. The original productions of these shows were often accompanied by interruptions from angry spectators, journalistic debates, outright threats, and eventual closings when things got too far out of hand. In the plays and in the media, Levin and other left-wing writers oppose Israel's occupation of the West Bank and Gaza and warn against reliance on military might and nationalistic fervor following the crushing victory over the neighboring Arab States. Most of all, these writers fear the corruption of age-old humanistic values and morality; Jews, who have historically been a victimized minority and in some way "the conscience of the world," have suddenly been thrust into the role of masters — in their view, even oppressors. Apparently disillusioned with politics, Levin turned in the early seventies to a unique brand of absurdist drama, which, though set in Israel, contains only veiled references to any identifiable reality. He did, however, return to politics in *Execution* (1979), *The Sorrows of Job* (1981), *The Great Whore of Babylon* (1982), and finally *The Lost Women of Troy* (1984). But, unlike the directness and bluntness of his earlier works, these are highly abstract allegories, some written in verse, and are set in biblical or mythical places, with biblical, mythical, or invented heroes. Overall, these plays are brutal indictments of authority, divine and human alike: gods are seen as cruel and merciless, and men in power, ruthless. In *Execution*, for example, the sun is veiled, the biblical "song of degrees" and ascent to the temple become instead a descent into the depths of misery. There is no escape, no redemption, only an accursed life on earth. In *Job*, the rulers are intolerant of any deviation from the law; disobedience results in violent death. Job alone dares defy the rule and ultimately pays dearly for his actions. Likewise, the Trojan women in *Troy* are subjected to inhumane treatment by their Greek captors: they are humiliated, degraded, tortured, killed at whim. In the end, the Greeks even manage to break the spirit of Hecuba, the proud Trojan queen. Given the political climate of Israel in the 1980s, in which the radical right, both religious and secular, was wielding increasing power, these outcries for individual freedoms, for decency and tolerance, are understandable. Levin's bleak view of life in these plays and in his dramatic output generally stands in direct opposition to traditional dogma asserting that man can control his destiny, that good deeds yield a good life and vice versa. Considering the human tragedy taking place in the West Bank and Gaza, it is no surprise that almost everyone viewing *Troy* sees Palestinians in the Trojans and Israelis in the Greeks.

In contrast to Levin's allegorical political drama, Mundy's political plays — indeed, the bulk of his work — are rather explicit. No lyrical, stylized language here; instead, plain street talk. While Levin disguises the action in his plays from easily identifiable Israeli reality, Mundy rarely leaves any doubt that the action, the characters, and the situations presented depict the here and now in Israel. While it is true that in *The Governor of Jericho* and *Messiah*, two expressionistic works from the mid-seventies, Mundy mixes in biblical and historical elements, the arguments are unmistakably about contemporary issues. *The Governor of Jericho* shows the frustrations of Israelis and Palestinians when confronted with such questions as peaceful coexistence, national aspirations, security, and justice. Some characters represent leftist views, others — most notably the governor — voice rightist ones. We also find moderates

and militants — like Aved, a young Palestinian, who refuses
to compromise, who will accept nothing less than a total
Israeli withdrawal from "Arab land." (It is not clear
whether he means only land conquered in the 1967 war or
Haifa and Jaffa as well.) A similar character, simply called
an "agitator," appears in Mundy's latest work, *Closing Up*
(1990), but here he is in the heart of Tel Aviv trying to stir
up Arab workers to rebel against their Jewish employers.
In *Closing Up*, Mundy shows a Jewish community divided
by ideology and religion, fighting what appears to be an
already lost battle against the Arabs outside as well as
inside Israel's borders — those thousands of Palestinians
from the West Bank and Gaza working in the country, in
some cases staying overnight illegally. The uncompromising, self-righteous, religious nationalism expressed by
the so-called Hassid is equally alarming.

As we have seen, Levin's mature political drama draws
its material from Jewish and universal sources. This drama
is highly allegorical and focuses on a variety of existential
problems, echoing some burning Israeli issues but appli-
cable to broader situations. These Levin plays, set in
unspecific times and places, peopled by invented, exotic,
or grotesque characters, sound like Kafkaesque parables
couched in Ionescoesque dialogue. Mundy, on the other
hand, though occasionally resorting to historical or biblical
settings, brings concrete, clearly identifiable political problems to the stage. In general, his drama attacks the radical-
ism of religious or secular nationalism while showing the
passivity and helplessness of liberal, humanistic forces.

No doubt Sobol's plays grow out of the frustrations he
shares with the other engagé playwrights dissatisfied with
the way the Zionist dream is being fulfilled. What is unique is
a deliberate attempt to demythologize Jewish and Israeli
history, to show heroes, moments, and events in a highly
critical light. For example, *The Night of the Twentieth* (1976),
Sobol's first major drama, recreates a night preceding the
takeover of a piece of land in Palestine by a group of
young settlers from Central Europe. The time is 1920. The

traditional image we have of these early pioneers is that of heroic, self-sacrificing, determined Zionists. Sobol, however, modifies this larger than life image by including human problems and conflicts. Thus, his middle-class Jews from Austria are beset by self-doubts about their mission and troubled about leaving behind Western culture and a familiar way of life for an unknown environment filled with dangers and hardships. In an attempt to justify their presence in the new land, they seek answers to questions of personal and national identity. In the process they also try to clarify the motives that brought them here. For most of these inexperienced youngsters this is very confusing, since both ideological and personal elements — alienation, anti-Semitism, family problems — were involved in their decision to leave Europe.

None of these young Jews, however, is as confused and troubled as Otto Weininger, the hero of Sobol's drama *Jewish Soul (The Last Night of Otto Weininger)* (1982). The play is based on the life of the brilliant Viennese intellectual who committed suicide in 1903 at the age of twenty-four, shortly after he received a doctorate in philosophy, published his controversial thesis, *Sex and Character*, and converted to Protestantism. In recreating this complex and fascinating person, Sobol focuses on Otto's inability to come to terms with his Jewishness, which he feels is antithetical to strength, nobility of spirit, and moral rectitude — qualities he finds embodied in the Aryan race. His obsessive adoration of the Aryan spirit and his utter self-loathing lead him to conclude that masculine, positive, creative, and aesthetic qualities belong to the Aryan group, while weakness, equivocation, femininity, destructiveness, and ugliness are inherently "Jewish" and must be expunged at all cost. The masculine/feminine dichotomy stems from Otto's struggle with his sexuality, specifically his homosexual tendencies. In his eyes homosexuality is a shameful "Jewish" disease that stands in his way of becoming an Aryan.

In light of the Holocaust, Weininger's fascination with Aryanism is acutely ironic. But beyond that, the play has been correctly seen as a critique of those within Israel's political spectrum who believe that the solution to the problems facing the country is military power, a kind of "Aryan" reliance on machismo and superiority. By revealing Otto's darkest and most embarrassing feelings about his Jewishness, some of which were historically used by anti-Semites to degrade Jews, Sobol unleashed a wave of controversy. Despite or perhaps because of this, the play has been performed successfully in Israel, Europe, and America.

A different, even more intense controversy followed with the production of *Ghetto* (1984), the first in Sobol's trilogy on the demise of Lithuania's Jews in the Vilna ghetto. As noted earlier, others too have tried to present the Holocaust on stage. Characteristically, these efforts, along with most major international Holocaust drama, such as Peter Weiss's *The Investigation* or Barbara Lebow's *A Shayne Maydl*, shy away from actually showing the horrors of the camps and ghettos. Not only does Sobol set his trilogy in the midst of the horror, but he goes one step further and creates almost human Nazis and less than morally pure victims. Ostensibly written to celebrate the courageous spirit of a Jewish theatre group in the ghetto, *Ghetto* delves into the soul of the ambiguous figure of Gens, the head of the Judenrat, the Jewish council. Vilified by many for working with the Germans, he maintains that thanks to his collaboration, lives are being saved. Then there is Weisskopf, a shrewd businessman, who occasionally places profit above human considerations. Finally, we find the "Jewish mafia", led by unscrupulous Hassidim trafficking in everything from food to medicine. On the German side, we find Commandant Kittel, who loves music, especially the banned Gershwin and American jazz. He encourages artistic events, but also kills people at whim. Kittel, however, does make sure the ghetto is not liquidated, as insurance that he will not be sent to the dreaded Russian front. In addition to depicting the complex moral problems confronting Gens and other Jewish leaders, *Ghetto* deals with a variety of ideological issues revolving around Jews and Communism and Jews and Zionism. For example, is Gens an immoral, power-thirsty politician or a true hero, one who must sacrifice both people and moral values to save some? The play has also been performed abroad—to rave reviews at the prestigious National Theatre of London and to mixed reviews at New York's Circle in the Square.

Adam (1989), the second play in the Ghetto Vilna trilogy, focuses on the Jewish resistance in the ghetto. We know that despite overwhelming odds, Jews did manage to stand up to the Nazis in some of the ghettos, Warsaw's Jews being the most effective. In Vilna, however, the revolt never took place, because the population was divided over the wisdom of such a dangerous action, its opponents hoping the Russian armies, which were gradually closing in on the Germans, would soon free them. Yitzik Wittenberg was the leader of the militants, and Adam, the play's protagonist, is fashioned after this legendary underground fighter. Here, too, Sobol goes "behind the scenes" to explore the personal and moral issues facing the Jewish community in finally deciding to hand Adam over to the Germans to avoid the collective punishment that would ensue if he remained in hiding. Like *Ghetto*, *Adam* touched off another storm, as survivors and historians argue Sobol's handling of history. The storm is kept alive by the author's public statements, interviews, and articles defending his plays. By comparison, Levin grants no interviews and is silent about the meaning of his works.

The final play in Sobol's trilogy, *Underground*, had its premiere in America, in the spring of 1991, at Yale's Repertory Theater. This drama focuses primarily on the fight by doctors in a special ward to conceal cases of typhus from the Nazis and thus save lives. As in *Ghetto*, doctors, Jewish leaders, and Germans are embroiled in a battle that transcends the matter of physical survival to raise delicate ethical questions. No doubt Jewish "collaborators" like Gens from Vilna and Rumkowski from Lodj will continue to be the subject of many historical debates.

In 1987, Sobol temporarily shifted his attention from the Holocaust to the Palestinians' and Israelis' seemingly endless armed conflict. His first play on this theme is *The Palestinian Girl*, also translated as *Shooting Magda*; the other is *Jerusalem Syndrome*. Written as a play within a play (actually a film within a play), *The Palestinian Girl* delineates the shooting of a movie about the life of Samira, a young Palestinian. The character based on Samira is called Magda in the film and ironically played by Dalia, a Jewish actress. Samira/Magda, a university student, falls in love with David, a Jewish student portrayed in the movie by Uddy, a young Jewish actor. Magda and David's relationship gives Sobol an opportunity to explore the complex and often painful question of Arab-Israeli coexistence. As expected, there are bigots and well-meaning people on both sides. The real problem is that some of Magda's Arab friends view Israelis as oppressors while David's Jewish parents consider all Arabs terrorists. As in *Romeo and Juliet*, this story of star-crossed lovers ends tragically. Most moving, however, are Samira/Magda's desperate attempts to hold on to her true self in the face of conflicting and often confusing choices. In the end, she wants to be regarded as simply a human being, but society insists on labels that do not fit her image of herself. She is frustrated and angry at being misunderstood by Jews and Arabs alike. Dalia, the Jewish actress playing Magda, is troubled as well, for this experience causes her to question her own values and the society she lives in, especially its attitude toward the Arabs.

While *Shooting Magda* focuses closely on personal feelings, *Jerusalem Syndrome* is a play about ideas and propaganda in a highly tense political atmosphere. Sobol's drama is set in modern Jerusalem, but the bulk of the action takes place in a play within the play — directed by a character called the Professor — about the great Jewish rebellion against the Romans. Again, by way of this device, the author can suggest parallels between the ancient situation and the modern, especially as they relate to the nation's attitude toward war, the way the military and political leadership behave, and the factionalism engendered by the hostilities. The plot lines of both the play and the play within the

play are fast paced, the action switches rapidly between
them, and chaos and insanity reign supreme. Stylistically,
the play bears traces of German Expressionism, agitprop,
and early Brecht. The audience is barraged with political
slogans and biblical passages denouncing violence, military
occupation, religious fundamentalism, and nationalism.

The Habima National Theatre has recently produced
Sobol's latest work, a play about Spinoza, the controversial
seventeenth-century Jewish philosopher, whose religious
scholarship put him squarely at odds with traditional
Judaism.

Not surprisingly, a great deal has been written about
Sobol's reading of history and current events, some of it
sharply critical. Sobol himself often engages in media
debates, a rather dangerous enterprise in a country where
emotions run high and almost anything goes in public
discourse. Regardless of a reader/viewer's position on the
man, his drama is consistently stimulating, provocative,
and challenging.

In assessing the work of Yehoshua, Mitelpunkt, and Bar-
Yosef, a group of playwrights labeled "domestic realists,"
we must keep in mind that differences in style, language,
and tone do exist, and virtually nothing Israeli can possibly
be free of some political dimensions.

That said, we turn to Yehoshua's dramatic output: *A
Night in May* (1969), *Final Treatments* (1973), and *Possessions*
(1986). (Two of his novels, *The Lover* and *Mr. Mani*, have
also been turned into dramatic monologues by Haifa's
Municipal Theatre.) The stage success of this world-
famous novelist stems largely from his masterful handling
of his characters' psyches, their family and social relationships. Like his fiction, his dramas usually develop around
a family unit, one on the verge of or already coping with a
serious crisis.

Thus, in *A Night in May*, extraordinary circumstances —
the impending Six Day War — force the protagonist, Tirza
Levin, to reexamine her relationships with her current
husband, a visiting former husband, and a brother. Faced

with the possibility that they may never again have the opportunity, these characters reexamine their past actions and motivations. This unraveling of the past is emotionally freeing, a denouement reminiscent of some of Ibsen's domestic dramas, especially *Rosmersholm*.

In a desperate attempt to suppress the past, the hero of *Final Treatments*, Mr. Herman, a bookstore owner about to retire, causes himself and others a great deal of suffering. By contrast, Shatz, a former patient of Herman's therapist wife, insists on reliving his younger years in treatment in order to regain hope and confidence in the future.

A great deal of *Possessions* too is a reexamination of the past, only here it is Ezra, the protagonist, who undergoes a cathartic experience. While pressured by his recently widowed mother to accept a variety of mostly useless family possessions, the forty-five-year-old literature professor is forced to confront some unresolved issues concerning his deceased father. Coming into contact with his father's belongings and sleeping again in his parents' home lead to a gradual demythifying of the image and a tempering of guilt, a guilt stemming from the gnawing sense that the old man's removal to the hospital might not have been for medical reasons but a decision motivated by selfish concerns. To illuminate the nature of the father-son relationship, Yehoshua weaves into the plot Ezra's comments on Kafka's *The Metamorphosis* and *The Judgment*, two classics about fathers and sons that have long preoccupied him. In Kafka's works the father is a dreaded, domineering figure with sufficient power to lower the son to the insect level of Gregor Samsa: a creature devoid of self-respect and self-confidence, a sexually repressed, guilt-ridden being. The bitter father-son power struggle in *The Metamorphosis* ends with the father's complete triumph and the son's grotesque death. In *Possessions*, on the other hand, it is the father who falls ill, becomes dependent on the family, and eventually dies in the hospital. Though Ezra and his father had rarely been close, his father's death makes Ezra question this detachment and eventually leads him to a keen awareness of his own fatherhood. In the Kafka story Gregor's demise

produces an (albeit grotesque) affirmation of life in the
final scene; in Yehoshua, the removal of guilt and the
eventual acceptance of death create an equally irresistible
affirmation of life manifested through Ezra's craving for
family closeness and sexual fulfillment.

In all of Yehoshua's plays, family ties serve as a backdrop
to the unleashing of unconscious or subconscious forces; in
Yosef Bar-Yosef's work, the family unit is a social institution
with a powerful hold on the individual. As in Lorca's *Blood
Wedding*, family honor plays a major role in *Tura* (1963),
Bar-Yosef's first significant work. In this tragedy, father
Tura kills his daughter because she has conceived an
illegitimate child. Tura's violent action must, however, be
seen within the context of the shocks to culture and values
experienced in making the transition from primitive,
patriarchal North Africa to the considerably more modern,
westernized Israel. (In *The Ewe* [1970], the author returns
briefly to the plight of the North African in the new land.)
With *Difficult People* (1973), Bar-Yosef seems to be moving
away from rather serious, lyrical social realism and larger
than life figures to "comedies of sorts" (the subtitle of
Difficult People) or domestic intrigues minus the earlier
intense drama and violence (1974's *Wedding*, for example).
In *Difficult People*, he focuses on the intricate maneuverings
of a brother and sister preceding a much desired but
eventually failed attempt to marry her off; *Wedding* is about
the nasty fights between two families after they have become
bound by marriage.

Still Bar-Yosef's best known play, *Difficult People* is
atypically set in England and features only one Israeli
character, Layzer, who comes from Jerusalem to be matched
up with Rachel. The success of this play lies in the sustained
liveliness of the dialogue and the honesty, directness, and
humanity of the central characters. Unlike the seriousness —
often gloominess — of Yehoshua's plays, this drama is only
"half serious." Like a Pinter classic, it is never melodrama,
always serious domestic comedy. Marriage is after all serious
business, but the way it is handled here — the "imported
suitor," the futile tactics employed to win him over

(especially the lie about the age of the bride, who is forty-four), Layzer's matter-of-fact, businesslike attitude — are pathetically comical.

A similar atmosphere dominates *The Orange Grove* (1985), only here it is the intended bride, an elderly ballet teacher from Russia, who responds to but in the end rejects the advances of Menashe, a retired widower living inside an orange grove with an older brother. It is to Bar-Yosef's credit that an otherwise unappealing subject — two old men's bitterness, suspicions, and frustrations — can become so engaging. Indeed, he makes even the most banal situations dramatic and entertaining. On a thematic level, the attempt at blissful union fails in both plays, although the emotional experience does lead to some behavioral and philosophical changes: Rachel has a chance to vent some deep-seated frustrations and perhaps see herself in a more positive light, Menashe realizes that there is more to life than the orange grove and material things.

Essentially Bar-Yosef's aesthetic lies in extremely well drawn characters, usually middle-aged or old, speaking a slightly stylized, lightly poetic language and even displaying a touch of the absurd.

In sharp contrast, the style of Hillel Mitelpunkt, the third and final playwright in the "realist" group, rests on faithful reproduction of street language — the speech of lower-class (even criminal) elements — and, at the other extreme, the language of sophisticated, educated people, replete with foreign terms and slick clichés. Thus, Mitelpunkt's early dramas, *The Swamp* (1979) and *Buba* (1982), take place in urban-center slums, the kind found in Tel Aviv or neighboring cities. The characters are either performing menial work, attempting to fulfill some glamorous dream of success, or stealing. Much of the action in *The Swamp*, the dramatist's first major success, focuses on the power struggles of several criminal factions, confrontations sparked by the return from jail of Avram, a feared gang leader in the area. Poverty, prostitution, and frustration are everywhere. There is also a great deal of anger at the government and those in the well-to-do upper classes who live in the beautiful buildings across the swamp. Typically, these small gangsters are Sephardim, while "they," the rich, are supposedly Ashkenazim, European Jews who have historically dominated Israeli politics and economics. While obviously resonating with social criticism, the power of Mitelpunkt's drama resides primarily in the characters' intensity, the use of street lingo, the posturing, and the fierce competition.

Though tame by comparison, *Buba* too contains violence, intimidation, and criminal acts. However, the action here is more focused; it follows Buba's desperate struggle to find happiness amid deceit, greed, and selfishness. His marriage has failed over an aborted baby. His brother Elie, a former soccer star, has repeatedly let him down, and Rachel, the girl he loves, takes advantage of his kindness. Buba (in Hebrew, "doll," "honey") starts off the quintessential innocent victim, but he eventually learns to protect himself, fight back, and preserve his dignity. While this is evident from his behavior toward his brother and his associates, Buba's relationship with Rachel is ambiguous throughout. Most importantly, has he accepted the fact that the child she carries is Elie's? Given Rachel's reckless, irresponsible conduct, how safe is it to trust her? Most likely, she will never give him love and peace of mind. It seems that in matters of the heart, Buba has made no progress.

Struggling, working-class slum dwellers are the heroes of another 1982 Mitelpunkt play, *The Store*. The central characters are three generations of recent Polish immigrants to Jaffa who own a grocery store and live in the shabby rooms adjacent to it. Their hope is that by selling the store they will earn enough money to start a better life elsewhere. But all indications are that their move is going to be lateral, not vertical. Into their debates about selling the store, Mitelpunkt weaves a number of remarks about values in "the old country" compared with those in modern Israel. At the center of the storm is the hardworking Leytche; she is a Mother Courage, trying her best to steer a steady course as she mediates between her elders and her grown-up children. Not surprisingly, the members of the older generation believe in hard, honest work, while those in the younger are depicted as speculators, adventurers, some even morally corrupt. It seems that the new land and the modern life in it breeds unfeeling, disrespectful, irreverent people. Clearly, grandfather Dov Ber's tragedy in *The Store* is not unlike that of Tura in Bar-Yosef's drama, even though the two come from different ends of the world. Geographical and cultural disparity notwithstanding, patriarchal authority, social status, and material success were regarded with a similar degree of respect in North Africa and in Poland and Russia.

Mitelpunkt's *Temporary Separation* (1985), an Israeli *Who's Afraid of Virginia Woolf*, signals a turning point in his career, especially with regard to subject matter. The heroes are a Tel Aviv couple, college professors. The setting is a Tel Aviv hotel that they've checked into in order to discuss their decision to separate. The language, naturally, is that of academics, replete with literary allusions, foreign terms, and trendy expressions. The dialogue is full of cynicism, biting irony, and sarcasm.

His *Driver, Painter* (1988) features two totally opposite characters: Aharon, a truck driver in his thirties recovering from a severe accident, and Mira, a sixty-year-old painter who returns to Israel from South America after forty years and several marriages. She meets him unexpectedly in her childhood home, a secluded house Aharon bought from her brother, who died some months earlier. At first she is enraged and suspicious, but she gradually begins to trust him and to accept the situation. As time passes they realize that opposites need not always clash; they can complement each other, even merge. These opposites are on one side practical, unimaginative, uneducated (Aharon) and on the other impractical, creative, well educated (Mira). Ironically, he, who lives on facts and details, suffers from loss of memory, and she, who paints, is gradually losing her eyesight. One thing unites them, however: both have struggled to succeed and failed, she as an artist and a woman, he as an enterpreneur and a man. It is no coincidence that

each is still single and has no family. But in this rundown,
secluded house, they eventually gain the freedom to unburden themselves, to appreciate each other's qualities,
and ultimately to give each other the emotional support
they so sorely lack.

The political drama of Hanoch Levin and Nissim Aloni,
discussed earlier, is essential to their development as artists;
the mainstays of their dramatic output, however, are, in
Levin, a special brand of drama of the absurd and, in
Aloni, stylistic ecclecticism. The term "absurd" is widely
applied to Levin's work because in his typical plays (*Heffetz*
[1972], *Yaacobi and Leidental* [1972], *Suitcase Packers* [1983])
the characters are two-dimensional figures, often named
after a personal trait (Heffetz, "object") or function
(mother, father, son). Time and place are vaguely the
present and the south side of Tel Aviv, a working-class,
somewhat dangerous area, but one that Levin knows well,
since he grew up there. The dialogue comprises short, fast-
paced lines spoken in highly idiomatic Hebrew and is very
difficult to translate. While Beckett's drama is devoid of
psychology, Levin's deliberately subverts psychology. He
achieves this by having a character enunciate the implicit
as well as the explicit, the expected and the unexpected,
the proper and the improper thing, thus producing a mixture of black humor, cruelty, and grotesquery. Some of
Levin's favorite themes are marriage, death, lost illusions,
and social failure. For instance, a typical hero—Heffetz,
Elchanan (of *Suitcase Packers*), Yaacobi and Leidental (of
the play by the same title)—finds himself stuck at the
bottom of the socioeconomic ladder, tries desperately to
escape, but fails miserably. The futile attempts, the humiliation and degradation accompanying the process, elicit
pity as well uncomfortable laughter, the kind one might
experience while watching Sisyphus roll that rock uphill.

It is only fitting to conclude this introduction with Nissim
Aloni, the much revered "old man" of the Israeli stage. As
mentioned earlier, Aloni has not written a play since 1980,
but his impact continues to be felt, in dramaturgy of

course, but in production and direction as well. Aloni is unique in Israeli drama because he has written mainly about non-Jewish, non-Israeli topics, striving to create truly "universal drama." Thus, he rewrites works from other mediums for the stage: Hans Christian Andersen's *The Emperor's New Clothes* saw new life as *The King's Clothes* (1961). *The American Princess* (1963), a play about a deposed king living in Buenos Aires, is a retelling of Sophocles' *Oedipus Rex*. *The Gypsies of Jaffa* (1971) concerns a troupe of vagabonds performing near medieval Cracow and is a modern version of a medieval pageant play. Finally, *Eddy King* (1974) another retelling of *Oedipus Rex*, is about Sicilian mobsters in Brooklyn.

A typical Aloni show — he also directs his plays — contains a play within a play and many audiovisual devices (e.g., recorded sound and on-screen projected images). Sets and scenery are extensive, often exotic, always lively and colorful. The language is highly stylized, tension and ambiguities are punctuated by short, cutoff lines that emphasize the sonoric quality of words. The action is often confusing, the borders between fact and imagination, the conscious and the unconscious not always delineated. Time and again, the world of his characters is governed by the elemental Oedipal conflict between father, son, mother. In two plays, the father figure is a king, the embodiment of ultimate power and authority. Don Laios of *Eddy King* is the "king" of the underworld, head of a Mafia family, until his son, Eddy, kills him in a bar. As in the Greek classic, Eddy marries Donna Jocasta, Don Laios's wife and Eddy's mother, but here the audience knows early on that Eddy is the murderer. As in the Greek model, the new king's ascent to power brings suffering to his "people": divisiveness, treachery, deceit, and greed ultimately lead to the gradual disintegration of a crime empire. This modern fallen empire suffers because of weak, inexperienced leadership. While in Sophocles the punishment results from Oedipus's inadvertant transgressions, Eddy King's demise is simply a matter of failing to fill Don Laios's big shoes, failing to learn the system, especially failing to adapt to

America. For Aloni's hero America is a totally new place, a much more complicated world than his native Sicily. Essentially, the new immigrant is unconsciously competing with his father and fails; naturally, the competition applies to sexual performance as well, since he marries Donna Jocasta, his father's wife, who tragically is also his mother.

In *Eddy King*, destiny brings father and son face to face in mortal combat; in *The American Princess*, the role of destiny (or perhaps that of a cruel god?) is played by a mysterious and invisible Dolly Kokomakis (note the Greek-sounding name), the "American Princess" who finances a movie about the exiled King Bonifacius and his son, Crown Prince Ferdinand. While in *Eddy King* the Oedipal forces are unconscious, in *The American Princess* they are played out in the open — on the "real" level between father and son, and on the fictional level between father and son as actors on the set of a movie about their lives. Here, the queen, Ferdinand's mother, is dead, possibly gone insane over the king's callous philandering, an issue son Ferdinand refuses to lay to rest. But the sexual competition exists nonetheless, because each has a secret liaison with the same high-class Buenos Aires prostitute. On an unconscious level, the idea of regicide/parricide is reinforced by suggestions regarding the script made by the movie director and the actor hired to play the old king. The king's murder by the son as someone "accidently" loads live bullets into the stage gun is actually the fulfillment of a suppressed wish to do away with an archrival, not unlike Dostoevski's Smerdikov, who in his own twisted way serves as a tool of parricide for the brothers in *The Brothers Karamazov*. It is worth stressing that while Don Laios is a powerful figure, Bonifacius is a rather pitiful, almost clownlike character, which reinforces the parodic nature of the play. The ancient myth is likewise parodied by the substitution of the mother/wife/queen with a prostitute.

Two short farces, *The Bride and the Butterfly Catcher* (1967) and its sequel, *The Deceased Goes Wild* (1980), round out Aloni's long theatrical career. Written for two speaking parts — a young woman and a middle-aged man (Mee and

Ghetz in the first play, Mee-Mee and Offenbach in the second) — these works are a tour de force of dialogue and wordplay. The text consists of extremely short, fast-paced lines (interspersed with lots of pregnant pauses), mostly construed around double entendres (often sexual), evasiveness, innuendo, and ambiguity. This unique style gives the play an air of surrealism and a sense of the absurd, as fierce verbal duels unfold in quick succession. The dramatic situation in both plays is rather absurd too; in *The Bride*, the eponymous Mee refuses to attend her wedding because the groom fails to pronounce her name correctly. Instead she spends the afternoon with Ghetz in a park where once a week he comes to catch butterflies. In the sequel, Mee-Mee (Mee ten years later and now a widow) is unable to speak to a certain Offenbach without her dead husband's voice interrupting, mostly to accuse her of immorality and deceit. Physically absent in both plays, the husband's presence is manifested by his voice, either heard naturally or amplified over a loudspeaker.

This introduction has provided a general background to the major trends in Israeli drama today, and has placed the featured playwrights and plays in their proper literary context. The contemporary scene is ongoing: styles and trends are constantly evolving and changing. Critical, evaluative remarks have therefore been kept to a minimum to allow the plays to stand on their own. The plays have been selected on the basis of artistic achievement, popularity, and consistency, all of course filtered through my subjective preferences. I chose these plays to suit the English reader; because of translation difficulties and other technical problems, some excellent scripts were not available. It is especially regrettable that Yosef Mundy, a dramatist discussed at length in this introduction, is not represented in this collection.

I conclude with a few words about Herbert Joseph's 1983 anthology, *Modern Israeli Drama* (Fairleigh Dickinson University Press). Joseph's book is a valuable first, an inspiration for mine. It features Moshe Shamir and Aaron

Megged, major fiction writers whose plays were popular in the 1950s and 1960s, but who since have not been theatrically active. Sobol's first significant full-length play, *Night of the Twentieth*, is there, as is *Cherli Ka Cherli*, by Daniel Horowitz, an author who *is* still active in the theatre. Finally, Joseph's volume includes the original translation of *Difficult People* and the one-act monologue *Naim*, an adaptation of A. B. Yehoshua's novel *The Lover* (although Yehoshua did not write the adaptation).

By contrast, the present anthology features one of the most important works by Hanoch Levin, Israel's undisputed national playwright. One also finds here original contributions by two other major contemporary artists absent from the Joseph volume: A. B. Yehoshua and Hillel Mitelpunkt. *Jewish Soul* marks a decisive turning point in Sobol's career, and is most associated with his style in the past decade. Aloni, the most dominant figure in the pre– Levin/Sobol era, is still one of the most influential figures in Israeli theatre: hence *The American Princess*. Finally, thanks to a fine new translation of *Difficult People* by Barbara Harshav, Bar-Yosef's drama is reintroduced to the English reader minus the problems of the earlier version.

MICHAEL TAUB
Judaic Studies Program
State University of New York
  at Binghamton

hanoch levin

the sorrows
of job

TRANSLATED FROM THE HEBREW BY

BARBARA HARSHAV

characters

JOB

GUESTS

SERVANTS

BEGGARS

MESSENGERS

BAILIFFS

FRIENDS

SOLDIERS

ENTERTAINERS

CORPSES

chapter 1: the beggars

I

A banquet in Job's house. The revels have ended and the guests are glutted, stretched out, exhausted. Leftovers are strewn on the tables.

JOB. What is a man who has eaten his fill?
A man who is finished, done for it, nil.
What hope can he wield?
It's all delivered, signed, sealed.
He sprawls inert, barely taking in air.
Life lies like a rock on his heart,
Can I describe such despair?
Darkness like that can't be found anywhere.

But two hours later?
Two hours later, despair despairs.
Though less clear-cut, the horizon grows brighter.
The man doesn't budge, his belly still presses,
But his breath is lighter.

And four hours later?
Four hours later, hope begins to creep
Into his belly. Not yet a peep
Of appetite but some idea steals in
And the man who lay on his back an hour ago like a
        turtle,
With no feeling,
Aiming belches of sorrow up at the ceiling,
Wakes up a bit, turns over on his belly
Like a block
And shifts the job of honking from front to backside.
Whoever said that life is a rock?

And six hours later?
Six hours later the rock turns into a bird;
For life is light, colorful, spreads its wings,
Little chirps in the belly and the man once more springs,
Soars, fresh and wide awake, salivating to the table.

A new man is born every six hours.

FEMALE GUEST. For me it works out very nice:
Every six hours, I'm born twice.

II

SERVANT. My Lord, the beggars ask leave to come to the table.

JOB. Blessed art Thou O Lord Our God who feedeth all His
creatures. Let them in.

*Enter the beggars. They swarm over the table, gnawing on the
bones.*

BEGGARS. Bones. Nothing but gnawed bones.
Think that's the end of the meal? Wrong!
They open a bone and suck it
Chew on it a bit and chuck it.

But we are not like you, we suck and suck.
We go to it with devotion, diligently, deliberately,
Almost tearfully. You'd be amazed—
You who gorge yourself on meat
And leave the bone with a lick so hasty—
How fat and juicy it still is, how tasty.

Part of the juice, of course,
Comes from your spit.
But that's just it—
To suck a bit of bone
That was once in the mouth of a contented swell—
That's not just a bone, it's a pedigree as well.

They finish and exit.

III

SERVANT. My Lord, the beggars of the beggars ask leave to
come to the table.

JOB. What! Another round on that heap of bones?
Blessed art Thou O Lord Our God who feedeth all His
creatures. Let them in.

Weak and disfigured beggars enter and attack the table.

BEGGAR A. Second-tooth bones. The left behind
Of leftovers. Never mind,
What was sucked once and satisfied twice
Won't disappoint when served up thrice.
Of course there's no marrow, no juice.
But the bone, on the other hand, is already ground,
It's soft, falls apart, just like porridge
And is ready to eat, easily downed.

We gorge ourselves on warm bone gruel.
For the rest, we let the stomach rule.
BEGGAR B. Sometimes they forget a bone
With a little marrow and fat,
For, in time, some high-class beggars
Assume the habits of genuine lords, put on airs
Sucking sloppily here, skipping something there —
Then we come . . .

They suddenly bring out a neglected bone and fight over it. One of them wins and chews it while the others watch him. They finish and exit.

IV

SERVANT. My Lord, the most beggarly beggar of all the beggars
asks leave to come to the table.
JOB. What will he eat, the table?!
Blessed art Thou O Lord Our God who feedeth all His
creatures. Let him in.

Enter the most beggarly beggar, a frail old man; he totters and lands on the table.

BEGGARLY BEGGAR. Empty. Not even a bone. And if there was,
How would I chew? I've got no teeth.

The only time I get food is when
One of the middling beggars gulps down
The bones too fast, his gorge rebukes,
A bone sticks in his throat and he pukes.

I can swallow what he pukes without having to chew
And easily digest the thrown-up stew
Which is already half digested.
And if I have luck, I find in the mess
A piece of what was once potatoes, beets, or cress.

Of course, it happens not every day,
So I'm always weak, almost fade away.
Yet, never mind—you get used to it.
Be patient, my friend,
And somebody will surely puke in your hand.
Well, somehow we manage to live.
There's a God in the sky,
Tra-la-la, tra-la-lie.
Maybe they'll throw up for me on the way,
Tra-la-la, tra-la-lay. (*Exits*)

V

JOB. What did we see here? Miracle? The ways of nature?
One chicken bone fed a whole gang
And the last one of them even sang.

Two things we've seen, it's clear.
First, there's a God!
GUESTS. Blessed be He and blessed once again!
JOB. Second, God gives!
GUESTS. Amen! And amen!

chapter 2: messengers of poverty

I

Job and the guests drowse off. Enter messenger of poverty 1.

MESSENGER 1. Bad news, my lord. (*Pause*)
My lord, bad news.

Job is dozing. The messenger raises his voice.

My lord, very bad news.
Very very bad news. (*He shakes Job*)
Forgive me, my lord, for persisting but that's how it is
With bad news — I didn't invent this —
You're usually sleeping when it comes,
It's always at night,
They wake you up so you don't lose,
God forbid, a minute of life
Without knowing the bad news.
(*He shakes Job harder*)
My lord, I have very bad news,
It's for your ears, it's yours,
I have to give it to you, nothing will help.
JOB. I'm digesting, don't yelp!
MESSENGER 1. Try digesting, my lord, what I have to tell.
An earthquake struck Lebanon,
Your iron mine caved in.
A hundred and eighty slaves buried alive.
JOB. (*Sitting straight up, stunned*) Deny it! If you have a shred of
        humanity — deny it!
MESSENGER 1. And if I do —
Will the stones in your mine jump back up
And stand on top of one another once again?
JOB. My little iron mine!
My little iron mine in Lebanon!
This is how a man feels when they rip off
His hand and foot. The iron mine was half my wealth.
        (*Stands up*)
MESSENGER 1. Where are you going, my lord?
Whatever has to be done — was done.
The police are investigating. My lord's accountants
Are balancing the books. My lord's lawyers
Are drawing up claims for the imperial treasury in Rome.
The Emperor himself guaranteed investments in imperial
        development. (*Exits*)
JOB. Now it's happened to me, what always
Happens to somebody else.
The most awful thing of all has happened to me.
Nothing could be worse.

And if we all were called on to bestow
Our share of suffering and sorrow —
I've just given mine, be it nice or mean.
Thank God — now I'm clean.

II

Enter messenger of poverty 2.

MESSENGER 2. Bad news, my lord.
JOB. They already told me.
MESSENGER 2. Who? I was sure I was the first . . .
JOB. They were already here.
MESSENGER 2. Well, when more information comes in
    From Alexandria, they'll tell you right away.
JOB. Alexandria?!
MESSENGER 2. Alexandria. Of course, Alexandria.
JOB. What happened in Alexandria?
MESSENGER 2. You said they told you . . .
JOB. What happened in Alexandria?! What happened in
    Alexandria?!
MESSENGER 2. A dreadful storm. The port was flooded.
    Your docks sank, your ships
    Shattered on the rocks.
JOB. What am I? A player in a farce?
    This is my life! My life!
    Those docks and ships you destroyed with your breath
    Were the other half of my fortune! Now I have nothing!
        (*Pause*)
    Everything?! Nothing's left?! You're sure?! (*Pause*)
    Two fruits of my life, two beloved children
    I bore and tended and raised up.
    What do I say children?! —
    It's me, my own flesh and bones,
    My arms and legs, my sweat and blood!
    Didn't I give myself there,
    My youth, the best years of my life!
    They killed me! Slaughtered me!
    Sliced my carcass in two! I'm buried,

Half of me in Lebanon, crushed in the ground,
Half in the port of Alexandria, drowned! (*Turns to leave*)
MESSENGER 2. Where are you going, my lord?
Whatever has to be done — was done.
The police are investigating. My lord's accountants
Are balancing the books. My lord's lawyers
Are drawing up claims for the imperial treasury in Rome.
The Emperor himself guaranteed investments in imperial
     development. (*Exits*)
JOB. I thought the most awful thing happened to me before.
I was wrong — it happened now.
(*To the guests*) Forgive me, everything is falling apart.
I have to go to my office. (*Turns to leave*)

III

Enter messenger of poverty 3.

JOB. Perhaps you have some bad news for me?
MESSENGER 3. Yes.
JOB. (*Frightened*) Forgive me, I'm just joking.
MESSENGER 3. I'm not.
JOB. Lebanon?
MESSENGER 3. No, my lord.
JOB. Alexandria, then?
MESSENGER 3. No, my lord.
JOB. Something else?
MESSENGER 3. Yes, my lord.
JOB. (*Laughs*) I don't have anything else, I don't
Have any more businesses. Go
Tell your news to somebody else.
MESSENGER 3. No, you.
JOB. Somebody else.
MESSENGER 3. Only you.
JOB. I don't have anything. The two messengers before you
Already wiped out everything.
MESSENGER 3. My lord, listen ...
JOB. Don't keep me. I have to get to the lawyers
To collect the guarantees from the Emperor of Rome.

MESSENGER 3. That's just what my news is about.

JOB. Something happened to the lawyers?

MESSENGER 3. The lawyers are fine.

JOB. Then what?

MESSENGER 3. Rome. A military coup.

JOB. Hey, man! What are you talking about?
Military coup?! The Emperor won't let it happen.

MESSENGER 3. He already did.

JOB. Not as long as he's alive!

MESSENGER 3. That's right. That's why he's dead.

JOB. Dead or alive — he won't let it happen! (*Pause*)
Dead?! The Emperor of Rome?! There's no Emperor?!
The most immortal man in the world, two thirds
Of the trade in iron and lead, eight tenths
Of the production of iron and lead, the steel safe
Of the Empire, the great, infinite trust
That we mortals are just its compound interest —
He's dead?!
If he's dead — who's alive?! Who's alive?! (*Pause*)
I still have one lot left that I bought once
In Jaffa, not far from the port ...
That's all I have left ...

MESSENGER 3. The new Emperor also decreed ...

JOB. ...I can build a shop on it ...

MESSENGER 3. ... with regard to all lands in strategic
places ...

JOB. ... not a big shop ... a little hole in the wall ...

MESSENGER 3. ... absolute confiscation ...

JOB. ... just a stand ...

MESSENGER 3. ... with no financial compensation.

JOB. Not even a stand. (*Pause*)
What do my lawyers have to say?

MESSENGER 3. You don't have any lawyers, my lord.

JOB. What do the accountants and clerks say?

MESSENGER 3. You don't have any accountants or any clerks.

JOB. I'm going to my office to clarify things for myself.

MESSENGER 3. You don't have an office either, my lord.

JOB. It's *my* office! There's my chair,
My beloved desk,

All my little toys . . .

MESSENGER 3. It's not yours anymore.

JOB. To hell with you! Don't tell me "It's not yours!"
Who are you?! Who are you and what are you —
"This is yours, this isn't yours" — to hell with you!

MESSENGER 3. My lord is not in a position to talk to me like
that.

JOB. What?!

MESSENGER 3. Lower your voice.

JOB. (*Raises his hand to him*) Varlet! Dog!

MESSENGER 3. (*Pushes him*) Dog yourself. From dog you came.
Dog is your father. Bitch is your mother.
Son of a dog. Phooey! (*Spits in his face. Exits*)

IV

The guests begin to withdraw slowly.

JOB. You're going? Well, it's late, good night to you all.
Too bad it suddenly grew late.
We could sit some more and leisurely reminisce:
Remember how once, five minutes ago,
I was a rich man?
Not so long ago, five minutes. Remember?
Like a lord I strode upon the earth. And once,
Five minutes ago, in this place,
Who would have dreamed of calling me dog
Or spitting in my face?!
(*He bursts into bitter sobs then stops*)
Suddenly it grew so late — Oh, just a phrase.
Remember? Five minutes ago. Those were the days.

The last of the guests avoid him and exit. He remains alone.

chapter 3: the bailiffs

I

Enter the bailiffs.

HEAD BAILIFF. We're the bailiffs come to carry out the decree.
You're bankrupt.
We've come to confiscate all you own,
Except for you yourself—skin, hair,
Body, soul and underwear.
(*To the other bailiffs*)
Take the tables, take the benches, take the chairs,
Take the plates, take the cups, take the forks,
Take the knives, take the spoons, take the jars,
Take the pans, take the bottles, take the corks,
Take the corkscrews, take, take, take, take the cases
Of the corkscrews, take the candlesticks, take the jugs,
Take the tablecloths, take the napkins, take the vases,
Take the sofas, take the carpets, take the rugs,
Take the bowls, take the plants, take the frills,
Take the screens, take the curtains, take the stocks,
Take the shutters, take the glass, take the sills,
Take the bolts, take the keys, take the locks,
Take the doors, take the floors, take the ceiling, take the
walls,
And if I forgot something—without violating any rights—
take that too, take it all.

The bailiffs empty the hall and strip Job down to his underwear.

JOB. You forgot my gold teeth.
I've got some gold teeth in my mouth. (*He opens his mouth*)
HEAD BAILIFF. Don't be ridiculous.
Don't try to make us into monsters.
We're all just human, part of the group,
We all go home to our wives at night,
To our slippers and a hot bowl of soup.

The bailiffs exit.

II

JOB. Naked came I from my mother's womb and naked came
        my mother
    From her mother too,
    Shuddering, we emerge, one from another,
    A long line, naked and new.
    "What shall I wear?" asked my mother in the morning,
    But when the day was done,
    Naked was she borne to the pit.
    Now I too stand naked, her son.

*The head bailiff sneaks in, approaches Job, grabs him by the
throat and takes out a pair of pliers.*

HEAD BAILIFF. Open your mouth and don't say a word
            Or — you die!

*Job opens his mouth wide. The head bailiff pulls out his gold teeth.
Job is about to shout in pain.*

    Here's a tooth — one!
    Another tooth — two! Three!
    Not a sound! Swallow your shout!
    It hurts? Your mouth in bleeding?
    Bite your lip! Swallow your shout!
    Help me get through with this job and get out.

The head bailiff exits. Job makes muted cries.

III

JOB. My sons and daughters, fruit of my loins,
    Look at this hand — with this hand,
    Your father fed you.
    Like magic, infinite plenty he drew —
    Bread and honey and butter, flowers and clover,
    The charms we thought would never end. Now it's over.
    The magic is gone. The hand is empty.
    Now it's stretched out to you.
    Congratulations, my children.
    Unto you a new father is born!

Look at him. How sweet. Just like a babe,
Naked, weeping and wetting. Skin smooth as silk.
Helpless, toothless. Take him in your arms,
Rock him, feed him on porridge and milk,
Put him to sleep with lullabies, keep him warm.
He needs your love.
Oh, my children, the hand is empty,
The father who gave is no more.
A new father is born unto you — a father who takes.
Congratulations!

chapter 4: messengers of death

I

Enter messenger of death 1. He stands silently, facing Job.

JOB. The house is empty. And you don't burst in
As if you came to take something.
You reach out your hand, hesitantly.
You want to tell me something. (*Pause*)
If you had bad news to tell me,
You would look squarely in my eyes.
But you're trying hard to be human,
So, I see it's not bad news you bring,
It's dreadful tidings. (*Approaches him*)
I'd like it better if you looked at me coldly.
Those eyes, full of pity
Can mean only one thing . . .
(*Suddenly he groans*) Which one?!

MESSENGER I. The firstborn. At his own banquet. At noon.
Suddenly a mighty wind struck the house.
Fire quickly spread to all corners, mounted the stairs.
Shrieks of fear and pain were heard.
When the fire died, the shrieks did too.

*Two stretcher bearers enter carrying a body covered with a blanket.
They put it on the ground and exit with messenger of death 1.*

JOB. This is my firstborn.
    The baby who would fall asleep in my arms,
    Calm and trusting. The baby who called me at night,
        "Papa!"
    He knew I'd come and put him on my lap
    When he ran around the room
    Shrieking, shrouded in smoke,
    When all the years suddenly fell away
    Like a shell. When he became once more a frightened
        child.
    "Papa!" he called to me. "Papa, Papa!"
    He screamed and couldn't understand
    How the flesh, so dear to his papa, was burning up:
    "Where is Papa?" he called to me. "Papa! Papa!"

    Here is my firstborn son. His face turned to me
    But his eyes were already fixed
    On something beyond me.
    Disappointed perhaps, he turned away from me,
    Walked off, left me alone
    With the burden of my guilt.

II

Enter messenger of death 2.

JOB. I cannot bear any more tidings.
    Two daughters and a son are left.
    Take pity on me.
MESSENGER 2. God will take pity on you
    Who took your two daughters from you.
    Your firstborn invited
    To that feast, it seems,
    All his brothers and sisters.

*Enter four stretcher bearers carrying two bodies covered with
blankets. They put them on the ground and exit with messenger of
death 2.*

JOB. My daughters, my little girls,
    I'm just beginning to grieve

For your older brother.
Now you come too, two dead girls,
Mute, obstinate, demand
Your share of grief. As once,
When you jumped up to hug me when I came home,
Rejoicing, shouting, prattling away, kissing my
Cheeks with warm lips. Your breath was so fresh
And you called out: "Papa, see our new dresses!"
"Papa!" you call to me now, "See how we lie here,
Still. See how we have no breath!
Papa, you think this will pass
Like the measles and mumps of our childhood?
When, Papa? When will we get up? When will we go out
To the garden? When will the doctor
Let us see the sun again? And if we don't get up, Papa,
Weep for our lives! Weep for the golden days of our
        childhood,
A foretaste of the great joy to come. Where, Papa,
Where is that great joy?"

Just a minute, my daughters, wait.
I haven't yet finished with your older brother.
How will I have enough grief for all of you?
Even if I turned into
A torch of grief and wrath, how long can I burn?
How long can I shout "I have lost my firstborn son and
        my two daughters,
I have lost my firstborn son and my two daughters!"
The land is so big
And heaven so far away   .
And I have only one throat to shout, one throat!

And I haven't yet forgotten my grief for my lost riches,
I loved my wealth too.
Oh, my wealth and my money, oh my children, my children,
Oh, how much labor of grieving I must do.
(*Pause. Suddenly*) He invited *all* his brothers and sisters to
        the banquet?!
My youngest son, was he there too, at that table?!

III

Enter messenger of death 3.

MESSENGER 3. No, your youngest son wasn't there.
   He was late ...
JOB. I still have a son!!
MESSENGER 3. And death was waiting for him on the way.
   In an earthquake
   A rock came loose from a mountaintop,
   Rolled down to the path beneath
   And crushed the passersby, your son included.

Enter two stretcher bearers with a body covered with a blanket.
They put it on the ground and exit.

   It may comfort you to know that death was instantaneous.
   No suffering, no agony. (*Pause*)
   It may comfort you to know that the calamity isn't yours
      alone.
   Other people were killed, a bride and groom, children.
      (*Pause*)
   I don't have any other comfort for you.

Exit messenger of death 3.

JOB. My youngest son, my favorite child.
   Grief for any one of them
   Would have drowned me like a flood.
   Grief for all four of them —
   I don't have the strength to bear it.
   Hence, my youngest son, I defer the tidings of your death
   For another time. May I live to see the day
   When I have strength for the hard labor
   Of grieving for you.

   Now I'll say only this: Welcome back.
   They all came back. All my children are here.
   My little boys, my little girls, you came home.
   And the house is filled once again. Welcome back.

IV

Job sits stunned, facing the bodies. Almost insensibly, he begins to feel an itching, first in one place, then another. He scratches absentmindedly. The itching is relentless. He scratches some more. He begins to feel itching in various parts of his body, and it grows worse. He scratches madly. He tears off his underwear so he can scratch more easily. He rolls naked on the ground, scratching and thrashing around. Suddenly horrible animal screams come from him. He rolls around and screams until his strength fails him. He remains on all fours, barely whining and then falls on the ground, rolls up like a fetus and lies unmoving. Every now and then, his body is convulsed by a spasm.

chapter 5: the friends

I

Enter Job's friends, Eliphaz, Bildad, and Zophar. They see him from afar.

ELIPHAZ. We're looking for a man by the name of Job.
　　We're his best friends. We heard
　　That calamity befell him.
　　We have come to give him comfort.

Job doesn't respond.

BILDAD. We're looking for a man by the name of Job.
　　We're his best friends ...

ZOPHAR. Friends, here's our companion Job.

The three of them stand still, shocked, for a moment. They approach him slowly.

ELIPHAZ. Job, here are your friends, Eliphaz, Bildad, and
　　Zophar.

JOB. (*Groaning from the itching*) This itching! Itching! My skin is
　　burning all over!
　　I could be a happy man if not—
　　For this itching. Just this itching!

I'll tell you, gentlemen, you itching beasts,
Without this itching — the world would not be the same.
Why complain? — Everything's fine, splendid, a game,
So well-balanced, life, death — the world goes on, it seems.
But this itching ruins our happiness, spoils our dreams.
You know what brought down the grand
Roman Emperor? Itching. The Emperor of Rome lifted his
    hand
To itch his nose and lost his neck.
Listen to the words of an experienced man, my boy,
It is only itching that separates man from his joy.

The three friends weep silently.

II

JOB. Why do you weep? You itch too?
ELIPHAZ. Our good friend, Job, do not condemn us
    For not being stricken with your plague.
    We too are at the mercy of God's wrath
    Or His grace
    And if God should turn His face
    From me, too,
    I would be itching and naked over there instead of you
    And you would be standing here, blessed,
    Giving me pity — and dressed.

    God chose you to suffer
    And us — to bring you consolation.

    My friends, let us now rend our garments,
    Cover our heads with ashes
    And pray humbly to God.

    The three friends sit facing Job.

JOB. What are you talking about — "God"?
    What does God have to do with this,
    The wreck of my life?
    If that's God's doing,
    What's His game? What are the rules of His play?
    Why does He return my sons as carcasses all in one day,

Why does He crush my mines in Lebanon,
Sink my ships in Alexandria and bring down the Emperor
   of Rome?
Maybe you'll tell me why, for dessert, a sweet,
He gives me this itch for a treat?
Why is He punishing me, this God?
That's a reward? Divine justice? An even rod?
No, my dear friends,
The world of Job
Does not include God.

ELIPHAZ. Dear friend, Job, we do not intend to prate
   Morality to you in your present state.
   We always keep in mind that things are good, for us now,
      it's true —
   Though who knows for how long — and bad for you.
   Nor do we want to hint
   That God is punishing you for your sins.
   The whole world knows
   That Job is a righteous man. And yet.
   There is a "yet."
   Scratch around inside yourself a bit.
   Maybe you once committed a sin, a crime? No?
   Try to recall, now's the time. No?
   Maybe many years ago?
   Never? Well, let's say.
   Maybe you were once on the verge of sin? No? No way?
   Not even that? Well, let's say.
   But maybe you sinned only in thought?
   Not even there? Let's say.
   There's a lot of "let's say" here.
   That really ought to make you a righteous man, so
   Maybe God is simply testing you, like long ago
   Abraham, another righteous man (so much greater) —
   And like him, He will reward you richly (generations
      later)?

   Who can know the mind of God?
   We are only small details
   But only God can see it whole.

Man makes small accounts, one, and one, plume and
   broom
And the Lord above sits and sums up all the brooms,
All the plumes, the heaven and the earth.

Look at the world. Don't rip pieces —
Look at all of it. See how correct it is, how right.
Embracing everything, in beauty and in might.
Into this world, our lives are poured
Like water from a dark pitcher
Suddenly bursting out onto the open field.
Here is the ground, here the sky,
Here are trees and fruit and birds that fly,
A world splendid, colorful, a world filled with sores
But also with solace and healing,
A world familiar as our home
But also filled with mystery and concealing,
A world where darkness is encircled by a great ring of
   light.

Job, it takes greatness of soul to ponder
The whole world. If you have the magnanimity now to
   wonder —
This is the time. Lift your eyes up.
Leave off your sufferings, accept God! Rise up!
JOB. My good friend, you're tormenting me!
   You talk to me about justifying God,
   First, prove you can justify man.
   Don't torment me. Let me scratch in peace.
   I don't know the grace of creation, I don't know God.
BILDAD. You knew Him when things were good.
JOB. When things were good — things were good. Now
   Things are bad. I don't know God.
ELIPHAZ. Does God exist when we're content
   And disappear when happiness is spent?
   Is God a bubble of soap
   That we blow with a puff of air,
   And then burst with a little poke?
   People in torment like you and even worse
   Call to Him in their distress.

They see no confliction
Between belief in God and their affliction.

For who are you with all your pain?
A hundred yards away
No one hears your scream or plea.
A thousand yards from here, you look like a flea.
What do you think you look like from the stars?!

JOB. Let the stars accept the existence of God! Let he
Whose notions of right and wrong haven't gone awry,
He who believes the arms of God embrace him —
Let him embrace God!

I am small and blind and groping like a mole
In a dark burrow. In darkness I live,
Total darkness, a hole.
And I hear of light only in tales!

ELIPHAZ. The blind man doesn't know the sun
But he does know it exists.
You're steeped in your itching but you know
Under your skin that God exists.

JOB. No! I exist! You exist!
The gap between us exists! God does not exist!
The itch on my skin exists!
The death of my sons exists!
The loss of all my wealth exists!
All I do not have —
That's what exists!

BILDAD. You're quite arrogant, you know? A little humility.
Just because you're suffering
And we show complete understanding of your plight
Does not mean that you are right.
There's the demagoguery of the contented man;
But there's also the demagoguery that suffering and torment
    bring.
You're not allowed to do everything, not yet everything.

You think if you yell "My itching exists!" day and night
That wipes out God. Your world today is itching — right.
God is long-suffering and generous, He's not mean.

You're not the first itcher He's ever seen.
But I'm not generous like God.
I'm just an impatient man, I mind —
I won't let you spit on all that is holy, divine.
JOB. I see the world through itching —
How do you see it?
Through your belly? Comfort? Fat? You stand
On the firm base of your lives,
Feel the ground solid beneath your feet.
How will you see the fact that it's all fluid, built on water?
You need someone to guard your safe
And you hired God to do the job;
I don't have a safe anymore —
I fired God from my world.
ZOPHAR. Friends, from the guts of our dear Job
Comes an awful shout. The eyes of our dear Job
Are dimmed with blood and tears.
How can he see God? Give him a day or two,
I'm sure it will all become clear.
For in a man's soul, as in a pond, anger and woe sink
And the limpid water once again reflects the image of
    God.

Let us go now. Let us leave him alone with his sorrow.
We shall return again on the morrow.

III

BILDAD. I'm not sure I'll come back. Let's be frank:
Philosophizing about God didn't start today.
The pros and cons are known. But I'm not
Talking now about philosophy, just life.
The everyday life
We mortals — with a safe or without a safe — lead
In a society which upholds law and order.
Yes, law and order.

Who gives our laws meaning?
Who endows our life with sense?
In our society — God is the significance.

If God does not exist, it will follow —
Life has no meaning, law is just hollow,
Empty, with no rhyme or reason.
If God doesn't exist, life's just a game —
To steal or not to steal, it's all the same.

JOB. You're scared of thieves. So you
Burden my suffering with meaning.
But what is meaning except suffering?
I itch and itch
Try to dig into suffering, find meaning in it.

And I tell you: There is nothing
In the depths of suffering — only suffering!
I see only suffering filling the world!
Every block of suffering composed of a thousand slivers
Of suffering and every sliver of suffering is built
Of millions of atoms of suffering!

Suffering exists! I exist! You exist!
The gap between us exists! God does not exist!

BILDAD. *You* don't exist! *You* don't exist!
Not one member of our society
Would emit such dirty garbage! Not for a moment!
Not if he is a member of our society!

JOB. "Our society"?! What society is "our society"?!
(*Points to the bodies*) Here is my society. With them I live
And socialize. For them and for me —
For our society — there's no room for God!

BILDAD. Huddle together and you'll find room! Four corpses
And a poor wretch smitten with boils won't crown
And won't drown our God!

It's easy for you. You talk like a man who has
Nothing to lose.
I have. I'm not stricken like you.
I have to choose
Life. And it's not easy to keep
Holding to the fragile pole
Of life. I'm tired, too, I want to drop the role,
Lie on the ground, beat my breast. But I refrain.

I won't let you sit and shout there is no God!
I won't let you. You're insane!
JOB. You won't let me?! What will you do? Pull out
My tongue?! Kill me?! Please! Be my guest:
There is no God! No God! No God!

His shouts sound like barking, especially since he is on all fours.

BILDAD. Look at this dog of God, on all fours, lying
At the feet of God, barking: "No God!"
God swings His foot, kicks the dog in the snoot
But the dog sees only the boot
And whines: "No God!"
JOB. It suits you, standing there with the boot
Ready to kick my face. You're at your best.
You never looked so perfect, so slick.
All your words were just a preface to the boot.
You were born to kick — so go on, kick!

IV

ZOPHAR. But, my friends, what of pity?
Not only is justice holy and divine,
So is pity. Did you forget? Let me remind.
It is not for us to be more harsh than God.
The man is drowning and we're standing on the shore.
Not holding out a rod? (*Approaches Job*)
In this world we're all simply
Frightened orphans seeking our father.
Did we forget the father's mercy for his sons?
And you who lie at our feet,
On your heap of corpses, itching,
How did we forget your father's mercy for you? (*Kneels
next to Job*)
JOB. My father? Yes, I once had a father.
ZOPHAR. And you called out to him at night when you had a
bad dream.
You woke up scared, drenched with sweat and you called
out: Papa!
JOB. Papa! I called out: Papa!

ZOPHAR. And he was always there, he came to you and leaned
      over you
    Picked you up in his arms,
    Held you in his embrace
    And you felt his warm breath on your face.

JOB. (*Tears begin to flow from his eyes*) Papa ...

ZOPHAR. You buried your frightened face in his neck,
    A smile of relief hovered over your lips,
    Your breath calmed down and you fell asleep.

JOB. (*Sobbing*) Papa ... Papa ... Where is he, my father?

ZOPHAR. (*Hugging Job in his arms*) There, up above.

JOB. I'm his little boy and it's so bad
    I had a bad dream in my bed ...

ZOPHAR. He hears you. You had a
    Bad dream. Call to him.

JOB. I had a bad dream, Papa,
    And I'm scared and drenched with sweat ...

ZOPHAR. Hold out your hands to him.

JOB. (*Lifting his hands*) Take me in your arms and bury me in
      your neck ...

ZOPHAR. He's holding out his hands to you. Don't you see?

JOB. My eyes are dimmed by tears ...

ZOPHAR. He's answering you. Don't you hear?

JOB. Yes, I think I do. He's answering me.
    Now I see clearly
    His hands reaching out to me.

ZOPHAR. He'll never desert you.
    He's hugging you ...

JOB. He's hugging me ... I feel
    He's hugging me now ...
    (*Suddenly he bursts into bitter wailing*)
    Papa, look what happened to me, Papa!
    Look what happened to me in this world
    You brought me into with joy!
    Look what happened to your boy!
    Look what happened to the joy.

ZOPHAR. You were dreaming, I told you,
    The world is a bubble of a dream.

JOB. (*Gradually calms down*) Yes, a dream. I was only dreaming.

ZOPHAR. Now you wake up in the arms of your father
    And he rocks you slowly,
    Up, far above the world,
    Stars here, the moon there,
    Softly and gently and your eyes are shut tight
    And you only open them ever again to see light ...
JOB. (*His eyes are shut*) And I only open them ever again to see
        light ...
    (*A silent joy begins to fill him*)
    Papa's alive, Papa's not dead,
    From the cradle of his death, my papa arises,
    My sons and daughters will do the same.
    For the world's just a dream, a bubble of a dream,
    And death, like the snow, washed away in the stream.
    Farewell suffering, farewell sorrow,
    Goodbye to my dead daughters and sons,
    I'm a baby again, warm in Papa's lap,
    Above the world, he carried me far away,
    Softly and gently and my eyes are shut tight
    And I won't open them ever again to see light ...
    (*Zophar rocks him in his lap*)
    Rock me, Papa, rock me, like that ...
ZOPHAR. Call him, talk to him: Our father who art in
      heaven ...
JOB. Our father who art in heaven ...
ZOPHAR. Who sits in the highest ...
JOB. Who sits in the highest ...
ZOPHAR. Into your hands I entrust my spirit ...
JOB. Into your hands I entrust my spirit ...
ZOPHAR. And in the shadow of your wings will I take
      refuge ...
JOB. And in the shadow of your wings will I take refuge ...
ZOPHAR. Hear my voice ...
JOB. Hear my voice ...
ZOPHAR. May your ears heed the sound of my suppli-
      cations ...
JOB. May your ears heed the sound of my supplications ...
ZOPHAR. For you are good and forgiving and merciful ...
JOB. For you are good and forgiving and merciful ...

ZOPHAR. God of all the world.

JOB. God of all the world. (*Pause*)

ELIPHAZ. Behold, my friends, the heavens are opening.
　　See how great is his love for us,
　　For he called us the sons of God.
　　My loved ones, are we not the sons of God?
　　And the heavens are opening.

chapter 6: the soldiers

I

Enter five soldiers led by an officer.

OFFICER. In the name of the new Emperor,
　　Emperor of great Rome and her colonies,
　　These are the words of the Emperor:
　　I am God, that is he, the Emperor.
　　You shall have no other gods
　　Except me, the Emperor.
　　All prayers and sacrifice to other gods —
　　Are forbidden. Religious rituals in the temple — are
　　　forbidden.
　　The idol of the new god
　　Will replace all other idols.
　　No temple priests, no attendants,
　　No rabbis, no cantors, no sextons. The new god
　　Will send his own sextons.

　　For these are the words of the Emperor:
　　The god of the Jews is null and void, wiped out.
　　All who believe in him are heretics and rebels.
　　To reinforce the new belief and make it crystal clear:
　　All those who believe in the god of the Jews will have
　　A spit stuck up their rear.

II

OFFICER. (*To Eliphaz*) You, c'mere. (*Eliphaz comes to him*)

Does the Jewish god exist or not?
(*Pause. To the soldiers*)
This man is a rebel.
Put him on the spit.

BILDAD. Esteemed soldiers, why do you draw
Such hasty conclusions from his silence
Which emanates from his great excitement
At the rise of our new Emperor,
Whose most devoted servants we all are?

OFFICER. (*Pointing to Eliphaz*) Has his excitement passed? We're
waiting for an answer.

BILDAD. Eliphaz, my friend, surely you recall how,
When we came here an hour ago now
And saw the calamity that befell
Our dear Job, itching in his hell,
How you said to me: A world so full of such suffering
Is empty of god. (*Pause*)
Esteemed soldiers, all of us here will confirm
That he said to us: There is no god.

OFFICER. We want to hear it from him.

BILDAD. (*Quietly, to the officer*) Let's go off to the side. He'll say
what you want
But not in front of everybody.

OFFICER. The confession is in public. That's the Emperor's
decree.

BILDAD. Eliphaz, my friend, the esteemed soldiers want
You to repeat what you said before.
(*Pause. He embraces Eliphaz*)
Eliphaz, my friend, when you consider the subject deeply
now,
Think, not about Job's dead children, think about
Your own children, they're alive.
Think about your fields under the plow.
They produced a splendid crop this year, right?
Think of your house, of dinner,
That wonderful dinner after a day of toil
Of slippers, a glass of wine, a chat with friends around the
table at night.
The lovely routine of our lives, the seasons, the days,

The holidays. Did you swim in the sea this year?
Warmed your bones on the soft sand, in the sun's rays?
Eliphaz, my friend, my comrade true,
Will you eat the rich, wonderful dinner tonight?
Or will everyone sit at the table — but you?!

ELIPHAZ. (*Weeping with him*) Tell me some more. About the
children, tell me.

BILDAD. Like fruit on a tree. You're the sturdy trunk
Where hang the red hearts of your children.
The coarse spit that slices your flesh also pierces their soft
skin.
They wait for you. Eliphaz, I am become the mouth of
your children,
The small, sweet mouth gaping at the horror of the world.
With so much trust.
Hear how it screams this mouth:
Will you let the spit be thrust?!

ELIPHAZ. Oh, my children, sweet little mouths!

BILDAD. Oh, Papa, hear the sobs that burst
From our sweet little mouths. Not like Job's
Children frozen for eternity, our bodies are warm, it's not
yet too late,
The last, irretrievable step has not yet been taken,
Don't abandon us, Papa, redeem our fate!

To die for your god, Papa, is a great sacrifice;
Now we call on you to make even greater one, strive,
Sacrifice for your children — stay alive!

ELIPHAZ. (*Still weeping a bit, wipes his tears*) Among the things
you said, Bildad, my friend,
So vivid, so concrete,
My heart was touched by the appeal to sacrifice.
Not the sun or the crops or the dinner —
Which, indeed, is fast approaching
As I sense by my appetite's encroaching —
But the plea of my dear ones.
On that, I couldn't turn my back
That alone led me, after serious thought,
To take the inevitable tack:
(*To the officer*) There is no god.

III

OFFICER. (*To Bildad*) You, c'mere. (*Bildad comes to him*)
Does your god exist or not?

BILDAD. I have never made a secret of my opinions.
I have always insisted and I continue to insist on the
importance
Of social law and order.

No doubt, the innocent attempt to engage
The base of social order
With the god in heaven was necessary at some past stage
Of human development. God was a rung,
A means to rise to the highest step,
Where the Emperor is hung.
In the middle, wretched people stuck.
Happy are they at the top, where I now stand,
Peeping at the hem of the Emperor's frock
And calling out in gratitude: There is no god!

IV

OFFICER. (*To Zophar*) You.

ZOPHAR. (*Approaches him*) There is a god . . .

OFFICER. Put him . . .

ZOPHAR. . . . in my ass.

OFFICER. Who?

ZOPHAR. God. (*Pause*)

OFFICER. You make things a bit complicated for me.
On the one hand you claim there is a god.
That is, you don't deny his existence.
On the other hand,
I'm not such an idiot to think you really believe in him
If you shove him up your ass.
On the third hand, if god
Exists everywhere, he also exists in your ass, that is,
You still believe in him.
On the fourth hand, if you do believe in him,
Can't you find a better place for him
Than your filthy ass?
In short: either you're poking

Fun at me or you're joking
To curry favor with the brass.
But I have precise instructions and I need
A simple answer to a simple question:
Does god exist or not?

ZOPHAR. "A simple answer to a simple question." Ah,
What a triumphant military sense of humor . . .

Gives the officer a friendly pat on the shoulder. The officer hits him in the face. Zophar falls down, his nose bleeding. He gets up, still trying to joke to save his honor, shakes his finger humorously at the officer.

Naughty, naughty . . .

Tries again to pat the officer on the shoulder, the latter again hits him in the face, Zophar falls down, gets up, comes to the officer, has trouble standing, again shakes his finger clowningly.

Listen, people are liable to think
We're quarreling . . .

The officer hits him a third time, knocks him to the floor.

My, my, aren't we lively today . . .

The officer scolds him for continuing and hits him. Zophar cannot go on any more and bursts into bitter weeping and shouts.

There is no god! There is no god!
We all see there's no god, don't we?

V

The officer and his soldiers turn to go. Suddenly he notices Job curled up on the floor. Comes to him.

OFFICER. You. Get up. Does your god exist or not?
JOB. My dear fool, don't you see him
Stretching out his arms to hug me?
OFFICER. (*To the soldiers*) Put him on the spit.
ZOPHAR. (*To the officer*) Don't waste your precious time
On this human pile of weeds.

The man went mad because of a calamity—
He's not responsible for his words or deeds.
OFFICER. Clown, you talk more than you have to.
  Anyway, when is madness an excuse? That nut
  In the next village who claims to be the son of god
  Already has twelve disciples. So? Are they
  Nuts too? Should the imperial army sit on its ass
  And leave the world alone because it's a nuthouse?

  I'll be honest with you: My men
  Are hungry for fun, they haven't seen blood on the spit yet
    today:
  And looking at it from the spit, sane or crazy,
  The difference in asses is pretty hazy.
ZOPHAR. Job, my friend, it's time to open your eyes.
  We dreamed a little that there is a god,
  Now wake up, get up to your suffering, to yesterday's
    suffering.

  Bark, bark at the empty skies,
  Bark as before "There is no god!" For nothing has changed.
  Remember death, recall your poverty,
  Remember your itch, rolling on the ground, all of it.
  And most of all—remember the spit!
JOB. But my loyal friend Zophar, why are you
  So upset? What is it?
  Did someone lose his four children and is he weeping?

  You know, from up there, from the bosom of the lord,
  A weeping man looks like he's sneezing.
  The shrouds—
  Like handkerchiefs. Grief, joy—all movement
  Is the same and quite absurd. From up there, my friend,
  It's all so amusing.
  Who separated me from my father?
  Who brought me down
  From the bosom of the lord?
OFFICER. He's right. Help him get back up
  To the bosom of the lord on the spit.

VI

Zophar takes some money out of his pocket and gives it secretly to the officer.

ZOPHAR. Take fifty dinars and let him go.

OFFICER. You're trying to buy the army—so cheap?

ZOPHAR. (*Returns, puts the money back in his pocket*) Well, I tried.

OFFICER. Make it double. Maybe it'll work.

ZOPHAR. (*Looks at Eliphaz and Bildad. They don't respond*) No. It's not worth more than fifty

To me. I did what a man

Must. My conscience is at peace.

OFFICER. (*Angrily pointing at Job*) Come on, put him on the spit!

VII

The soldiers spread Job's legs and bring the spit.

SERGEANT. You found the ring? Yes, in the center. Good.

Even a blind man on a dark night, they say,

Will find the entrance to the ass.

SOLDIER. You can't mistake the smell.

SERGEANT. Now shove it in, yeah, like that.

JOB. Oh! My arse! My arse! Oh, god!

My arse, my arse! Oh god, my arse!

OFFICER. That man's whole being

Is now concentrated in his ass.

All family ties, instincts,

Feelings, loyalties and opinions

Are all mixed up in a shapeless mass—

A heavy fog and the awful pain in his ass

Flickers like the beam from a lighthouse.

As the spit ascends to his belly

The pain in his ass will dissolve in the fog,

Give way to a new focus of being.

JOB. Oh! My guts! My guts! Oh, god!

My guts, my guts! Oh god, my guts!

OFFICER. Now he makes his god pass
    To his guts from his ass.
ZOPHAR. (*Shouts*) Deny god, Job!
    Say there is no god!
    Deny god!

*The soldiers raise the spit Job is impaled on, putting the end on the
ground.*

JOB. Papa, they raise me up to you on an iron pole.
    On poles and crosses and spears and pyres they raise us,
    Our arms stretched out to our Father.
    I'm riding up to my papa, on a knife.
    How dreadful is the trip but how great the grace,
    How sweet the repose at the end of the journey —
    To look my Papa in the face. (*He falls silent*)

VIII

The three friends stand looking at Job on the spit.

BILDAD. See how he's looking at me. His tormented eyes
    Stare at me with the boldness of someone you owe some-
        thing to.
    What's wrong? What did I do and what do I owe him?
    Does a spit in your belly make you a saint?

    And why do you look at me from above, from the heights
        of the spit,
    With such pride? The god you believe in
    Doesn't love arrogance. The god you believe in
    Loves me, the humble, the fearful, lower than a weed, the
        mud.
    Here I stand, the soft human mud to mold into great faith.

    And if I were in your place
    On the spit, staring at me — what then?
    Would you come sit in my place?
    So, what's the difference?
    What's the point? What would change? And why
    Do I even stand here defending myself?

Does somebody owe you something?

So take those pleas out of your eye!
I told you: You are you and I am — I!
You hear? You are you and I am — I!
You are you and I am — I!
Shut your eyes! Or lift them to the sky,
Villain! Look for your papa in the sky,
Shout to the sky and cry to the sky,
Go weep in the bosom of your god that here on earth —
O horrors — you lost your drawers!

The three friends exit. Job calls to them.

JOB.   Don't leave me alone with god!
My friends, don't leave me
Alone with god!

chapter 7: the entertainers

I

Enter the ringmaster.

RINGMASTER.   Too bad about this one, isn't it? Bad taste
For such a performance as this to go to waste.
All those potential tickets mutely crying out
Like the souls of unborn children dying out.
Not to mention the educational worth
For those who still think god exists on earth.
I've run musical circuses in all the most
Important capitals of Europe.
I can even say that I've run Europe.
I've got a stripper and I've got dwarfs,
I've got French cooking,
And drinks and dance music to go with it.
What I don't have is just that —
An ass flambé on a spit.

Five hundred dinars to the royal treasury
For the right to put this man

In my circus.

OFFICER. If the Emperor sold tickets himself,
He could make at least five thousand.

RINGMASTER. What? You're joking. We missed the part
Where you shoved in the spit
And pulled down his pants;
The shrieks of fear, all
The humiliation and scorn —
The juiciest part.
The pole's deep in his belly,
He hardly has another hour
Of silent agony.
How many tickets do you think you'll sell for an hour
Of inner agony? Who's interested these days
In a man suffering in silence?
The audience, you know, pays
To hear a little singing, something gay.

OFFICER. This man will live for another six or seven hours
And, with a musical comedy, maybe even till morning.

RINGMASTER. Really? And can somebody guarantee
That a hemorrhage or a fit
Won't carry him off any minute?

OFFICER. A hemorrhage in the belly — yes;
But until the pole pierces his diaphragm,
If it does, toward the heart . . .

RINGMASTER. I don't know much about anatomy.

OFFICER. Thirty percent to the circus, thirty to the Emperor.

RINGMASTER. And the other forty?

OFFICER. I'm a human being too.

RINGMASTER. So, forty to the circus, forty to the Emperor
And twenty to the human being.

OFFICER. No less than forty percent to the human being.

RINGMASTER. Listen, we're all human beings.

OFFICER. I don't know much about philosophy.

RINGMASTER. Enough. Fifty percent to the circus,
Fifty to the human being.

OFFICER. And the Emperor?

RINGMASTER. The Emperor doesn't speculate in asses.

OFFICER. You're right. (*They shake hands*)

RINGMASTER. (*Turning to the audience*) Ladies and gentlemen,
the sun now is setting, another
Weary day of buying and selling
Comes to an end.
Now as you wend your way home
To potatoes and soup in a bowl,
Be sure to throw a little crust to the soul.

Have you closed the shutters? Dimmed the light?
Did you lock the store up tight?
Ladies and gentlemen, five minutes for art. All right?

II

*The circus performers enter and surround Job. These include a
dwarf who chases the stripper and sings.*

DWARF. Once when I was the age of three,
What a wonderful time.
No one thought that I was wee
And nobody called me dwarf.
The future belonged to you and me,
When we saw eye to eye,
Happiness waited for you so free
And happiness too—for me.

But you grew up and left me far, far behind in the notch,
And now your face comes up to the sky and mine comes
up to your crotch.

Don't call me dwarf,
Call me eternal child,
For with warmth is my heart all aflood
And I still have such passionate blood
And so much feeling, so much warmth in stock,
And perhaps it may please you to know
That I have a very long cock.

STRIPPER. In Africa, I spent some years
And I know what long is. And I also know, it appears,
What hard is. If I say so myself, my cunt
Is fit for African dimensions, not some runt.

And I don't want to stuff it with noodles.
This is what comes
Of living in Africa.
DWARF. Judge us not by African pricks.
We live in Asia. Judge us by Asian dicks.

The stripper dances and strips in front of the dwarf.
When she is naked, she examines his erect penis.

STRIPPER. Well, even on that wretched scale
You don't fit the accepted tale
That nature made you topsy-turvy —
A short body with a long prick.
No, nature fucked you barrel, stock, and lock:
Short body, short life, and short cock.
You have something long?
Suffering, we may regard.
Your suffering is long, long and hard.
(*Looks at Job then at the spit*)
Here here's something fit for my tail,
Even on an African scale.

The stripper spreads her legs, puts her crotch to the spit, rubs
against it and moans with pleasure as if in response to the groans of
suffering Job emits stuck on top with his legs spread to the sides.
Their spasms and groans ostensibly resemble a fornication in which
the spit serves as a penis.

JOB. (*In agony*) Papa ... Papa ...
STRIPPER. (*In ecstasy*) Mama ... Mama ...
(*She sings as she rubs against the pole*)
Between my legs there's a hole that is black,
Between my legs there's a hole that is black,
Who will fill it up tonight there
Who will bring a little light there
Who will go in from the front
And come out from the back.
Between my legs there's a hole that is black ...
DWARF. (*Masturbating and singing*) Don't call me dwarf ...

The two songs blend into one another; the dwarf and the stripper
are shouting and making violent movements.

III

The spit slices into Job's lungs and it becomes hard for him to breathe.

JOB. Oh! Air. Oh, god!
    Air! Air!
RINGMASTER. Why are you standing around like jerks?
    Where's your sense of humanity?
    Give him some water. We have to stretch out
    His death throes a bit!
    There's still a lot of people waiting in the doorway.
OFFICER. Too late. The spit pierced the diaphragm
    And penetrated the lungs.
JOB. There is no god—
    Take me down from the spit! There is no god!
OFFICER. Too late, pal. Death
    Has struck root in you. Go
    With death!
JOB. Air... there is no god ...
    I swear to you there is no god!!!
OFFICER. Too bad. For the same price, you could have died
    As a man of principle.
JOB. Take me down from the spit!
    There's no god—and that's final!

IV

Two clowns climb ladders on either side of Job and paint him like a clown.

SOLEMN CLOWN. "That's final," he says and who will remind
        him
    Of all the final things he pronounced in his life.

    For what is man? Here's a man for you:
    Now he cries "my son, my son," now he shouts "my ass,"
    At night roasted doves in his mouth, at dawn a poker up
        his toot.
    Then he sang, now he weeps, soon he'll be mute.

What is man: What he said yesterday?
What he cries now? His silence, soon?
Is he his memories? His hopes?
What he does or what is done to him?
His last scream on his deathbed?
Or his first scream between his mother's legs?
Or is he that awful, ridiculous muddle
Between one scream and the other?
Where is the thread that binds it all,
Where is the thread and what is meaning?

What is man? And what is life?
And the thread, gentlemen, tell me, where is the thread?

CYNICAL CLOWN. "What is man? What is life?"
What is hemorrhoids? What is a fly?
Who cares where the thread may lie?
Who cares what is a man?
What is the world? Who gives a damn?

Ladies and gentlemen, you see
A man fall off a high roof, you stare —
His arms waving, spinning in the air,
His shattered scream reverberates in space.
You step back a bit so the blood won't spatter your clothes
    and face.
Hypnotized by his fall like lead
Your expressions a blend of yearning and dread
For that final, unrepeatable moment when his body hits
    the ground.
Don't search for a meaning,
Don't ask for a moral. Why try?
Just watch: a man falls, soon he'll die.

V

Job gargles his death rattle.

RINGMASTER. (*To Job*) You won't leave me right in the middle,
    will you?
You look like a reasonable man, you're bread for my

children tomorrow.
Listen how they cry out to me, Papa ... Papa ... in
  sorrow.
You wouldn't take bread out of the mouths of babes,
  would you?
OFFICER. Too late. This is death.
RINGMASTER. He could easily have gone on for another hour.
OFFICER. I don't tell you how to train elephants,
Don't tell me how to smell death.
For ten years, I've lived with death, like a little monkey
Sitting on my shoulder, playing with my ear.
Gentlemen, this is death.

*He holds out his hand for the money. The ringmaster gives him his
share.*

JOB. Death? Death itself? This is the famous moment
I've heard so much about? It's here?

*The officer and the soldiers exit. The ringmaster tries to divert Job
and keep him from dropping dead.*

RINGMASTER. Hey, man! What are you thinking about now?
Is there a god? You see something there? Huh?
Or is it just
A black hole, about the size of Africa?
Huh? Hey, man, tell us! Tell us! Tell us!
(*He hits him in despair*)
SOLEMN CLOWN. This man is now far above us.
He knows something we do not.

But he will not say a thing. He is now
In those dizzy heights where a person recognizes no one.
  All the plains
And hills are behind him, the story of his life and his
  deeds, the people and tools
That bound him to the world—all severed from him,
At long last, he has slipped out of his father's tight clasp,
  left it
Far behind and now he is all alone. Alone. Enveloped like
  a high priest

In the simple shirt of the mystery of his death.
Which each of us will have his turn
To don
Someday.

JOB. (*Whispering with the last of his strength*) What is a man on a
    spit?
A man who is finished, done for it.
Can I describe such despair?
Darkness like that can't be found anywhere.
(*He retches vomit and blood and dies*)

RINGMASTER. (*Angry*) "Anywhere!" You couldn't have waited
    another hour?!
"Anywhere!" Phooey!

*He spits on Job's corpse and exits. The circus and the audience
disperse and exit.*

chapter 8: the dead

I

*The most beggarly beggar of all the beggars enters and licks Job's
vomit.*

BEGGAR. Just like I said: A little patience
And somebody finally pukes. Yes,
Somehow we manage to live.
There's a god in the sky
Tra-la-la, tra-la-lie. (*Exits*)

II

The dead sing.

THE DEAD. But there is mercy in the world
And we are laid to rest.

Thus the dead lie patiently,
With silence are we blessed.

Grass grows on our flesh,
The scream dies in our breast;

But there is mercy in the world
And we are laid to rest.

joshua sobol

jewish soul

(the last night of otto weininger)

TRANSLATED FROM THE HEBREW BY

MICHAEL TAUB

characters

OTTO WEININGER: twenty-three

LEOPOLD: his father, forty-nine

ADELHEID: his mother, forty-six

BERGER: his friend, twenty-three

TIETZ: his teacher, between thirty and forty, carouser, changes masks

CLARA: his friend, twenty-two

FREUD: forty-five

ADELE: concierge, twenty plus

OTTO'S DOUBLE: played by a woman

PROSTITUTES

CABARET PERFORMERS

setting

The setting is a large living room. The walls are actually semitransparent, back-lighted mirrors. Each mirror is a revolving door, making it possible to enter the room from practically any direction. The address is Schwarzspanierstrasse 15. The apartment has been empty and neglected for years as luxury mixes with decay. Certain objects and pieces of furniture are covered with white sheets. The apartment symbolizes any place in Otto's mind. Scene changes are made without moving furniture around and without blackouts.

time

Real time—the night between the third and fourth of October, 1903.

Internal time—from Otto's early childhood to the night of October 3, when he commits suicide. We are shown Otto's memories and visions, as he lies dying, after shooting himself near the heart in the apartment he rented to commit suicide.

act 1

SCENE ONE

A shot. Complete darkness in the theatre. The curtain goes up on a dark room. In the right corner — a piano covered in a white sheet. In the left corner — a large covered sofa also covered in a white sheet. A pile of boxes blocks the entrance door. In the back of the room a partition reveals a bathtub. The play begins with Adele, the concierge, trying to open the door from the outside. Muffled voices are heard from there.

ADELE. Damn it, the door is stuck. Has the gentleman perhaps changed his mind? (*More muffled noises from outside*) Something's blocking the door. (*Adele and Otto push the door. The boxes begin to move; the door opens about an inch. A ray of light penetrates through the crack*) Together! Together! Push! (*The door opens wide*) Ffui! What an awful smell! Like a tomb!

OTTO. Maybe there's a corpse inside.

ADELE. Holy Mother, how you speak! A corpse! God protect us! It's only mildew and dampness.

OTTO. A little more and we're in.

ADELE. You go. I'm not going in.

OTTO. (*Sticks his head through the crack*) Give me the candle!

ADELE. (*Gives it to him*) This is the first time I've opened this door since I began working in this building. The windows and shades must have been closed for years.

OTTO. (*Shouting*) My head! I'm choking! Open up!

ADELE. (*Pushing the door hard*) Stop kicking.

OTTO. Air! I need air!

ADELE. It's your punishment.

OTTO. I'm suffocating.

ADELE. I told you this apartment is not fit to live in.

OTTO. Help me!

ADELE. Use your shoulders! Yes! A little more! Yes! It's moving! Harder! Together! (*The pile of boxes suddenly collapses. The door opens wide. The two come flying in, landing on top of the boxes. A cloud of dust. Adele laughs while trying to get up*)

OTTO. (*Shouting at her*) Get off me! You're squashing me!

ADELE. So it's you! (*Laughing*) Stop tickling me there!

OTTO. Help me get up!

ADELE. God you're clumsy ... (*Gets up, offers him a hand*)

OTTO. You almost killed me!

ADELE. You're so clumsy. Stubborn too. (*Mimicking him*) "Show me the room! Just show me the room!" (*Laughs*)

OTTO. Stop it, you idiot!

ADELE. I'm an idiot all right, coming up here with you. I don't understand how you made me do this. (*Mimicking him*) "I must rent a room in this house!" Why it had to be here is beyond me. Why? Where's the candle?

OTTO. (*Gives her the candle that has broken and gone out by now*) Here ...

ADELE. You're really something! Why did you break it?

OTTO. It broke by itself.

ADELE. We're lucky it's not lit, otherwise we would have had a fire ... we would have burned to a crisp. Do you have a match? (*He shakes his head no*) I guess you're not the right person to ask for a match. (*Takes one from her apron pocket*) Hold the candle straight! (*He holds it, she lights it and takes it away from him. She looks at him*) You're some character ... what a face you have ... did your girlfriend leave you?

OTTO. No.

ADELE. I know your type. I always get in trouble with types like you ... the kind that make you feel sorry. Are you Jewish?

OTTO. Why?

ADELE. Never mind. You're here. Now have a look for yourself and tell me if this place is fit to live in.

OTTO. It suits me just fine.

ADELE. Listen, young man, there's an empty apartment across the street. Why don't you take it if you must live in this rotten neighborhood?

OTTO. I want this one.

ADELE. What's so special about it?

OTTO. You.

ADELE. Careful, my boyfriend's in the cavalry. He's very jealous and also an excellent sharpshooter. He could hit you right between your eyes from a hundred yards. He may be in

Hungary now, but I wouldn't make him mad if I were you!

OTTO. You're not from Vienna?

ADELE. I'm from the country, from Schteier. I came to Vienna about five years ago. So what?

OTTO. You really don't know what happened in this house?

ADELE. No.

OTTO. I suppose you've heard of Beethoven?

ADELE. A relative of yours?

OTTO. He died here.

ADELE. (*Scared*) When?!

OTTO. Seventy-six years ago.

ADELE. Ffff ... who cares what happened in this rotten place seventy-six years ago.

OTTO. Woman, why should I be surprised ... when my father, who's a devoted music fan ...

ADELE. What?

OTTO. When I left home to come here, I pleaded with my father to accompany me to the bus station. We waited in the station and talked. A bus arrived, but I didn't take it. Then another, and another. He didn't understand ... I told him ... "Father, I'm going to rent a room at Schwarzspanierstrasse 15 ..."

ADELE. You make me laugh. What if there were no rooms available?

OTTO. Certain things, it makes no difference where one does them. With those that count, those which capture people's imagination, they must be done in the right place and time, and there's always only one such place!

ADELE. And then you got on the bus?

OTTO. When the eighth bus arrived, I said, "Father, remember Schwarzspanierstrasse 15?" "Yes, yes, I'll remember," he said. He could have grabbed my arm and prevented me from leaving, but he didn't. So I hopped on the bus and left ...

ADELE. It's only a story, you don't have to get all worked up! It's only a story!

OTTO. I haven't laughed in years. I was already sure I'd die without ever laughing! But thanks to you I smiled ...

goodness is found in everything and not just in some individual thing ...

ADELE. Sorry ...

OTTO. Which proves that the individual is totally without value ...

ADELE. I don't understand you!

OTTO. I'm talking to myself. I repeat things to myself to remember to write them down. This sentence is a death warrant.

ADELE. (*With a shrug*) Would you like to see the kitchen and the bathroom?

OTTO. No. There's no need for that.

ADELE. So you've given up the idea of renting this tomb?

OTTO. Yes ... the ego doesn't exist either ...

ADELE. Great. Now help me arrange these boxes.

OTTO. A falling star, that's the individual ...

ADELE. I can't do it by myself!

OTTO. Don't bother ... and there's no meaning ...

ADELE. I've got to do it before we leave and lock up.

OTTO. Young lady, you're mistaken!

ADELE. What? Help me put these boxes back, then we'll lock up and leave.

OTTO. Leave? Where?

ADELE. If you want, you can have some coffee in my place, then catch the first bus and go home.

OTTO. I'm staying here.

ADELE. You said you weren't interested.

OTTO. When?

ADELE. You don't know what's going on, sir, and don't know what you're saying!?

OTTO. Sorry. I'm renting this place. It's self-evident. Give me the key.

ADELE. You're not thinking of sleeping here tonight?

OTTO. I certainly am. (*Extends his hand for the key*)

ADELE. I told you this apartment is not livable in this condition. I need a week to clean it and air the rooms.

OTTO. Please, just give it to me!

ADELE. If you're in trouble with your family, you could stay at my place for a while. There's room in the hallway, I won't

throw you out, in the state you're in. Come, let's put back
these boxes.

OTTO. No, no. Leave it. I must stay here tonight. I must.
Don't ask me why. If I told you it would become a lie
simply by virtue of my telling you, understand? (*He reacts
to her bovine look*) This is the type of truth which, if revealed,
can't be realized; therefore, premature revelation would
inevitably turn it into a lie ... my head ... (*Presses his
forehead to lessen the pain*) Give me the key, and good night!

ADELE. No!

OTTO. (*Suddenly grabs her aggressively*) Give it to me!

ADELE. Leave me alone ... (*Hits him hard on the arm, breaks
loose*)

OTTO. Woman!

ADELE. Don't come near me! (*Grabs a stick, threatens him with it*)

OTTO. Don't shout ...

ADELE. Get out! You hear?

OTTO. Listen, if I leave now because of you, you'll become a
partner in a horrible crime. A crime to be remembered a
thousand years from now; your name will forever be connected with it.

ADELE. Get out of here right now!

OTTO. The only way to prevent this despicable crime is for
you to give me the key and say nothing to anyone until
tomorrow morning!

ADELE. What do you want from me?

OTTO. What's your name?

ADELE. Adele ...

OTTO. Adelheid? Impossible! This is the name of the woman
who brought me into the world ...

ADELE. Please, sir ... don't start any cheap tricks now, don't
get any perverted notions ... I'm a simple girl, but honest
and decent.

OTTO. If I had any perverted notions would I have refused
your invitation to spend the night at your place?

ADELE. I didn't invite you!

OTTO. Woman! Not only did you invite me, but you even
bothered to inform me that your boyfriend, the dangerous
cavalry man, was stationed God-knows-where in

Hungary, hundreds of miles from here!

ADELE. It's the truth! Honestly ...

OTTO. I turned down your invitation and now you accuse me of perverted intentions? Listen to me: the man standing before you has lived the last six months in extreme torment and in total abstinence! Woman! Never in your whole life have you been or ever will be in the presence of a man with such pure intentions. Listen, everything in life symbolizes something spiritual, every encounter between man and woman symbolizes the meeting of good and evil. And you hold in your hands the key to a fateful night, a night when good and evil battle to the end. Adelheid ... give me the key!

ADELE. (*Hands it to him*) Here ... sir, tomorrow morning you'll come to sign the register as required by law.

OTTO. No! Do it now: Otto Weininger, doctor of philosophy, born April 4, 1880.

ADELE. The gentleman is only twenty-three?!

OTTO. And a half, to be exact.

ADELE. Sir, about the fee, will you come to pay it tomorrow morning?

OTTO. We'll take care of that now, too. Tomorrow I won't be able to. Here. (*Gives her a large sum of money*)

ADELE. But, sir, this is too much!

OTTO. Keep the rest. If anyone asks about me, if anyone looks for me — you never saw or heard a thing. I'm not here. No one should interfere with my work tonight. Is that clear?

ADELE. Yes, sir ...

OTTO. And tomorrow morning promptly at nine-thirty please knock on the door.

ADELE. Yes, sir ...

OTTO. Have a restful night, Adele.

ADELE. Good night. (*She leaves. Otto closes the door behind her and locks it*)

SCENE TWO

The light behind the back wall turns the mirrors into transparent glass. We see a forest: it's a park in the Tietz family estate. Clara appears from the woods. She's wearing a white, semitransparent summer dress; across her chest, a string of colorful flowers. Otto observes the scene from the room but in fact he's looking at a picture from his memory.

CLARA. Berger! (*Shouts in the direction of the woods*) Ber-ger! (*Whistles a tune, their signal*)

BERGER. (*Whistles back the signal, shouts*) Cla-ra!

CLARA. I'm here, Berger! Here! (*Berger appears from the woods, a mandolin hanging from his neck. He, too, is wearing white summer clothes*)

BERGER. Are you alone?

CLARA. Come, stay with me. Otto took off, disappeared. He left me alone with Tietz.

BERGER. Where's Tietz?

CLARA. He follows me everywhere. He's looking for me. When we're alone he whispers in my ears all kinds of silly things. I keep telling him: you're not a boy, Tietz! He answers: around you I feel sixteen again! At our last student ball he suddenly came up to me: "Come to my apartment!" "Tietz, are you mad? Is your wife here? I don't understand you, you're respected at the university, you have money, status, your beautiful wife Bertha, everything, and yet keep chasing a girl like me."

BERGER. Another mistress for his collection, that's what the old sinner wants!

CLARA. Luckily we were hidden from the crowd; the loud music swallowed up our voices. He was drunk. He whispered in my ear all kinds of crazy things about my hair, my skin, my misty, penetrating Jewish eyes, and my Jewish sensuality that is driving him crazy ...

BERGER. They're crazy about Jewish women!

CLARA. He swore he would give up everything, right away, if I only would come with him ... I was forced to be cold as ice and deaf as a wall to his entreaties.

BERGER. The philanderer is truly in love with you! What do you care? Why not have some fun with him?

CLARA. He's so big, and his wildness frightens me ... ready to give me anything I want!

BERGER. All you have to do is whistle and he'll give you this entire estate. We'll have a place for the summer.

CLARA. Luckily Bertha and the children are here with him. This way, at least in the evenings, when we all meet in the castle, I can relax a little. You know, just a few minutes ago he wanted to drag me to his hunting lodge. I didn't know how to get out of it so I told him I wanted some wine. Right away he ran to the castle to get it ... I want to go back to Vienna!

BERGER. When?

CLARA. Today!

BERGER. And what excuse will you offer him?

CLARA. I don't know, you make up something ...

BERGER. He'll be hurt. He's very sensitive. He'll understand right away ...

CLARA. While we're having fun here, the anti-Semites are meeting tonight in Vienna.

BERGER. Here he comes ...

CLARA. Berger, you'll know how to explain this. I'm not staying here ... (*Enter Tietz: a big man, face of a carouser, wearing a long oriental robe, the kind worn by Arabs. He carries a wicker basket filled with sausages and wine*)

BERGER. (*Walks towards him joyfully*) Hey, Tietz! Where did you disappear to?

TIETZ. Our Ondine, our heartless Ondine, was suddenly thirsty for some Austrian blood. (*Shakes the bottle*) I also brought some hot sausage to awaken your taste buds and get your stomach juices going!

CLARA. Tietz, your descriptions make me nauseous.

TIETZ. Cold Ondine, soulless Ondine! Bertha's fixing a royal feast — roasted lamb! We'll sit in front of the fireplace, drink, and sing until the morning light! Hand me your glasses. (*Pours wine*) Where's Otto? Hiding in the woods? (*Calls out*) Otto!

BERGER. We won't be able to stay; we must return to Vienna.

TIETZ. When?

BERGER. As soon as this evening ... Karl Lueger's anti-Semitic pigs are holding a meeting tonight in Rosenau Tavern. We must go and start a debate among the people there ...

TIETZ. You're going to Vienna because of Lueger and his hoodlums?

BERGER. We have to ...

TIETZ. Forget about him! You take him too seriously!

BERGER. He demands to restrict the rights of Jewish citizens.

TIETZ. So, let him demand! He can demand until doomsday. The Kaiser won't allow anyone to harm his Jewish citizens. Leave Karl Lueger alone and stay here!

BERGER. Tell me, did the Kaiser block handsome Lueger's election as mayor of Vienna? You know the Kaiser's no longer all that powerful. He too must abide by democratic rules.

TIETZ. Austria has been and will remain a liberal democracy!

BERGER. If Karl Lueger wins the majority of votes in the elections, liberalism will be separated from democracy, and anti-Semitism will assume power in a democratic way, if that's what the majority wants.

TIETZ. The majority of Austria will never feel that way! Life in Austria has never been more peaceful, beautiful, safe, joyful, and rich than it is today. Austria is Europe's paradise! Stay here, enjoy the country air, nature, the view ...

BERGER. This paradise sits on a very thin surface. Lava is gathering underneath ... the peasants, the craftsmen, the artisans, and the small merchants are watching with fear the emergence of modern factories and big stores, and new banks popping up everywhere. Life is changing rapidly and the petite bourgeoisie is running scared. Enter handsome Karl's new anti-Semites to tell the people: "Who's destroying Austria's beautiful, old way of life? Capitalism and international finance companies. And who's behind it? The Jews! And what allows them to carry out their work? Austrian liberalism and the excessive freedom they enjoy here!" They've already started to spread this propaganda on campus ... we can't let them win over the students! We must go to Vienna.

TIETZ. Bravo, Berger! You convinced me! I'm going with you! Let's go! If we hurry up we can catch the four o'clock train.

CLARA. What about Bertha and the children?

TIETZ. Bertha's staying here, we can't drag the children back and forth to Vienna ...

CLARA. Why don't you two go, I'll stay here with Bertha and help her with the children ...

TIETZ. Bertha doesn't need you. She has the servants. She'll manage.

CLARA. But it's not nice: she cooked, cleaned ... no, you go, I'm staying here with her.

TIETZ. Clara! If you paid attention to Berger like I did, you would know that tonight you must be in Vienna!

CLARA. You men go. You argue, fight ... I'm staying here, with Bertha.

TIETZ. I was sure you'd be going too.

CLARA. You were wrong, Tietz. You two can manage without me, isn't that right, Berger?

BERGER. We will ...

TIETZ. But you must go! (*Otto bursts in*)

OTTO. She doesn't have to, Tietz! Can't your male Aryan head grasp that? If you tell her now that you're staying, she'll go!

CLARA. (*In an outburst; cuts him off abruptly*) We came here to enjoy nature. These are the last days of summer and since we arrived all we do is argue! (*She turns her attack on Berger*) Bertha worked all day. She cooked, she cleaned ... if you want to go, go, and miss the exhilarating feeling of this country air, quickening the senses, the warm caressing sun burning the skin, the wonderful wine sliding down your throat like velvet, filling your stomach with tingling butterflies ... how many more sun-drenched days like these are left before the autumn winds? Who wants to drink with me?

BERGER. (*Raises his glass*) To youth, joy, to our friendships!

CLARA. Tietz! My gloomy teddy bear, what about you?

TIETZ. (*Lifts his glass*) To beauty, wine, and our unique and unifying love. To freedom!

CLARA. Otto!

OTTO. To truth and faith, without which there's no life ...

CLARA. Berger and I have prepared a surprise. Berger composed a tune to a small poem Otto once dedicated to me when

we were in high school ... Otto, I'm sure you forgot ...
but I didn't. This poem is dearer to me than any emotion
I've had since ... (*She signals Berger to start playing. She
sings*)

The Butterfly

The small head rocks; half-laughter wells,
Timid, in eyes where tears are thronging.
The voice that was sweet with the sound of bells
Trembles and shakes with longing.

Learn, little maid, learn wisdom's way:
Loose to the winds the winged creature.
Broad the world stretches, colored, gay
With butterflies flying, for you to capture.

Ever, forever, will they emerge
From their dark cocoons with courtly bearing.
While the world lasts, while eons surge,
They will come forth, in sunlight faring.

Laugh, little maid, with the joy of flame.
Be strong and glad as the running water.
Take comfort: Butterflies stay the same—
They flutter away. What matter?

TIETZ. Bravo! Bravo! (*Applause*) It's as good as young Heine's
youthful poems!

OTTO. (*Mumbling*) For me that is no compliment!

TIETZ. And to the singer—a bouquet of flowers! (*Gives her a
flower, kisses her cheek*) Clara, decide: are you or are you not
going to Vienna?

CLARA. (*Ignoring him*) Otto, you didn't like the tune?

OTTO. Tietz, Tietz! ... all this inviting us to your family
estate, honoring us with your fine food and wine, opening
your house and heart to us ... and what about us?

TIETZ. What's the matter?

OTTO. In Vienna, Karl Lueger the anti-Semite wants to restrict
the rights of Jews and Tietz the humanist invites three of
his Jewish students to his family estate to breathe the fine
air of Austria's generous outdoors. Life goes on as
usual ... and the truth is buried deeper and deeper ...

BERGER. What do you mean?

OTTO. There's more truth in Lueger's open hatred and blatant anti-Semitism than in this idyllic liberalism ... (*Reacting to their puzzled looks*) What is it that attracts Tietz to us? What attracts us to Tietz?

TIETZ. You are not clear, young man ...

OTTO. Tietz! You're naive! If you really knew, if you really understood the Jews, you wouldn't think them worthy of your love! First of all we lack nobility of spirit, we have no self-esteem ... no faith ... we are all slaves at heart ... when the world grants us freedom, like here in Austria, our slavish nature makes us impudent ...

BERGER. Otto, what are you saying?

OTTO. How can you look into each other's eyes? One has only to watch you to know right away that the moral, rational man is dead ... and what's left in his place? A kind of a psychological being ... a man without qualities ... a product of cheap journalism and stolen sexual pleasures ... two adult males dancing to the tune of a girl. (*To Tietz*) You want to go to Vienna to fight the anti-Semites, or to spend a night with her in your apartment? And you? (*To Berger*) Pimping in all directions. She turned you into a woman. And you? (*To Clara*) Going around seducing men, planting in them hope and illusions, relishing the power you have over them ... and all this talk about liberalism, democracy ... a wonderful liberal trio indeed! You despise me now, right? (*To Tietz*) Underneath your thin liberal crust you're saying to yourself: who is this creature—uncouth, crude, loud, impolite, impudent, tearing down fences, violating good taste, lacking respect for individual rights, an idea alien to him, a man who increases the value of his individuality by humiliating that of others ... in a word—a Jew!

BERGER. Otto, enough, shut up! (*Motions him to stop. Tietz wants him to go on*)

TIETZ. Don't shut him up! Otto, speak! This man speaks from the heart!

OTTO. So here you are standing before me, patronizing me ... despising this Jew carrying on before you like a wild goat in such an unmanly fashion. At the same time, though, this wild Jewishness brings out the noble Aryan in you, helps it find its true meaning ... it reminds you who you are, and in what ways you are different from me. I make you want to spit on me, but you control yourself, so in fact the Aryan in you should be grateful to the Jew in me. Thanks to me you know what you should guard yourself against: Judaism as a potentially destructive force inside you! So you see, we're bound to each other like life and death!

TIETZ. I love you!

OTTO. Why can't you admit your true feelings? It's disgusting, isn't it? You stand there, watching me, knowing that I know things said about you which concern you; you'd like to know them but you're too polite to ask! This is spiritual death! Ask! Ask what this woman is doing to you! Ask me why she wanted to go to Vienna, then suddenly changed her mind! And you, Berger, if you took your Zionism seriously, would you concoct this stupid Jewish plot? And you (*To Clara*) how can you take love seriously if that's how you behave? Do you take anything seriously? Do you take yourself seriously?! How can you possibly keep your dignity if you play with your beliefs and opinions as if they were little schemes. Beauty! Love! Truth! Liberty! Liberalism, Humanism, Zionism ... you're great experts in self-deception, that's what you are! All of you! Not one of you is sincere, not one! (*Suddenly the spiritual energy which sustained him gives out. He leaves. The rest leave too*)

SCENE THREE

Otto's back in his room. He stands in front of a mirror and speaks to his reflection. His double appears briefly in the mirror.

OTTO. Flea! Cockroach! Once again you've made a mess with your preaching! And they ... dumb animals ... they should have stuffed your ... they should have locked you up somewhere to choke in your own stench! Mouse ... worm ... are you better than they? Who are you anyway?

(*Twisting his face*) Look, look! You are gazing into the emptiness in you ... into this nothingness, changing forms and masks. When you die, this nothingness will simply become nothing. No more posing. No more trying to pretend to be someone else, a kind of nothingness without trying to be one. The face of an adaptable Jew. Death is the exterior form that fits the emptiness in you. Who are you, Otto? Are you me? A different me? I'll be someone else. Someone completely different. So different I won't remember anymore who you were, and won't understand how you were once me ... how I was you ... one day I'll be so different that I'll look at myself and won't want to be another, and say to myself: stop! That's how I wanted — that's how I want to be! (*Poses, looks briefly at his reflection, spits on it, wipes it off, walks away*)

SCENE FOUR

Enter Berger. He visits Otto in his room.

BERGER. Otto, I want to talk to you about what happened at Tietz's ... I couldn't tell you there, but I feel it's important that you know: I really meant to go to Vienna and confront Karl Lueger's anti-Semitic hoodlums! It has nothing to do with Clara's schemes! Even if she hadn't asked me to help her get away from Tietz, I would have suggested that we go! In any event, I certainly would have gone. Otto, you're not the only person in the world who takes his convictions and opinions seriously. Other people too are prepared to sacrifice their lives for things they believe in! It's true, I'm not sure yet where I'm going ... for me, too, Judaism is a problem, not a solution ... believe me, it would have been much easier if I had been born a German. I know I'm not religious. I don't believe in the beyond and hereafter. The beyond and the hereafter are in our heads, too. But, if I decide that my path is Dr. Herzl's Zionism, I'll follow that path to the end with the same seriousness you'll follow yours!

OTTO. Tell me, Berger, what would you do if at this very

moment your double suddenly showed up here?

BERGER. What? ... Who? ...

OTTO. A person who knows everything about you, even things you never told anyone, things you'll never tell anyone.

BERGER. Do you mean a living person or just an idea?

OTTO. One who watches you when you talk, observes you from a certain point after your death ... what would you do if at this very moment he appeared as if out of the blue, stood before you and asked you to confront the most terrible things you've ever done in your life? Would you have the courage to follow him?

BERGER. And if I suffered from a sickness people tend to hide out of shame, would you advise me to see a doctor or to hide it and go on as if it never existed?

OTTO. Why do you ask me? You're no longer seeing Dr. Freud?

BERGER. Yes, I am. We're meeting tomorrow.

OTTO. Excellent! Excellent ... I'll give him my thesis on sexual attraction. I want him to read it.

BERGER. You finished it? When did we speak about Fliess's thesis? Maybe a month ago! You said then you had just started.

OTTO. I worked at it day and night.

BERGER. You really need a rest ...

OTTO. I must see Freud. You'll get me an appointment with him.

BERGER. Absolutely! (*Changing the tone*) Absolutely ...

OTTO. Well, then, what in your opinion is the disease that I'm hiding, a disease people are too ashamed to admit they have?

BERGER. You know which ...

OTTO. You think so? ... (*Berger vanishes in the dark*)

SCENE FIVE

Otto walks toward the back of the room, then to the mirror he had faced earlier. Otto's double bursts forth from behind the wall. He mimics Otto's movements as he walks about the room. Otto notices him momentarily, but ignores him like a shadow. This game is repeated a few times.

OTTO. To be different! Another! Another!

DOUBLE. Another! Another!

OTTO. Who are you?

DOUBLE. Who are you? "A bug ... a flea ... a mouse ... a worm ..."

OTTO. Big hero!

DOUBLE. Big hero!

OTTO. Let's see you stand before me!

DOUBLE. Let's see you stand before me! Why were you afraid to stand up to Berger?

OTTO. (*Mimicking him*) Why were you afraid to stand up to Berger?

DOUBLE. You can only repeat after me ...

OTTO. You can only repeat after me!

DOUBLE. So you went to your friends, told them a few petty lies, and already you're scared and run to me!

OTTO. You run to me!

DOUBLE. What will you do when Tietz comes, or Clara?

OTTO. What will you do when Tietz comes, or Clara?

DOUBLE. Every piece of truth that comes out of your mouth terrifies you to death? And you intend to be a prophet, a heralder, with so little courage?

OTTO. What do you want?

DOUBLE. What do you want! That's the question. That's a good start! Where average people remain silent and become partners in crime, you speak your mind. However, this is only the beginning. Now they're asking: Are these merely squeals, soon to turn into barks, or are these the first sounds of a roaring lion! Sounds that will terrify the foxes and the hyenas and send them running for their lives!

OTTO. Do you believe in me?

DOUBLE. Do you believe in me?

OTTO. What could I know?

DOUBLE. What could I know?

OTTO. What should I do?

DOUBLE. What should I do? (*The double starts the metronome on the piano and leaves*)

SCENE SIX

Clara comes in dancing. She makes the room into her own — a studio apartment. Otto stands still watching her. She suddenly discovers that he's there, and is surprised by his coming in unnoticed.

CLARA. Oh, Otto!

OTTO. Don't stop.

CLARA. It's too bad you didn't come with us to Rosenau's Tavern. You'd understand what's going on. You would have seen Professor Strasser, who dissects with such analytical talent the basics of Roman Law, sitting there surrounded by students, his face all red, choking with enthusiasm: "The Jewish Vampire is lurking outside the narrow windows of Germany's peasants and artisans."

OTTO. You're so beautiful!

CLARA. Sorry?

OTTO. Nothing. I was talking to myself.

CLARA. "We demand from the Parliament immediate legislation restricting the rights of the Jewish parasites exploiting our people! If we die fighting before we rid our country of these roaches, we are confident that avengers will rise up from our bones. To the oppressive, Semitic terrorists and their liberal cronies we must respond in the only language they understand: a tooth for a tooth, an eye for an eye."

OTTO. What do you want now?

CLARA. Attend student meetings and you'll know what's going on in Vienna. The Jewish elite live on Olympus. Yesterday in the tavern I overheard Stephan talking to Hugo: "This movement won't survive!" "Yes, no doubt a passing fad." (*Otto grabs her waist. She freezes; is silent. Both remain silent. Suddenly he lets go of her and walks away*)

OTTO. Go tell Berger about it ...

CLARA. What?

OTTO. Nothing! What's between Berger and you?

CLARA. Me and Berger? Otto ...

OTTO. Don't answer! Just pretend I said nothing.

CLARA. But Otto, you did ask ...

OTTO. I don't want to know!

CLARA. All right ...

OTTO. Using my poems!

CLARA. We thought you'd be happy ...

OTTO. "Otto's a little sad lately ..." "How do we cheer him up?"

CLARA. A person's allowed to be sad, no?

OTTO. I'm not "sad!"

CLARA. Why are you torturing yourself? Let's go and have a glass of wine!

OTTO. They'll make me a Viennese song writer!

CLARA. If you don't want to ...

OTTO. No! I don't want to!

CLARA. You're angry at yourself.

OTTO. Yes!

CLARA. Is it because of my strange behavior at Tietz's?

OTTO. God, no! (*She walks toward him*) Don't come near me! I don't want pity!

CLARA. I'm fed up!

OTTO. So am I.

CLARA. I'm fed up with this life.

OTTO. What life?

CLARA. They hate us here. If we stay ...

OTTO. Who is "we"?

CLARA. We, the Jews.

OTTO. I'm not a Jew.

CLARA. A Jew, just like me.

OTTO. I'll decide who I want to be.

CLARA. Better listen to handsome Karl: "I'll decide who's Jewish and who's not."

OTTO. I don't give a damn about Karl Lueger and his anti-Semites! Which, by the way, is a typical Jewish trait.

CLARA. He doesn't give a damn about you either, but he's more powerful than you are.

OTTO. What is a Jew? What does it mean to be Jewish? Being part of the Jewish faith and observing the Commandments? If so, I'm not Jewish. Is it being part of the Jewish family tradition? Is it celebrating the holidays? If so, I'm not Jewish!

CLARA. Come with me, Otto!

OTTO. Where?

CLARA. If we continue to swallow this hatred, we'll just end up hating ourselves.

OTTO. Whom are you quoting now?

CLARA. You're not listening to me. You don't understand me. You don't want to understand.

OTTO. What's the point? Anyway, I can't stand myself.

CLARA. Come with me!

OTTO. Where? Where?

CLARA. Join the Zionists.

OTTO. Isn't Berger enough for you?

CLARA. Berger again! Forget Berger. I'm talking about you, Otto!

OTTO. I see you're trying to keep your options open: if not one, then the other . . .

CLARA. Why don't I have the strength to go alone? . . . I want to leave this place so much.

OTTO. Zionism doesn't stand a chance.

CLARA. This world, Otto, is about to collapse on top of us. We must abandon Vienna. We must leave Europe behind us . . . leave this world before it's in ruins.

OTTO. Clara, you must understand: Judaism is the abyss, the gaping abyss inside the Jewish soul. And this abyss will swallow anything we try to build on it.

CLARA. What Judaism, what . . . I feel terrible. I feel terrible here in Vienna. I feel terrible around the anti-Semites on campus, around this false culture so elegantly hiding the truth, around my friends who live in a fool's paradise! Yes, Otto, I feel terrible! Come with me! I know you want to! Both of us want to! So why fight it? Come, let's go! (*She touches him. He's excited and confused. He embraces her. He suddenly screams, pushes her off and walks away*)

CLARA. What happened to you?

OTTO. A pig . . . I'm a pig . . .

CLARA. Otto?

OTTO. Must you awaken the beast in me? Is this how you get satisfaction? Now you'll run to tell your girlfriends that Otto is a beast just like Berger and Tietz, right?

CLARA. You find me that repulsive? Why is that?

OTTO. It's not your fault, actually; it's the woman in you

trying desperately to attain happiness.

CLARA. So that's my defect? Is that a sin?

OTTO. "Come with me, come with me!" Why this need for other people? You're looking for salvation, that's what you're looking for.

CLARA. We could love each other. We could fill a whole lifetime with our love. Otto ... I love you!

OTTO. Don't say that word! "Love." Say "murder!" And if murder, then by knife!

CLARA. I don't understand you.

OTTO. How could you? The need for salvation is immoral, understand? You won't drag me into the abyss! All I need now is a mix of Jewishness and femininity!

CLARA. Even Tietz can't understand your ideas on the Aryan spirit.

OTTO. Even Tietz! How could a liberal like him, his brains softened by alcohol, grasp the tremendous powers awakening within the Aryan soul?

CLARA. He's Aryan, isn't he? Or is something wrong with him, too?

OTTO. Maybe he's good in bed, you certainly know that better than I.

CLARA. I don't, all right?

OTTO. I'm not interested.

CLARA. You're mistaken, totally mistaken.

OTTO. I don't want to know if you're sleeping with him or not.

CLARA. I'm not talking about Tietz or about sex, if that's all you can think about when you're with me. "The Aryan spirit." Another thing you know nothing about. Or about me.

OTTO. Of course, you know. Going to taverns and listening to some drunken students cursing Jews you think you know something about the German spirit!

CLARA. Nietzsche said: "The Germans are responsible for everything that exists now—the sickliness and stupidity that oppose culture, in the name of the neurosis called nationalism, a mental disease from which Europe suffers; they have robbed Europe itself of its true meaning and its intelligence. They have led it into a blind alley." End of quotation. And rest assured, I never slept with Friedrich Nietzsche either!

OTTO. Quotations and more quotations! All you have is quotations! A receptacle, that's what you are ... from the womb to the soul. A receptacle capable of absorbing only what men excrete. The mere thought that you could pull me into the mire these excretions have left inside you disgusts me!

CLARA. I can't believe it ... can't believe it! Otto, you can take away everything from me, your face, your body, but you can't take away this longing for intimacy, the hope you brought when you came to me filled with love. Otto, what's happening to us?

OTTO. You're asking me to deny myself, to neglect my responsibilities toward myself and run with you to your strange land, to seek salvation. This is cowardice. Weakness. Evasiveness. This is impossible! Don't look at me like that! I'm sure all you're thinking about is how to seduce me. Now don't lower your eyes! I'm talking to you. Don't play the modest innocent with me, because it's false. Your feminine tricks don't impress me at all. You talk to me about Zionism because you know I consider Zionism to be the last remnant of nobility that's still left in Judaism. So all this talk is merely meant to ensnare me. No chance! You'll give up Vienna? You're only scheming how to dominate me and drain me! You'll never go to Asia, and the Jewish nation won't go with you either.

CLARA. I will go. And the Jewish nation will, too. You shouldn't hide behind excuses. Be frank and tell me what you have against me. I can handle it.

OTTO. Yes? You'll seduce them?

CLARA. Seduce whom?

OTTO. The Jewish nation you plan to drag with you. Why should they go?

CLARA. Otto, I know what's troubling you. You feel guilty. Just like Berger and me.

OTTO. Don't compare me with you two! What do you know of my guilt?

CLARA. All Jews are guilty for the way they live. You too!

There's only one way to get rid of this guilt ... we must return to the place where we sinned against ourselves, where the greatest guilt originated. There we could live in a way totally different from that which brought destruction and ruin on our heads.

OTTO. Jews acting out of a sense of guilt? A Jew never admits guilt. A Jew only wants to blame it on others. If Jews had any sense of guilt they would have left exile long ago, during the Second Temple when they had a country of their own. But the Jew prefers to live in exile because exile is his natural habitat, he chooses it voluntarily.

CLARA. This will change.

OTTO. Nothing will change!

CLARA. Zionism will create a new Jew.

OTTO. Nonsense! Zionism too will sink in the Jewish abyss like a stone in a swamp. "A new Jew ..." character is fixed, it's unalterable! The Jew believes in nothing: himself, guilt, true penance, nothing. Jews always look at the pocket, at what brings them material gains. Judaism served its purpose two thousand years ago, when it gave birth to Christianity, a force that somehow managed to overcome the abyss underneath it. Since that time Judaism has had no more messages to the world. I agree with Dr. Herzl on one point: One bright, sunny day, the sun at its zenith, Jews should get up and march in line to Church and convert.

CLARA. Why don't you do it, if you believe in it?

OTTO. I'll do it. I'm converting.

CLARA. You're not because you know how meaningless such an act is to people like us. Besides, if character is fixed and unalterable, Christianity won't change you a bit. You'll still be the same person!

OTTO. I'll convert, but you, you'll never go to Eretz Israel. We'll see then who's willing to pay the full price for his convictions and who's only engaging in empty gossip.

CLARA. We'll see! (*She starts to leave*)

OTTO. Clara! ...

CLARA. (*Stops; walks towards him*) I'll wait for you.

OTTO. Go out and dance! (*Clara leaves*)

SCENE SEVEN

The stage becomes a house of prostitution, a Viennese cabaretlike performance in progress. Enter Otto's double accompanied by dance music. He urges the audience to enjoy themselves. Cabaret performers present a medley of vignettes without words. The show depicts absurd scenes of temptation and seduction. Otto's double leads the performance while singing a profane version of a prayer.

DOUBLE. My Lord, God of this, the most
Jewish, Feminine age.
Blessed and hallowed be Thy name.
Eternal provider of copulation.
My Lord, God of copulation,
Fortify my spirit in copulation.
Give me vigor in copulation.
Bless my deeds in copulation.
God, oh merciful God,
Devise the right position.
God full of copulation,
Fill with copulation,
Our spiritual void.

(*Continues to accompany himself while speaking to the public*) The author of this prayer is a contemporary of ours, one who raised sex to heights of sacred ritual, not in order to lose himself in it like a Greek or Roman bacchanal, but to find himself through bodily excretions ... as our distinguished guest Otto Weininger put it! (*While the double continues to sing, a young prostitute undresses Otto, notices he's circumcised*)

PROSTITUTE. (*Shouts at an older prostitute*) What's this?! Lotte! What is this?

LOTTE. Can't you see? He's Jewish. (*Looks at him*) A Jewish boy!

PROSTITUTE. Does it look like that from birth?

LOTTE. They cut it.

PROSTITUTE. Poor creature! It's so completely naked, nothing to protect it.

LOTTE. Go away, you idiot. You want to ruin his life forever? Come here, my Jewish boy, don't mind her, she's a stupid peasant. Come here, my boy. (*She fondles him, while another prostitute does the same to his father, Leopold, who is a guest there as well. While being fondled they converse, pretending they are sitting in some high-class drawing room or a coffee house*)

LEOPOLD. Otto!

OTTO. Yes, father.

LEOPOLD. I hope you've decided to do it.

OTTO. What?

LEOPOLD. The Consular Academy for Languages.

OTTO. No, father. I have decided to study at the University of Vienna.

LEOPOLD. We're not rich, you know. As a correspondent in foreign languages, you could support yourself. I started my career like this too. And, if you're successful, you can become a diplomat.

OTTO. I'm not interested in the Consular Academy, in a career in foreign languages or in the diplomatic corps. I'm enrolling at the University of Vienna. I want to study philosophy.

LEOPOLD. So why did I teach you seven languages?

OTTO. Must everything have a purpose?

LEOPOLD. You can't make a living from philosophy.

OTTO. I'll give private lessons in Latin and Greek.

LEOPOLD. Jewish teachers are not very popular these days.

OTTO. If that's true then I have another good reason to convert.

LEOPOLD. Not a bad idea, from a practical point of view!

OTTO. Money! You see everything from a Jewish point of view.

LEOPOLD. I see everything from a Jewish point of view? Me?

OTTO. You! You! (*Leopold hums a tune from Wagner's Meistersinger while staring at Otto*) Religion was only intended to make life easier! A solution to every problem! An escape when you're in trouble! Only Judaism could come up with such a utilitarian, practical attitude to religion! (*Reacting to his father's singing*) You're distorting Wagner's sound! It's not like that, it's like this. (*Sings more dramatically*)

LEOPOLD. You could sing it either way, it's a matter of interpretation.

OTTO. You're softening, dissolving the form. You're ruining the German in it with your Jewishness. Wagner conquered this Jewishness.

LEOPOLD. What do Jewish and Germanic have to do with it? Otto, this is music. Pure art! Universal art!

OTTO. What do you mean by pure art? What is pure art?

LEOPOLD. Otto, not everything must be put in words. You should allow the beautiful moments in life to be as they are, let them be!

OTTO. Feminine romanticism!

LEOPOLD. Listen, Otto, I happen to have a client who's a Russian prince, a collector of precious objects, a man with very refined tastes. I asked him once why he loved my jewels so much. He answered with a popular Russian saying: "A song needs beauty, but beauty doesn't need the song ..."

OTTO. This folk saying really explains Wagner!

LEOPOLD. Wagner doesn't need explaining. Wagner is simply a genius.

OTTO. "Genius, genius!" You completely melt when you speak about him. The woman in you takes control ... you're like a woman!

LEOPOLD. Oh, yes? You still have a lot to learn about women ...

OTTO. There's nothing for me to learn! I know everything!

LEOPOLD. Of course, a lady's man like you ...

OTTO. A genius doesn't need experience. A genius has within him all of humanity. And if you want to know, I'll tell you the secret of Wagner's genius. The secret is that two of life's fiercest rivals, Judaism and Aryanism, waged a mortal battle inside his soul. This is the reason he was able to give the German spirit such a lofty and unique expression in history, why his works are so beautiful and rich!

LEOPOLD. Otto, you have too many theories! (*The two recite in unison*) "Theories are gray, only the evergreen tree of life is forever green." (*Leopold alone*) It's exactly like that, Otto!

OTTO. I've heard this before ... how many more times will I have to hear this quotation! People should be ashamed of repeating the same thing twice! It's immoral!

LEOPOLD. Morality?! Watch what you're saying: "One doesn't

tell modest ears things the modest must do." God, I can see myself in you, Otto ... live, Otto, live!

OTTO. Despite everything you're a Jew! (*Leopold turns away and starts to leave*) Only a Jew can mix everything up so badly! Only Jews! (*Adelheid, his mother, appears from among the prostitutes*)

ADELHEID. Otto?

OTTO. Only Jews!

ADELHEID. Otto, my Ottoleh! (*The prostitutes leave, the cabaret vanishes. Leopold picks up his suitcases and rushes out while Otto runs in an opposite direction, remains hidden in a corner*)

SCENE EIGHT

The stage becomes the home of Otto's parents. Adelheid paces back and forth, talking to the walls while Otto remains hidden in his corner.

ADELHEID. Otto, must you speak to your father like this? Is this what he deserves? Is this how you show your gratitude for all he's done for you? I remember you as a baby playing on the floor, and your father would come to you and say, "Little Ottoleh, listen!" and sing the *Meistersinger.* (*She hums a few notes, a bad cough interrupts her. She recovers, goes on*) I can see him reading to you in Latin from Terence, you repeating after him, your baby voice still ringing in my ears: "Homo sum, humani nihil, a me alienum puto ..." (*Chokes again*)

OTTO. Enough, mother, you must relax.

ADELHEID. (*Dismissing it, goes on*) Thanks to him you were always ahead of your class ... even your teachers had a hard time keeping up with you ... so why do you treat him like this? Answer me, Otto! (*He's silent*) I know why, I know you even better than you do. I've known you since you were born, even before that. Deep down, you're a good soul, Otto. Deep down, you're sorry and wish you never said these things, right? You don't have to say a word. I can see every change inside your soul. I even know things you don't know yourself. Remember the time, when you were a child, you saw me hand the butcher a chicken to be slaughtered, and before you knew what was happening, the knife had slashed the chicken's neck and the blood gushed out ... you ran home and cried bitterly for hours. You refused any comfort ... you didn't eat meat for months ... you see, you're not an extremist, after all; you're not stubborn ... so why this stubbornness when you know that your father's right? I'm not asking this for myself. I'm not important. But your father, that's a different matter altogether. He's a very proud and stubborn man. Be a good son. Let him have his way. Deep down you've already given up anyway. It makes no difference to you if you study at the University or at the Consular Academy for Languages ... anyway, deep down, you're already sorry for being so harsh! After all, you and I, we are made of the same stuff ... must you imitate your father's cruel stubbornness? You know how important it is for him that you go to the Consular Academy. So why are you hurting him? Go to him. He's waiting in the other room. I know he's anxious to see you. Open the door, and you'll see how his face will light up. Why not make someone you love happy, especially if it requires such a small effort? After all, deep down, you want to please him ... I know you ... there's no greater pleasure in the world than pleasing father ... so go and tell him! Father, I decided to join the Consular Academy ... do it, Otto. Believe me, you won't regret it. Otto, go ... I know it's hard for you to admit you've made a mistake because you're like your father. You're both stubborn ... well, it doesn't matter. Forget it. That's why I'm here, no? I'll do it for you. (*She goes to the door but a bad cough makes her bend over. She knocks*) Leopold! Leopold! Open up, Leopold! (*Waits, no reaction*) All right! So don't open, Leopold! I know that afterwards you'll be sorry ... at least let me know you can hear me, Leopold. (*Otto covers his ears*) Otto wants to tell you he's sorry ... he asks forgiveness. He's decided to join the Consular Academy, you hear, Leopold?

OTTO. Enough! Enough!

ADELHEID. You men are like children. Leopold! Your father's not an easy man. My whole life I cooked, cleaned, ironed, and scrubbed for you and this is my reward?

OTTO. Everybody's to blame ...

ADELHEID. Who's blaming? Am I blaming anyone? I accept my lot without saying a word. I was gifted in languages, just ask your father. You inherited your linguistic talents directly from me. I could have been a bilingual secretary if I hadn't had to raise seven children. I gave up many things ... I have my rewards — a warm family ...

OTTO. Tension ... Quarrels ...

ADELHEID. There are always some disagreements between husband and wife. The rewards make it worthwhile. I admired your father all my life. The first time we met I knew he was my shining comet, my idol! How he lifted me up! He introduced me to opera, classical music, the theatre ... but what a price we paid for this. Just look at this place. Every time my in-laws bought a rug, a dining set, clothes, I'd say to Leopold: material things are not important to me. (*Shouts in the direction of the locked door*) Leopold, tell me if I'm lying! I always said, Leopold, take the few pennies we have and go to Bayreuth to watch Wagner operas. (*To Otto*) You were only six when he took you to see Weber's *Freischutz*. At eight you went to see Wagner's *Meistersinger*. (*Talks in the direction of the door*) I was so happy to see you returning from Bayreuth! I could see the joy on your face! It really lit up my life!

OTTO. (*Bursts in*) You're talking to the walls!

ADELHEID. (*Breaks down, cries*) What else was there for me in life ... what ... what thrills. What relief ... while other women bought fur coats, I kept patching up my old coat so he could buy books, sheet music, complete scores. We always saved up for the next trip to Bayreuth. (*Deep sigh*) And what do I get? Arrogance, impudence, blatant scorn ...

OTTO. (*Shouts at the door*) Sadist, answer her! Stop torturing her!

ADELHEID. How dare you talk like that! He's your father! Leopold! Leopold! (*To Otto*) He locked himself in there and won't come out for two days. He's punishing me.

Why? Because you defy him, because you don't obey him like a lap dog. Adelheid, you deserve it! Stupid one! You spent your life without a decent skirt so he could go to Bayreuth! He had to go! He needed Wagner's music! (*Shouts at the door*) If we had been Aryans from birth— Austrian or German, in our position, in our poor economic situation, you would never even have thought of going to Bayreuth. I know, you're taking revenge on me, the children, and on your being born Jewish! You went to the concerts so you could brag to your Aryan friends: "I went to Bayreuth," "I saw Wagner . . ." In fact you were saying: "You see, I'm more German than you are!"

OTTO. Mother, that's a lie! If there's anything he loves in this world it's Wagner's music!

ADELHEID. (*Whispers to Otto*) I'm only kidding him. I only want to infuriate him, to make him talk! (*Shouts at the door*) Deep in your heart you hate Wagner, you only like to torture yourself and us with this ugly lie of yours. (*Bangs on the door with her fists*) Leopold, come out, come out, out, out! (*Turns to Otto*) Please Otto, do me a favor, go talk to him, if not for his sake then for mine. He could stay there for a whole week and say nothing, just to torture me! Otto!

OTTO. It's better not to be born at all than to come into the world as some fruit of repressed sexual nausea. (*She leaves through one of the revolving doors. Otto goes to his meeting with Freud. On his way he meets his double*)

DOUBLE. (*Crosses his path*) If man didn't get lost at birth, he wouldn't need all his life to look for himself . . . (*Otto walks away*)

SCENE NINE

Berger enters and meets Otto.

BERGER. Otto, listen to me, forget Freud.

OTTO. Did you give him my thesis?

BERGER. I did. Don't go to him!

OTTO. Did he say anything about it?

BERGER. No, except, "I read your friend's paper."

OTTO. That's all?

BERGER. He added, "Interesting . . ." Otto, forget it, don't go!

OTTO. You got me an appointment with him, didn't you?

BERGER. I did. But Dr. Freud is a busy man. He'll be glad to cancel it. I'll tell him you got sick and I'll bring back your manuscript.

OTTO. (*Grabs Berger's arms*) Berger, don't lie! Did Freud tell you what he thought of the paper? (*Shakes him. Berger is silent*) Berger . . .

BERGER. Perhaps there was something ironic in his voice when he said "interesting."

OTTO. Something ironic . . .

BERGER. He said "interesting" twice . . .

OTTO. Twice? How exactly?

BERGER. (*Imitating Freud*) "Interesting . . . interesting . . ."

OTTO. Like that exactly?

BERGER. I'm not quite sure . . . anyway, the first time he said interesting, but the second time, it seemed he objected to it, had some reservations about it . . . maybe he scoffed at it, contradicted it, or, on the contrary, reinforced it!

OTTO. Did he object, scoff, or reinforce?

BERGER. What do you want from me? He said twice, "interesting." If you want my advice, you'll cancel this meeting.

OTTO. A typical Jewish trait — say everything twice: once white, once black. This is what I learned from my mother's family: when you say something, make sure you say it so that you can't be held responsible for your words. I must see him now . . . I must . . . (*Otto leaves Berger*)

SCENE TEN

Otto walks toward his double, who gets off the sofa and comes to greet him.

DOUBLE. Why so late?

OTTO. What are you doing here?

DOUBLE. You didn't notice but I was following you in the street. I passed by as you stopped to talk to yourself.

OTTO. I talked to Berger. (*The double bursts out laughing*) I talked to Berger.

DOUBLE. You'd better pay attention to yourself: you walk around talking to yourself and think you're talking to people. Anyway, I've been waiting a quarter of an hour already. A little nervous before the meeting?

OTTO. I need to concentrate!

DOUBLE. After all, Freud is not just anyone . . .

OTTO. Freud is not just anyone . . .

DOUBLE. Otto, it's beginning to look like a war! The question is who represents the spirit of the twentieth century, you or he? There's no room for both of you.

OTTO. I'm not competing with him.

DOUBLE. Oh, yes you are: a life and death competition. (*The double walks over to a pile of books on the floor, picks up one book at a time, shows it to Otto*) Did you see his library? Huge! And all the books about you! Look! *Otto Weininger — The Prophet of the Masculine Age* (London: 1905); *Weininger and the Copernican Revolution in Psychology* (Stockholm: 1930); *Otto Weininger — Liberator of the World from Jewish and Feminine Rule* (Berlin: 1945); *Moses, Jesus, and Otto* (Rome: 2040); *Otto — A Thousand Years of his Birth* (Paris: Theological-Scientific Symposium, 2880). They're all about you, Otto! Not one on Dr. Sigmund Freud . . . he's livid. He doesn't show it but he's livid. You'll see, he'll try to get you to lie on his couch. (*Lies on it, demonstrates the procedure*) He'll dig up secrets from your childhood.

OTTO. I'll tell him only what I want to!

DOUBLE. I trust Otto. (*They sing and dance to a German nursery song*)

> Aya, papaya, was raschelt im
> Stroh?
> Die Gänschen gehen barfuss
> Sie haben kein Schuh.
> Der Schuster hat leider kein Leder
> dazu
> Darum gehen die Gänschen
> barfuss,
> Sie haben kein Schuh . . .

SCENE ELEVEN

Suddenly, Freud appears behind Otto's back, surprising him.

FREUD. Otto Weininger? (*Otto turns around. Freud wants to shake hands. At this moment the double sneaks out*) Sigmund Freud. How old are you?

OTTO. Twenty-one.

FREUD. And you know Latin, Greek, English, Italian . . .

OTTO. Also French, Spanish, Norwegian . . .

FREUD. You learned them at home?

OTTO. From my father.

FREUD. Is he a professor of classical and modern languages?

OTTO. He's a goldsmith.

FREUD. A craftsman.

OTTO. (*Corrects him*) An artist. A master. One of Vienna's last great masters of this rare and noble art. (*Reacting to Freud's skeptical smile and amused grin*) The day will come when he'll be known even outside the Austro-Hungarian Empire, I'm sure of that!

FREUD. So, your father's a craftsman, what else?

OTTO. A refined, sensitive musician.

FREUD. Composer or conductor?

OTTO. My father's a devoted fan of Richard Wagner!

FREUD. Aha . . . he likes music . . .

OTTO. He goes often to Bayreuth to see Wagner's operas!

FREUD. (*Points to the manuscript*) Has he read your thesis?

OTTO. Oh, no! You're the first. (*Reacting to Freud's astonishment*) I like him, I admire him a lot, but he's very strict and uncompromising . . . he frightens us . . . I mean his children . . . even Franz-Richard.

FREUD. Who is Franz-Richard?

OTTO. My brother.

FREUD. Why "even . . ."?

OTTO. He's different.

FREUD. Different from whom?

OTTO. From me! From all of us.

FREUD. How so?

OTTO. He lives like all young people today: an epicurean . . . a carouser . . . a pleasure seeker.

FREUD. Likes women?

OTTO. He does. Very much. He's a dandy. Spends hours before the mirror before going out, loves to be adored. And how he comes home at night whistling those Strauss waltzes, Johann that is, right away, totally satisfied ... Franz is frivolous, full of self-love. He'll never amount to anything ...

FREUD. And your father lets him deteriorate like this without saying anything?

OTTO. My father can be a strict disciplinarian and a very harsh critic ...

FREUD. Then how is it that he failed to educate him?

OTTO. He never admits failure! We two argued about this for years.

FREUD. Franz-Richard is younger than you.

OTTO. Of course! The problem is that my father, the harsh judge, can unfortunately become a divinely generous man.

FREUD. Why "unfortunately"?

OTTO. Yes! There's something about Franz-Richard that softens him. It's his charm ... there's something feminine about Franz. His smile alone can disarm my father in an instant.

FREUD. How old is he?

OTTO. Twenty. A year younger than I.

FREUD. No, no, your father ...

OTTO. Aha ... My father is forty-seven.

FREUD. Two years older than I. And your mother?

OTTO. (*Shows sudden frankness*) She always looked younger than her age, although in spirit ...

FREUD. No, I'm asking if she read it — (*Waves the manuscript again*)

OTTO. No, not mother ... (*Tries quickly to correct his inadvertent slip*) My mother, she's a simple woman. (*Correction upon correction*) A good woman! But she's a housewife. (*Correction upon damage*) Mother is mother! (*Apologizes for the pathos*) She had to raise seven children. Had no time to develop ... she's very talented ... but ... didn't have the time ...

FREUD. (*Leafs through the manuscript*) So, you chose me to be your first reader.

OTTO. Yes, I've read everything you've written.

FREUD. You mean everything I've published.

OTTO. Yes, of course.

FREUD. Not everything I write do I rush out and publish. There are many things on my desk ... in the process of being carefully analyzed, revised, and rewritten. Unfortunately, I'm not very quick with the pen ... it takes me a while to formulate a sentence more or less the way I like it.

OTTO. I can see that from your style.

FREUD. Honestly, what is your opinion of my style?

OTTO. I can't answer that. I would have to reread everything more carefully.

FREUD. No, no, I mean generally speaking ... just tell me the most obvious faults that come to your mind.

OTTO. With your permission, a few critical comments on the style ...

FREUD. Shoot, young man. Go ahead, open fire! (*He lies down on the couch*) I hope you don't mind if I lie down a little ...

OTTO. Sir, your style ...

FREUD. Please address me as you would a friend, your friend, Berger, for example.

OTTO. Your style is a little heavy ... awkward ... the sentences are ... too long-winded. They don't aim directly at the target. Sometimes I read a sentence two or three times before I get your meaning: some sentences are weak and even contradictory ... as if you tried to say something and refuted it in the same breath. I think I know the root of the problem ... your thought processes are influenced by your ethnic mentality ... it's an influence you're not even aware of ... I'm talking about the spirit of Judaism ... it's the Jew's failure to believe in anything ... the failure to see value in anything that is not material ... the need and urge to nip everything spiritual in the bud.

FREUD. Go on! I'm not sleeping. I concentrate better with my eyes shut. Interesting ... interesting! ...

OTTO. Today you hold an important and distinguished position among Vienna's pioneers in psychological research.

FREUD. No need to exaggerate: I'm not a professor yet ...

OTTO. Everybody knows you're not promoted because of intrigues. I feel compelled to tell you something ... but maybe this is too much ... I don't have my doctoral degree yet.

FREUD. Don't worry, this thesis will get you your degree.

OTTO. Also, I must tell you ... that in my opinion you're on the wrong track ... because of the Jewish influence ... but now I'm taking too many liberties ... after all, you could be my father.

FREUD. God forbid! Young man! As Chesterton once said, a thought not turned into words is a bad thought. Also, admirers and flatterers are a creative person's greatest enemies.

OTTO. Above all, Judaism views science as a means for achieving material gains.

FREUD. You mean to say that Judaism views science as something that must be useful and practical?

OTTO. Judaism wants to shove aside, to purify science from everything transcendental and intangible ... it wants to grasp things simply, mechanically, as if to annoy on purpose. To the Aryan spirit this is complete disrespect for the world's value ... the Aryan knows that it is precisely the wonderful and the noble, which cannot be grasped and studied, that endow existence with value and meaning. Since Appius, the Jew has shown disrespect and indifference to life's mysteries: he simply doesn't feel their presence. The Jewish spirit only wants to prove the miserable simplicity and weak probability of everyday experience. Like in the marketplace, where he elbows his way through the crowd, so too in the spiritual world, he shoves aside anything that interferes with his free movement ... that's why your psychoanalysis is a Jewish science because you made psychology into an empirical science, which means you turned it into Jewish science!

FREUD. If I'm not mistaken, empiricism comes from England.

OTTO. The English and the Jews have a lot in common! You can't build a deep psychology by ignoring concepts of good and evil; your psychology doesn't believe in guilt, only in guilt feelings. Man is therefore never really guilty —

he merely suffers from guilt feelings others planted in him to control him more easily. All your therapy does is help me discover who planted them in me, so I can turn around and lay the blame on him! If it's my father, my father is guilty, if it's God, God is guilty! And I, I'm forever innocent!

FREUD. Why can't you accept this situation?

OTTO. Because you leave no room for penance! Tell me, what's left of man's soul if you eliminate the possibility of doing evil and of guilt? You make it impossible to repent over a truly bad deed and revert to being good again. This psychology has no spirit, no soul!

FREUD. Let's assume you're right! But why is this science necessarily a Jewish science?

OTTO. Pure goodness and pure evil are foreign to the Jewish spirit just as they are to a woman. A woman lacks soul and moral standards because, to her, sexual pleasures are the ultimate value in life. Judaism is trying to impose its feminine spirit on western culture by destroying the Aryan spirit from within! After all, what is modern culture and the spirit of our times? Sanctification of sexual pleasure!

FREUD. This anti-Jewish chapter didn't appear in your article ...

OTTO. No. I developed it after the article came out.

FREUD. Too bad ... these days, when Karl Lueger's anti-Semitic party is gaining support — and not just among the riffraff, but also among Vienna's university teachers and students, a chapter like this could draw strong academic interest.

OTTO. The Jewish chapter will be included in a more extensive book, on which I am presently working.

FREUD. Don't you think your book will only deepen the hatred between Jews and Gentiles and add to the misery on both sides?

OTTO. I'm only interested in the truth!

FREUD. (*Gets up*) Listen Otto ... your comments on my style are indeed to the point ... as you noted, I say something, then right away I retreat from it, which makes my writing convoluted and difficult to comprehend. But a rabbi once told me: the moment you discover the truth, you've already lost it, so don't rejoice, but look for it somewhere else, in dark places ...

OTTO. That's exactly it — the Jewish sickness!

FREUD. (*Shouting*) No! (*Banging on the table*) This is its healthy side. The theory of incarnation is wrong. Truth is never incarnated, whether in life or in a sentence. You know what's scientific? That which can be refuted the next day. That which can't be refuted has no scientific value. I'll be frank with you now. Had I been a Christian, I would have felt compelled out of compassion and mercy to say to you: Otto, there's a lot of talent in you, even a spark of genius, continue on the path you've chosen and you'll go far. But we are Jews and will remain Jews. The world will continue to use us without understanding us, without respecting us, and they'll use you too. But let's get back to our business: sympathy in my eyes is not the highest value; seeking the truth is. In Berlin lives a hard-working, decent man named Fliess. He shared with me some of his thoughts about his work. In my innocence I spoke about it to Berger, a young patient of mine. I believe he's your friend. And Berger, in his innocence, told you about Fliess and his research. If I chose to use concepts of good and evil and guilt, concepts you so firmly believe in, I would have to say to you (*In an outburst, screaming*) Otto, you're a thief! All the ideas you so brilliantly developed in your paper were stolen from Fliess! You stole a key and broke into the treasure vault of the scientific world. Now that you're inside you don't know what to do, so you roam around like a wild, ignorant bandit in a room full of precious objects. You grab whatever tickles your fancy, and the rest you trample on, break, shatter! Get out! ... Otto, get out of this garden, it's not for you, or people like you! (*He switches abruptly to a quiet, rational tone*) I can see you abhor femininity and Judaism. Why precisely these two things? What do they have in common? Why are you so troubled by them? I can see that sex disgusts you. I wonder what the connection is between this and your attitude towards femininity and Judaism. Ask yourself this question. If you want, I'd be willing to see you again and talk about it.

OTTO. (*Shaking with anger*) If they remember you in a thousand years, it'll only be thanks to this conversation, if I ever bother to mark it in my diary.

FREUD. Why did you come to me first? After all, you knew that besides Berger I was the only one who knew from whom you stole your theory of bisexuality and how it came into your possession. So why did you come to me first? (*Freud departs*)

SCENE TWELVE

The double accosts Otto.

DOUBLE. You really gave him a beating! He was stunned! Speechless! One exception: why did you say that a thousand years from now he'll be remembered only thanks to this meeting?

OTTO. It's the truth. That's what will happen!

DOUBLE. These are your words . . . people shouldn't confuse imagination and wishful thinking with reality . . .

OTTO. Is he crazy? I assume full responsibility! If I go mad, it's because I deserve it. One should blame no one but himself if he goes mad!

DOUBLE. They say history will remember you, too. And it has nothing to do with anyone else. After all, it could happen to Freud, too, regardless of you.

OTTO. No! I'll show the world his true face, that he's actually dealing with stereotypes, that he's a shallow and superficial psychologist! Not at all a genius! I'll destroy him! I'll erase him from the memory of mankind. I'll alert the Aryan soul against the threat of Jewish spirit, the castration of Aryan masculinity and its dominance by Jewish femininity from within.

DOUBLE. I think you're taking on too much. Will you be able to carry this load all by yourself?

Otto looks at the double with apprehension. The double begins to hum "Aya-Papaya." Suddenly Otto collapses and falls into his arms. The double tries to calm him down. He caresses him, rocks him to no avail. Hums "Aya-Papaya" in his ears in a merrier tone.

This only makes him cry harder. He rolls on the floor. The double crouches over him, raises his head to the audience and motions with his arms as if to say, "I'm helpless," or "What can be done with him?" The scene freezes briefly, then darkness.

act 2

SCENE ONE

Otto's alone in the room. Enter Clara in a glittering evening dress. She tells him a story; the events described unfold before Otto's eyes as characters enter and exit accordingly.

CLARA. Yesterday, as I left the theatre to go home, Tietz suddenly came up to me. "I have a great Parma ham and Saint-Emillion wine." (*While she speaks, Tietz tries to seduce her*) I was too tired to put up a fight. Earlier Berger and I argued and shouted at each other for hours. (*Enter Berger. Tietz continues to fondle her. Berger and Clara argue*)

BERGER. (*Waving a newspaper*) I'm a Zionist like you are but there's a limit! I can't agree with this! Listen to what Theodor Herzl writes here: "You say that if the Jews prepared a mass exit from Europe this might provoke acts of violence and riots against them. This only proves that I was right all along! If this thing alone can raise the Jewish question and turn it into a burning one, then it is a potent means which, despite some of its ugly aspects, I'm willing to use." (*Stops reading*) You understand? He's actually hoping for a wave of anti-Semitism in Europe to raise Jewish consciousness and strengthen the Zionist cause!

CLARA. What else can he do against the apathy and animosity of the Jewish middle class?

BERGER. This means that Karl Lueger and his anti-Semites are Herzl's and the Zionists' best allies! They need the Jews just as much as the Jews need them?!

CLARA. Since I talked to you about emigrating to Palestine, you've been searching for excuses to quit the Zionist movement.

BERGER. I'm sorry, there's a limit! I won't accept this! It's Machiavellian!

CLARA. The only important question is whether liberal Europe is collapsing, yes or no! If it is, then we must rescue the Jews before the disaster occurs, and any means to do this is welcome and justified!

BERGER. Enough! Let's not argue anymore. All we do lately is argue ... (*He embraces her, tries to kiss her, while Tietz fondles her from the back. She pushes Berger away*)

CLARA. Leave me alone! I'm not in the mood now! (*Still pushing him off, then pushing Tietz away. The latter finds himself on the floor, staring at her*) That's what I said to Berger. We quarreled about it and went our separate ways. Then on my way to the theatre, I met Tietz. (*Tietz gets up, fondles her*) After a glass or two and a Parma ham sandwich he simply tried to get me to go to bed with him while I'm in the middle of telling him about my argument with Berger. I told him: "Tietz, stop it! I don't need you right now for sex."

TIETZ. But you came up to my room!

CLARA. I just wanted to talk to you! To unburden myself!

TIETZ. All right then, unburden yourself ... (*Tietz tries again to undress her*)

CLARA. Berger suddenly has doubts about Zionism because of something Herzl wrote in the paper ... he postponed his departure to Eretz Israel ... Tietz, stop it! I told you I'm not in the mood now!

TIETZ. (*Finally gives in*) What happened to all of you? The three of you were once so dynamic, so full of life! Then suddenly last summer everything began to collapse. No more parties, no more drinking with you. Karl Lueger drove all of you crazy! Otto's become an auto-anti-Semite, refuses to enter a tavern or a coffee house and walks around pale, tormented, and gloomy like a Jesuit priest. He needs only to be baptized and converted to join the ranks of the Church's Saints as Saint Otto! And you? You've become a Zionist militant looking for a traveling companion to Palestine. Finally, poor Berger, who was the most normal among you, is confused, running back and forth between you and Otto ... our handsome Karl and your handsome Theodor grew out of the same cracks in Austria's deteriorating liberal foundations ... while one speaks of an anti-Semitic Utopia, the other speaks of a Zionist Utopia where Jews would live in joy and happiness ... and Tietz, liberal Tietz, must drink and make merry all by himself.

CLARA. I left him. He was half drunk. He kept shouting after me ...

TIETZ. (*Leaving, shouting from a distance*) Clara! ... Clara! ... My heartless Ondine! (*Exits*)

CLARA. Come with me to Eretz Israel!

OTTO. When?

CLARA. Tomorrow.

OTTO. I can't. Tomorrow I'm converting.

CLARA. I don't necessarily need you there as a Jew. I want you there as a human being.

OTTO. About seven weeks ago, on May 28, I went to the office of the Jewish community and told them I'm abandoning Judaism. Before my eyes they erased my name from their list. So for two months now I've been without a religion.

CLARA. Why all these hassles? I never went to the office, never asked them to erase my name, yet I'm without religion too. So what?

OTTO. How can you compare? Do you know what religion and faith really are? How can you, you're a woman!

CLARA. Good-bye! (*Turns to leave*)

OTTO. Clara, Clara!

CLARA. I don't want to hear this idiocy anymore: "You're a woman." Understand? Keep these sick theories for your papers and those degenerates at the university who read them! By the way, when is your graduation ceremony?

OTTO. Tomorrow.

CLARA. Though you deserve a beating, I'll bring flowers.

OTTO. Straight to the Church?

CLARA. What?

OTTO. Right after graduation I'm joining the Christian faith — the Protestant Church.

CLARA. Why not the Catholic, they're more dramatic!

OTTO. I'm serious. Tomorrow I'm converting. If you come, you'll meet my friends there, at four in the afternoon. I told everyone. This is the most serious and most important step in my life.

CLARA. You always like to attract attention, to be in the spotlight. It's typical of your dramatic nature and our life here in Vienna. God, how boring! I feel so strangled in this slimy city.

OTTO. Boring? Just wait and see! You'll see the commotion when they find out! If I'm not mistaken, we once bet on who of us is ready to go the limit for his beliefs. I'm converting tomorrow. The day you leave for Palestine to pursue your Zionist ideas, I'll be happy to come to the pier and wave my handkerchief . . .

CLARA. Otto, Otto! You really believe that by joining the Church, by mumbling a few words and getting sprinkled with holy water, you'll suddenly be a new man, free of the curse? Are you so superficial? What do you know about guilt?!

OTTO. What do you know about it?

CLARA. I'm cheating on you with your friend.

OTTO. You can't cheat on me, you're not my wife.

CLARA. So, this is what matters to you! You idiot! I love you, and I go to bed with your friend whom I don't love. Is this any easier for you?

OTTO. Why? Is he more masculine than I am?

CLARA. (*Bursts out laughing; hopelessly*) I never know what goes through your head when you say "masculine." I don't need you just as another lover. I need you as a complete person. Complete. To be with me and share with me everything, freely, as we two could . . . to leave this imaginary existence before it's too late, before the world can't accept us anymore. Otto! Stop these dramatic gestures, this conversion, and such idiocies! After all, you're like me, a person for whom religion, faith, and God are like dead bodies that can't be resurrected. We're both condemned to live completely for one another, or die!

OTTO. What do you mean by sharing everything with you?

CLARA. Give me strength to leave this place. Come with me to

Eretz Israel!

OTTO. And there you'll finally bestow on me the supreme gift, like you did to others—sleep with me?

CLARA. (*Strips naked*) Here. Come. (*He strips too. They stand facing each other. Otto freezes. Lifts his arm but drops it right away. They stand still facing each other*)

CLARA. Otto, come.

OTTO. Someone knocked on the door!

CLARA. You're dreaming.

OTTO. Quick, get dressed! I'm telling you, someone knocked!

CLARA. So what? The door's locked. Come on!

OTTO. Stop it! (*He gets dressed; she does the same*)

CLARA. Did someone catch you when you were a boy?

OTTO. Catch me? You mean when I did something bad?

CLARA. When you did something bad?

OTTO. My father, or do you mean my mother?

CLARA. Your father or your mother.

OTTO. (*In an outburst*) I don't want you or anyone else to stick their noses in my personal problems! Nobody—no pimps, no psychologists! I'll be my own soul doctor! I know what's happening to me! I know and understand everything! Anyway, whatever one knows and understands about himself won't make him sick! (*Clara holds her face. She's distressed and tired. Maybe she cries. He wants to come near her, touch her, caress her, hug her, but only manages to move towards her in an awkward, lame, pitiful fashion. It appears he lacks the desire; it seems he's locked into his own spiritual impotence*)

OTTO. What a curse: not being able to love back when one is loved. To hate the love instinct itself ... this hardness, this barrenness ... an olive tree on the hardest granite! My soul can't free itself and join your soul!

CLARA. Otto!

OTTO. Don't call me by my name!

CLARA. Why?

OTTO. Because it terrifies me. (*Walks to front stage. It's dark except for a spotlight on his face*) I'm like a house with the shutters forever closed. The sun may shine upon the house and perhaps heat it, but the house does not open. Angry, sullen, bitter, it refuses the light. What does it look like inside the house? A wild, desperate activity, a slow, terrifying realization of the gathering darkness, an eternal clearing out of things — inside! Do not ask what it looks like inside the house — but the light shines on, and, amazed, it knocks on the door again and again. Yet the windows close ever tighter from within.

SCENE TWO

Enter Berger. Plays on the piano his arrangement of Grieg's "Solveig's Song." Enter Otto. He stops near him, listens. Berger is aware of Otto's presence but continues to play. Otto hums the tune, then becomes silent. Berger stops playing, turns to Otto.

BERGER. Your father told me yesterday that before you left the house you said goodbye to everyone in such a serious and touching manner that they became worried about you.

OTTO. Well, you can tell him nothing happened, that they shouldn't worry!

BERGER. (*After a pause*) What's the matter, Otto?

OTTO. What's the matter, Berger? What's really the matter?

BERGER. Everything's just fine.

OTTO. I'm happy to hear that. What about Clara?

BERGER. I think she's all right too, no?

OTTO. All right, all right! Everything's all right! Still, something's not all right with you, Berger, right?

BERGER. We see each other so little ...

OTTO. I think you gamble too much. (*Notices Berger's puzzlement*) You think God will just grant you everything you want. You depend too much on a woman's love ... a little loneliness wouldn't hurt you, you know. Sometimes loneliness is better than the company of people ... you should always try to be brave, any place you happen to be. (*Silence, then in a different tone*) You don't understand me? You're thinking: "My friend Otto has suddenly gone crazy ... he's a bit mixed up ..." as the saying goes. Life is a terrible and frustrating journey as man tries constantly to escape misfortunes ... he tries to escape the explosions from within ... you don't think so, Berger, eh? You think life is a nice, pleasant trip in which man glides continuously, from past joy to expected joy ... from one intercourse to another! (*Suddenly concerned*) You've been avoiding me, lately. You feel guilty towards me?

BERGER. My parents told me not to see you anymore.

OTTO. Why? Do I have some contagious disease? Or a disease that people are too ashamed to admit they have? (*Imitates Berger's parents*) "Surely Otto's epileptic, maybe consumptive!" Maybe they think I might lead you astray! Snatch you away from the bosom of the Jewish family and lead you into the arms of the Church? Ruin your appetite for the conjugal bed, a bed stuffed with the life savings of two petit bourgeois families? Interfere with mother Berger's wishes to become grandma Berger!

BERGER. Leave my mother alone!

OTTO. So what's the reason, or didn't you ask ...

BERGER. We're together despite all, isn't that what counts?

OTTO. Despite it all! An exceptional friend! (*Sharp shift of tone*) Berger, come move in with me. We'll live together. We'll share everything.

BERGER. Otto ... you don't look well. Your face is pale ... you look like you're at the end of your rope ... like you're going to collapse. Don't you sleep at night? Otto, what happened to you?

OTTO. Maybe if I could confide in someone I could get rid of this feeling.

BERGER. What feeling?

OTTO. I feel the coldness of the grave take control of me. Can't you smell the dead body?

BERGER. Did you read the morning paper?

OTTO. What's in it? Another attack on my article?

BERGER. There is a rumor that Knut Hamsun killed himself.

OTTO. He, too. ... (*Silence. Otto goes to the window, opens the curtain, looks outside*) Such low and black skies ...

BERGER. It's the end of November. It gets dark early.

OTTO. The weather is bad both outside and inside.

BERGER. I'll turn on a light!

OTTO. (*Turns to him, cuts him off abruptly*) No light! No light!

BERGER. Otto, do you have a gun? (*Otto's silent*) Do you? (*No answer*) If you do I want you to give it to me!

OTTO. You have no right to deny me my will.

BERGER. Otto! (*Walks towards him to search him*)

OTTO. You have no right to deny me my will.

BERGER. If you don't give it to me freely, I'll take it by force.

OTTO. You have no right! I forbid you to touch me! (*Berger attacks him: brief struggle, Berger pins him down on the sofa; with one hand he holds Otto's hands while pressing his knees against Otto's legs. With the other hand he searches him*)

OTTO. Berger, I haven't got a gun! (*Laughing*) I'm unarmed! (*Berger lets go of him. Otto remains on the sofa exhausted*) God, you're strong! (*Looks him over*) Apollo! Let me touch your muscles!

BERGER. Forget it! (*A dog barks in the distance*)

OTTO. What's that?

BERGER. What?

OTTO. You didn't hear? (*Berger shakes his head no*) You didn't hear?! ...

BERGER. You're shaking?

OTTO. I'm cold ... (*Berger takes off his coat, wraps it around Otto. He walks to the fireplace, starts a fire. The conversation continues as Berger starts the fire and Otto, covered in Berger's coat, lies on the couch. He's shaking, looks scared, talks only to lessen the fear*)

OTTO. How's our Dr. Freud?

BERGER. Fine. They made him professor.

OTTO. Yes. I heard. Thanks to the Baroness Ferstel, who used her influence on Hartl, the Minister of Education and Culture. I heard it cost her an Arnold Boecklin painting, which she donated to Hartl's favorite modern gallery ... what counts is that Dr. Freud is finally professor.

BERGER. You know he deserved it, Baroness Ferstel or not ...

OTTO. You never stopped admiring him.

BERGER. Freud finds the whole thing ironic.

OTTO. You're still seeing him?

BERGER. Twice a week.

OTTO. He knows I converted?

BERGER. Yes. I told him.

OTTO. What did he say?

BERGER. It's not important.

OTTO. You're afraid you'll hurt me?

BERGER. He hardly said anything. Only: "Well, and?"

OTTO. "Well, and?" That's all he said?

BERGER. Yes. (*He starts the fire. A golden, warm glow spreads in the room. The atmosphere is briefly pleasant. Suddenly, Otto bursts out laughing*)

OTTO. "Well, and?" (*Loud laughter. Berger looks at him briefly, stunned. Otto laughs while recreating an imaginary conversation with Freud*) "Otto Weininger converted ..." "Well, and?" (*Laughs again. Berger laughs too. The tension is broken. The atmosphere is more relaxed and pleasant*) You know, Berger, if you hadn't found me tonight I would have put an end to my life.

BERGER. Why?!

OTTO. Why?! The questions you ask!

BERGER. What's the reason?

OTTO. "Reason." I can't tell you that.

BERGER. What do you mean, you can't?

OTTO. I don't want to tell you.

BERGER. You must!

OTTO. I don't owe anything to you or anyone else, and no one is going to get it out of me by force.

BERGER. I must know!

OTTO. That's your problem if you must. Go find out!

BERGER. You're disappointed by the reviews your paper got. You thought your theory would shake the world, and the lukewarm reception has destroyed you. (*Otto shakes his head in disagreement*) Problems with changing religion? (*Otto waves his hand as if to say no*) Women? Otto ... syphilis? (*Otto's silent*) God, Otto, I warned you, didn't I? Must you see the filthiest, the most wretched prostitutes in town?

OTTO. I don't care what happens to my brain twenty years from now. Anyway, I won't have any children.

BERGER. I know an excellent doctor. I'll take you to him tomorrow.

OTTO. I don't have syphilis!

BERGER. What then? You can tell me, I won't tell anyone!

OTTO. I can't tell, even you ...

BERGER. I'm not leaving until you tell me the reason. You're important to me, Otto! More important than anyone else in the world! I won't let you go on like this! I won't be able to live with the thought that because of me ... (*Stops, recovers*) It's Clara! It's the tennis!

OTTO. Tennis?

BERGER. You know that ...

OTTO. (*Interrupting him, shouting*) No! I don't care who plays tennis with Clara! What do you think I am, a woman?

BERGER. Why did you want to commit suicide? I won't leave you alone until you tell me. If you're stubborn we'll be here until tomorrow morning, and if you persist, a whole week. We're not leaving this room until you open your mouth and tell me. (*He grabs Otto firmly, shakes him*) What's the reason!

OTTO. (*Shouting in pain*) You're hurting me!

BERGER. (*Presses Otto against the wall, knocks his head against it, shakes him, becomes Otto's torturer*) The reason! The reason!

OTTO. I'm a criminal.

BERGER. (*Suddenly lets go of him*) What?

OTTO. A criminal from birth ...

BERGER. You?! Why, you couldn't hurt a fly, you couldn't kill a roach, you, a criminal.

OTTO. My head is full of evil thoughts.

BERGER. You're mad. You've gone insane!

OTTO. I was alone one night in a hotel in Munich. I couldn't fall asleep. Suddenly I heard a dog barking. I was terrified ... it was a black dog. I knew it was the devil. I fought him bitterly. I bit the bed sheets. I tore them to pieces, trying to stop myself from going out and doing something ... I knew then that I was a criminal. I knew that this was to be my destiny, if I went on living. That's why I must kill myself. You see, I'm carrying a terrible guilt since birth ...

BERGER. I don't believe you ... and your guilt ...

OTTO. I belong to an accursed race ... you can't grasp that! You're different. You don't know what hatred is, what loathing is ... I hate everyone who loves me! I'm only capable of hurting ... all that I leave behind me is destruction and desolation ... I can only cause death ... I can only kill ... I'm the flutist from the tale ... you live in this city with its opera, theatre, art ... you have no idea how many rats, roaches, spiders, and worms crawl around you ... I should have been a musician! Yes, yes! I could run in the streets and play the tune of insane hatred on my flute. I'd drive the rats and the mice out of the taverns, the beer halls, and the University, and they'll rush out to follow me ... and as they're marching behind me, rows upon rows, on the street, honest, good people like you will surround them with cannons, fire, hatchets, rocks, anything you can get your hands on, and kill them, one by one, until not one damn roach is left alive!

BERGER. You are insane!

OTTO. What's everybody waiting for? Can't they see what happens under the surface? Can't they see the snakes, the dogs, the octopuses, the horses? What are they waiting for? For the corpses to start floating in the streets? Let me kill myself!

BERGER. You're going to live. You must live.

OTTO. Why make me believe in something you don't believe yourself?

BERGER. You're young ... you've just started ... you're so gifted ... you made a mistake or two, but who doesn't? You have so much to say, so much to contribute to humanity. You must live!

OTTO. I can't ... I shouldn't ... let me die before I commit an act from which there is no return. If I go now, no one will remember, no one will know. It's got to be, it must!

BERGER. I'll speak to Professor Freud. He'll treat you to an analysis.

OTTO. (*Jumps up as if bitten by a snake*) Psychotherapy? What kind of psychotherapy is this — a Jewish pimp sticking his nose into people's souls? It's filth, not therapy! I'm not going to lie on a couch just because this Jewish profanity is Vienna's latest fad! The Aryan spirit will throw up this filth, you'll see! The Aryan man will become his own diagnostician through the power of introspection. Anyone can learn about himself, anyone can be his own psycho-therapist! With God's help. If not ... he is helpless ...

BERGER. (*Collapses during Otto's speech. Gets up, sits down, holds his head in his hands and cries*) Why ... why ...

OTTO. (*Gets up, looks briefly at Berger, who is heartbroken and crying. Takes in the scene. Thinks he has had enough. Walks up to Berger, presses him to his breast, pats his head*) It's all right, Berger ... enough ... I'll live ... but you must be quiet. If you tell anyone about our conversation, it's all over.

BERGER. (*Raises his eyes toward Otto*) No one will know ...

OTTO. I must finish my project ... I'll put everything in the book.

BERGER. I'll stay with you.

OTTO. No! I need peace and quiet now. Solitude. I need to be by myself. For weeks or months. Maybe years. Until I finish. (*Walks away. On his way he stops front stage*) A man lives until he either walks into the absolute or into nothingness ... either his life deteriorates or else it leads him to eternity. (*Otto kneels front stage. It's dark except for a spotlight on his face. He's praying*) God ... I'm ready to give up everything they call "happiness": a woman's love ... family ... physical pleasure ... I'll abstain. But I don't know if I have the strength to stay at these heights or atone for my failures by taking my life, sinner that I am. God, I stand here before myself, ready and fearful.

SCENE THREE

Otto walks toward the rear of the stage. The setting shows the forest of Act 1, Scene 2: a couple of lovers — Clara and Berger.

CLARA. I was waiting for you.

BERGER. I've just spoken to Otto. He's in a state ...

CLARA. Don't talk about Otto now.

BERGER. But he needs ...

CLARA. Hug me. (*He hesitates momentarily*) Good. Then go to him if he needs you.

BERGER. Clara.

CLARA. Can't you see what he's doing to you? He's castrating you! But if this is what you want ... a man should be able to say: "No more. This is it!" You should put an end to this abuse. (*Berger hugs her. She pushes him off*) Not so hard!

BERGER. You're wonderful.

CLARA. We could both be wonderful.

BERGER. I can't understand Otto!

CLARA. Don't try. You're his total opposite. I love your skin. It makes me want to touch it. (*She touches him*) I dream about your body. I have such crazy fantasies about it, it leaves me breathless, it really does ...

BERGER. You're drowning me ... I'm drowning! (*She begins to walk away. He follows her while whispering in her ears*) I want to be with you when you're thirty, forty, fifty ...

CLARA. I want you. (*They leave*)

SCENE FOUR

Otto and his double explain to each other Otto's thesis, by egging each other on, driving each other crazy, in a sort of orgy of spiritual awakening.

OTTO. Everything was created in twos: one versus another. There's no light without darkness, no profanity without holiness. If it were not for life, we wouldn't have death. There's no "being" without "nothingness." Purity — impurity. Masculine — feminine. One against the other. One opposite another. We all possess in various proportions a mix of masculinity and femininity, femininity and masculinity. Each of us is unique in that sense. The ratio between the two constitutes character; it is fixed at birth and is unalterable ... until death. Femininity is chaos.

DOUBLE. Masculinity — creativity.

OTTO. Femininity is matter.

DOUBLE. Masculinity — form.

OTTO. Femininity is nil.

DOUBLE. Masculinity — existence.

OTTO. Femininity is zero.

DOUBLE. Masculinity — infinity.

OTTO. Femininity — absurdity.

DOUBLE. Masculinity — meaning.

Otto shifts to a mere mouthing of the words, eyes closed, lips moving as if praying. His parents appear in the rear, the farthest point from Otto. As usual, Leopold is with his two suitcases; Adelheid carries a child's sailor suit. She tries to prevent Leopold from walking over to Otto.

ADELHEID. Leopold, leave him alone. The book he's writing will get him a professorship: the youngest professor in the history of the Hapsburg Empire!

LEOPOLD. Get out of my way! Let me talk to my son!

ADELHEID. He'll also get a Church degree — doctor of theology!

LEOPOLD. Let me talk to him!

ADELHEID. Tomorrow morning!

LEOPOLD. He can't stay up all night writing! (*Until now they have not advanced more than a step with each exchange, in all no more than three feet from their original point. They go on arguing in whispers like a musical motif. Otto and his double resume their conversation, oblivious of their presence*)

OTTO. Woman needs man to be somebody. Woman employs sexual means to attract men.

DOUBLE. Woman is a sexual creature from head to toe.

OTTO. Man is only sexual around his genitals, otherwise he's spiritual.

DOUBLE. Man's destiny — genius.

OTTO. Genius is ultimate masculinity. Ultimate ego.

DOUBLE. Woman has no ego. Genius is impossible in woman.

OTTO. Woman's fate — to be attached to man.

DOUBLE. Woman's only goal — sexual pleasure. Constant pleasure. Nonstop.

OTTO. Woman is either mother, or prostitute, or both.

DOUBLE. A mother's goal in sexual encounter — children. A prostitute's goal — pleasure. A woman's being depends on the phallus.

OTTO. The phallus is the superior ruler of her fate.

DOUBLE. The phallus is her God.

OTTO. Woman is man's original sin. Her eternity is the eternity of sin. (*During this exchange Otto's parents come nearer. Otto shuts his eyes, concentrates. It looks like he's asleep standing up. His parents view him thus*)

LEOPOLD. Do you know what time it is?

ADELHEID. He can't hear you. He's sleeping.

LEOPOLD. I'm talking to you! Tomorrow you're becoming a professor. Go to sleep!

ADELHEID. Leave him alone! You want to kill him?

LEOPOLD. He'll collapse in the middle of defending his thesis.

ADELHEID. A baby! He looked like this when he would fall asleep after he nursed ...

OTTO. Judaism is on an even lower level than femininity. Woman believes in man; the Jew believes in nothing. The Jew is the enemy of form. The Jew is a born anarchist. The Jew elects to live in exile: it is his natural way of life. He felt this way even before the destruction of the Temple. The Jew will prefer this way of life even when he has his own country.

DOUBLE. The Jew, like woman, knows that
He is matter without form,
Creature without ego,
A human being without soul,
Nil and naught, moral chaos.
Therefore, the Jew
Doesn't believe
In himself, or
In law and order.

Otto and his double disappear behind the partition at the back of the room. Otto undresses, gets into the bathtub. The double leaves.

LEOPOLD. Scribbling all night long ... scribbling all night long!

ADELHEID. I'll stuff the crack under the door with papers.

LEOPOLD. This scribbling penetrates the walls!

ADELHEID. I'll stuff your ears with cotton ...

LEOPOLD. He's crazy! The critics will attack his theory and he'll fall apart!

ADELHEID. Father is worried that you're not getting enough sleep.

LEOPOLD. Go to sleep! You hear? Sleep!

ADELHEID. Your father's right. You haven't closed an eye in a week ... you keep correcting and revising. Go to bed, I'll finish it for you ...

LEOPOLD. You're not going to start copying now!

ADELHEID. Anyway, I can't get sicker than this ...

LEOPOLD. Normal people don't work at such hours! (*Adelheid walks up to Otto, puts the sailor suit neatly folded on the screen, lifts Otto out of the tub, wraps him in a big towel and starts to dress him up in the sailor suit as the scene unfolds*)

ADELHEID. My life is worthless anyway.

LEOPOLD. This whole family is crazy.

ADELHEID. Anyway, I won't live long. (*While putting on Otto's underwear*) Show me where you stopped and by tomorrow morning you'll have it copied in my neat handwriting, and your father will sleep quietly.

LEOPOLD. A grown-up behaving like a baby in diapers! You shouldn't change them for him!

ADELHEID. I see you're concerned about him. I'm glad you're finally showing your feelings. Don't be ashamed of them! After all, you're his father!

LEOPOLD. Doctor, professor, nobody works in my house after eleven o'clock!

ADELHEID. Twelve, Leopold. (*While putting on Otto's undershirt*) Promise you won't write after midnight.

LEOPOLD. Eleven! (*Adelheid points to Otto's socks; Leopold hands them to her*)

ADELHEID. (*Bends down to put them on his feet*) And a half! (*To Otto*) Oh dear, when is the last time you cleaned your toenails?

LEOPOLD. No halves, no quarters! Eleven o'clock sharp! Not a minute later!

ADELHEID. (*Puts on the other sock*) Do you want him to leave the house?

LEOPOLD. I don't care!

ADELHEID. Father doesn't really mean that. He just can't fall asleep thinking you're sitting here in this cold stuffy room for hours on end. Maybe if we had fixed the cracks sooner, I wouldn't have tuberculosis now.

LEOPOLD. Tuberculosis doesn't come from cold or dampness!

ADELHEID. Tuberculosis comes from dampness, malnutrition,

and lack of fats!

LEOPOLD. One day they'll prove how primitive this whole theory is!

ADELHEID. I'm sure I won't live to find out. While my in-laws were stuffing themselves with sour cream, butter, and goose fat, my family had to save up for your trips to Bayreuth. That's why we never fixed the cracks in the bedroom. I had to wipe the black mildew off the walls! (*To Otto*) Show some respect for your father. I know he's mad now, that's why he said eleven, but if you show some respect, and for a few days write only until eleven, and don't stay up late copying drafts, but leave them to me, I get up several times every night anyway, my cough, you know, I can never fall asleep again like a normal human being, you know, for a person like me the hours before dawn are a time of fear and cold sweat, father will let you work until midnight, maybe even one o'clock, right, Leopold? Poldy, look how you wear your shirt! Inside out! Put those things on the chair and fix it! (*Furious, Leopold takes off his jacket, shirt, reverses the shirt, gets dressed again. Adelheid resumes her speech while dressing Otto*) It's not healthy after one o'clock. Even Dr. Melchior said: "The heart can't take it, just look at the black, musty dust you're breathing!" (*Dusts and dresses him at the same time*) This is the same dust that killed my lungs! Now let's all go to sleep quietly and daddy and Ottoleh will say goodnight to each other like good boys. Poldy, your collar, your collar. (*Arranges his collar*) Poldy, good-night. Ottoleh, daddy says goodnight, right, daddy? You're saying goodnight to Ottoleh, 'cause tomorrow Ottoleh must get up early and go to school. Now Ottoleh says goodnight, daddy. See, Ottoleh says goodnight daddy, so nicely . . .

OTTO. (*Lets out a sharp, broken shriek*) E-nough!

ADELHEID. Poldy! The scream! Like when he was born! Remember? The midwife was scared out of her wits! She said: "Adele, this is impossible, he's talking! I'm sure he said 'enough!' Adele!" (*Checking Otto's neck*) Didn't wash it right! At fourteen months he already spoke perfect German — no mistakes, even used long complex sentences, difficult verb conjugations, plus cum perfectum! You are

dirty behind the ears. (*Spits on a rag, wipes him*) Ever since
that day, it's been quiet in the family, right, Leopold?
Your father read to me from your manuscript. (*To Leopold*)
Forgive me for telling him — in a healthy family there are
no secrets ... turn around! (*Otto does so. She tucks in his
shirt, combs his hair, etc.*) I'm glad you feel this way about
women so we don't have to warn you about it. Dad, see
how clever and wise our son is? There are many bad, bad
woman around. They're dishonest, indecent. They're bad.
I can't even say the word. Even worse! Shameless, like
Mrs. Schindler! Yes, yes, Poldy! Showing up here in her
tight skirt, you'd think it might explode any moment. And
how does she sit down in front of your father? First she
lifts her skirt up like this to show her well-shaped ankles to
him, then shoves them right under his nose, like this! And
you, Poldy, although you talk to her about music, you
look, I saw you. You think she cares about music? All she
wants is to use her charms to catch you in her net, like our
Otto here so correctly points out. Yes, yes! I always warned
you: children can and understand everything. If you
had any sense of decency you'd have shown her the door
instead of sitting there looking at her breasts and ankles,
discussing Wagner and the German genius, while she's
only thinking how to drag you to bed; that Mrs. Schindler,
and I'm very, very happy that Otto sees this. I'm glad
Otto understands these things and knows how to protect
himself from women like Mrs. Schindler. It's really a
scandal how that whore carries on! (*Holds a handkerchief to
Otto's nose. He blows*) And he has to hear this before school!
Harder! Yes! More! More! (*Her prodding and his blowing
become gradually orgiastic*) Yes, blow! Strong! Strong! Hard!
Here it comes. (*Sigh of relief and satisfaction*) Excellent.
(*Wipes his nose, sticks the handkerchief in his pocket*) You can go
now. (*Otto's dressed for the ceremony at the university. Walks
front stage, lectures. They stand behind him in awe*)

OTTO. Women and Jews, their goal is to make us feel guilty.
They do this by laying the blame for their condition on
someone else so they can control them through guilt. This
is Judaism. This is the abyss upon which Christianity was

founded. A Christian accepts the blame, he doesn't lay it on someone else. Jesus' victory over Judaism makes Him greater than Buddha, Confucius, and other founders of religions. Jesus is the greatest of them all because He confronted the greatest opponent. It is only out of Judaism, valueless Judaism, that values can grow; only out of Judaism and against it. Like creation out of destruction. Like salvation out of ruin. It is only out of the Jew who is at the bottom of the human race that a new man can emerge, complete, courageous, superior. Our Savior, the Herald of truth, must come from within Judaism just as man comes from woman and becomes her opposite! This is the book. God, I could have lived my entire life without ever writing it. Did I want that? Well, it's done! I emptied out my soul, transfused my spirit into this creation, in these words, which are now in the public domain. These are the facts, they stick to me like glue. I'll have to face them and accept the consequences: insanity, the scaffold, or such glory as no mortal has ever enjoyed. (*Someone knocks at the door. Louder*) Is anyone knocking? No. It's only an illusion. Nobody knocked. (*More knocks*) Yes. Someone's knocking. (*Opens the door*)

SCENE FIVE

At the door is Adele, the housekeeper, in nightgown, bonnet, and holding a candle.

OTTO. (*Walks up to Adele at the door*) Who are you?
ADELE. Adele!
OTTO. Who?!!
ADELE. Adele, the housekeeper! Last night you rented this room from me!
OTTO. What time is it?
ADELE. Between three and four in the morning.
OTTO. I asked not to be disturbed until nine-thirty.
ADELE. A gentleman is here to see you.
OTTO. I don't want to see anyone. Send him away.
ADELE. He came from far away, from Sweden.

OTTO. What does he want?

ADELE. He says it's important. Asked to be announced as Mr. Strindburg, or Stroindberg ...

OTTO. Strindberg? August Strindberg?!

ADELE. Something like that ... came from Stockholm especially to meet you.

OTTO. Show him in at once!

ADELE. Mister Strindberger! Please ... (*She makes way but Strindberg bursts in through another door: wild hair, a black cape flapping around, red cheeks from the cold. A cold wind blows in his wake, snow falls off his shoulder. Stops, clicks his heels at Adele who leaves and closes the door*)

STRINDBERG. (*Waving a book at Otto*) Doctor, I read your book! To be able, at last, to see the solution to the problem of women is a great relief to me. Therefore, please accept my reverence and my thanks.

OTTO. This is only an illusion. I mustn't believe it!

STRINDBERG. Sorry?!

OTTO. May I touch you?

STRINDBERG. Please! (*Strindberg extends his arm but doesn't move*)

OTTO. I want to make sure I'm not dreaming!

STRINDBERG. My hands are cold from the winter air.

OTTO. I'm amazed ... amazed! Your work inspired me so much. I was hoping you'd read my articles ... but to think you've come to see me all the way from Sweden!

STRINDBERG. Why not?

OTTO. How did I earn this honor? I don't deserve it! Except for my book, which, I don't know how, but it seemed to write itself, I feel empty and hollow. I have no more thoughts, no feelings, nothing! I don't even know what to say to you except some very banal things! I feel stupid!

STRINDBERG. We have a lot in common: I, too, was born with a guilty conscience ...

OTTO. You think, too, that your existence is totally unjustified? (*Strindberg nods yes. Otto can't accept it*) Is it possible? You?! An artist ... a genius ... a born Swede. Not a Jew like me.

STRINDBERG. What's Jewishness got to do with it?!

OTTO. Of course, you have no idea what it means to be fed up and disgusted with yourself, to hate yourself from the start, to be constantly persecuted and tortured by a bad, sickly character that poisons your life from within like a curse. I could understand being persecuted for my opinions and beliefs, but to be the eternal victim of a character I didn't choose, one I inherited, but can neither accept nor get rid of ... I understand my foes better than they understand their hatred toward me!

STRINDBERG. I also believe that I'm defiled and guilty!

OTTO. Your speech is so full of life!

STRINDBERG. I'm sorry, I don't understand!

OTTO. "I also believe I'm defiled and guilty!" I'm working now on a theory of symbolic connections. I've discovered that every natural phenomenon is symbolic of some human trait. Thus, the dog symbolizes malice, the octopus evil, the cat is not clear to me yet. But I also found out that the letter "L," which you use so often, symbolizes life, love, light, laughter.

STRINDBERG. Yes, and lust, lewdness, lechery ... some discovery!

OTTO. I had a vision, an awful nightmare, that I was responsible for a despicable crime: and you appeared before me at the last moment: I was about to commit suicide!

STRINDBERG. Because of the reviews of your book?

OTTO. Really ... this critic, his name is Möbius, wrote an article filled with personal hatred! Others are simply indifferent to my ideas.

STRINDBERG. They're all idiots. Ignore them! They represent the spirit of the past. In twenty years they'll understand you. Forty years from now you will reach your peak!

OTTO. I keep telling myself the same thing, but it's very difficult for someone like me to live with a wounded ego. So, instead of concentrating on my work, I walk around tearing this Möbius apart inside me ... I'm torn between bitter anger and total resignation, the desire to quit this game completely ...

STRINDBERG. A few years ago, I felt the same ambition you feel now: to give up! This is what I wrote in my diary: "Why do I go on? Cato gave himself up to death when he realized he couldn't stay clear of the swamp of sin. Therefore, Dante absolved him from his suicide. Now I am sinking and I don't want to sink, therefore ... bang!" (*Points a finger at his forehead*) I was on my way up until a woman dragged me down. Yet I went on living because I understood that connection with a woman was a sacrifice, a duty, a test. We must not live like gods here on earth; we must live in filth (*Rests his arm on Otto*) and still stay pure, and so on. (*Caresses Otto's head as he speaks*) Do you remember the Maeterlinck case? It was exactly the same! He was far above the material, when the earthly woman came along ... he fell so deep that he carried his naked earthly spirit around to exhibit it! (*His stroking grows more affectionate. He takes off Otto's cloak*) Is that not tragic? Or Dr. Luther. When he married he wrote to a friend: " I marry! Incredible! I am ashamed! But it seems that God wants to make a fool of me!" Twenty-three years ago I too faced suicide, almost! Then I made a discovery ... you made one too! You belong to the race of the discoverers. Only now, like every creator who strives for the essential, you are beset by doubts: Did I indeed betray the secrets of the gods? Did I steal the fire? Or, did I create ruin and destruction. This is the moment after the creation when you're left empty and exhausted and every idiot, every brute can come up to you, spit on you, throw mud at you ... like this Möbius. I know this kind of cynicism is too much for people like us. (*He pulls Otto towards him and kisses him on the lips; a long kiss that becomes very erotic. Otto returns Strindberg's embrace in total abandonment. They grab each other's groins, and suddenly Strindberg jumps back and removes his wig. He is a bald man with glasses. He bursts out in an evil laughter as Otto is stunned*)

MÖBIUS. Ha, ha! I caught you, you pederast! You can't escape now! We finally know what you really are! The great critic of womanhood! The herald of the new Aryan — masculine — age! A genius in the guise of a legislator of a new religion!

OTTO. Who are you?

MÖBIUS. I'm the idiot, the brute from whom you stole all those ideas in your book. I'm Möbius! Möbius, the critic! Why do you look so surprised?

OTTO. Me, stealing from you?

MÖBIUS. It's a fact. You read my book. Admit it!

OTTO. A genius like me plagiarizing banalities from an average man like you!

MÖBIUS. Genius? You're only fancy words, catchy phrases any idiot can quote ... merely the pretentions of a clever man nowhere near spiritual greatness ... it's all pretense and forgery.

OTTO. So you know what genius is?!

MÖBIUS. Your mediocrity shines in many colors. Like a well-polished diamond, only it doesn't throw light on anything! All your life you've been running from yourself, you want to be different, you want to throw what's yours on others while stealing from them, robbing them of everything they have! That's how you stole a religion not yours, that can never be yours. Worse yet, you stole from me my ideas about woman, and if that wasn't enough — you also stole the title of my book!

OTTO. Go away! Satan!

MÖBIUS. What's the title of my book? *Sex and Decadence.* And yours? *Sex and Character*! You forged with impudence the combination "Sex and ..."!

OTTO. You're nothing!

MÖBIUS. Here's my book: The Words "Sex and ..." appear on the cover five times.

OTTO. You're an insignificant, petty man.

MÖBIUS. Five times "Sex and ..."!

OTTO. Soul of a shopkeeper!

MÖBIUS. "Sex and ..." "Sex and ..." five times!

OTTO. I want nothing to do with you!

MÖBIUS. I admit it, I'm an average man, but so are you.

OTTO. My book will last thousands of years!

MÖBIUS. It won't because it only serves your personal emotional needs. Maybe a few perverts and soft-brained idiots will enjoy wallowing in your dirt.

OTTO. A new age! I'm announcing a new age! Whole nations will march behind the banner of Aryan masculinity!

MÖBIUS. So what? This age of yours is a brief, ugly age, one nobody will want to remember! A wretched mental disease!

It's true I express mediocre ideas, but you tried to deceive people by showing yourself in full mediocrity. You didn't tear yourself to pieces, you didn't deal with your personal problems seriously! Instead, you played games, you deluded yourself and others to appear interesting! An average confession by an average man! Now, other average men will start rummaging through your papers and letters. Height. Body frame. Schizoid or manic depressive. Bone structure. Muscles. Your monstrously ugly lips that look like the rear end of a baboon, your genital organs, yes, yes! They'll search for evidence in the archives of Vienna's houses of prostitution: were they developed or degenerated! They'll search and search! You don't have any special privileges, no more than Swift or Kleist had in their time. This is what they said about Kleist, the genius who committed suicide along with his girlfriend: "His genital organs ... degenerated."

OTTO. Deep down I always knew that the battle was lost from the start. Man cannot escape his character. I thought I was roaring loudly, when in fact I was only barking ... what will I do now?

MÖBIUS. Disappear! You're superfluous! Your existence is unnecessary! If you live you'll only make a fool of yourself! They'll ridicule you. "A genius, a genius!" If I were you I'd swallow all those pages you wrote on genius! Neither one of us will be remembered a hundred years from now, not even in fifty. There's only one genius in Vienna: Sigmund Freud! Only Freud! If they remember you in five hundred years it will only be because of a note in his *Collected Papers*: "Weininger (the young philosopher, who, highly gifted but sexually deranged, committed suicide after producing his remarkable book, *Sex and Character*), in a chapter that has attracted much attention, treated Jews and women with equal hostility and overwhelmed them with the same insults. He was swayed by his infantile complexes: and from that standpoint what is common to Jews and women is their relation to the castration complex."
(*Otto sits down defeated, his spirit broken. Möbius takes off his mask, reveals himself as Tietz*)

TIETZ. (*Walks up to Otto, strokes his hair*) Otto, enough ...
enough. No more Strindberg, no more Möbius ... it's me,
Tietz. Good old Tietz.

OTTO. (*Ignoring Tietz, talks to himself*) I have this terrible habit
of destroying every conviction right at its inception, of
contradicting it, of eradicating it ... is this the Jew in me,
the Jew rebelling against me?

TIETZ. Leave these thoughts alone. Words have no meaning
anymore. Jew. Christian. Nakedness rules the world now.
Come, live with me. You'll have your own room in my
family's estate on a mountain, facing Salzburg. I'll support
you, you can write, you can do anything you want. You'll
eat and drink only the best. We'll elevate physical pleasure
to an art. This is how things are and this is your situation:
you're a kept Jewish mistress in a rapidly decaying
and deteriorating Nationalistic–anti-Semitic Christian
world ... so make the best of it. It's neither an honorable
nor a terrible situation, but who knows, if you stop resisting
it, you might even enjoy it ...

OTTO. I should have died long ago. (*Raises the gun*)

SCENE SIX

*Distant shouts. Otto stops short of pulling the trigger. A couple of
old beggars approach him. The man looks terribly sick, like he's
falling apart. The old woman's wearing rags, her sparse hair is
disheveled.*

WOMAN. Otto! Otto!

MAN. (*Echoes her words, though clearly he doesn't know what's going
on*) Otto ... Otto ...

WOMAN. He doesn't recognize us! He doesn't remember us!
(*She signals the old man to play on a broken mandolin. He plays
the "Butterfly Song" from Act 1, Scene 2, and she sings the words.
They hop and skip around Otto in a grotesque dance*)

OTTO. Clara? Berger?

BERGER. Messiah! Messiah! (*Holds on to Otto*)

DOUBLE. (*In a prison-guard uniform, whip in hand*) Forward march!
March, Jew, march!

CLARA. It's Otto! Our friend!

BERGER. Otto ... our friend.

OTTO. (*To his double*) Leave them alone! I told them Zionism is not the solution. I warned you this adventure will end up in disaster. I told you you'd return to exile, I told you you can't defeat the Jewishness in you. (*In the meantime Clara and Berger throw away their masks and clothes and become two young, blond, healthy "Aryans"*)

BERGER. What do you mean by "defeating the Jewishness inside"?

CLARA. Do you mean we should turn the hatred of others into self-hatred? Do you mean we should commit suicide to make the job easier for the enemy? or maybe we should rebel against the hatred of our enemy?

BERGER. There comes a time when their deadly hatred leaves you with only your body — your flesh and bones. There is no being "another" anymore, no more escaping through clever schemes. They want our flesh. Jewish flesh. Layers of Jewish flesh with Jewish brains and Jewish blood in between. That's Europe for you: two thousand years of aesthetics and good taste. A room at 15 Schwarzspanier strasse, in the house where Beethoven gave up his ghost. Soon we won't be allowed to mention his name or play his music. They issued a death warrant against us. All of us. But when they come to get us, I'll strike back hard, right in their ugly faces. If they come asking for my flesh they'll have to pay with their own, their wives' and children's.

CLARA. Otto, it's you who were defeated by Jewishness, not us! You are the real Jew, a hundred percent so! You're trying to save yourself by joining the hangman? You've given them your body and brain, all for nothing. Why? For what?

OTTO. Zionism dreamed of something totally alien to Judaism. To fulfill their Zionist dreams Jews should have first gotten rid of their Jewishness once and for all, so that Zionism can indeed be fulfilled. You obviously didn't do it. No wonder your Jewishness defeated the Zionism within you. And in its victory it is leading you to perdition. (*Clara and Berger leave. Otto pulls out his gun*) Either I, or everything I have created, must die! Evil spirits did it all!

SCENE SEVEN

DOUBLE. Ha, ha! What have we here? A gun! Trying to impress us? What indulgence! Otto, I'm not mother! Isolation, taking vows, abstinence! You don't scare me! Otto, cut it out! Where are your friends? Where are they? Gone! They're fed up! We're alone — you and I. Face to face. Otto, I'm begging you, Otto, you're healthy. And how! You hardly eat, you write all night long, write, write ... look how strong you are. You could live to be one hundred and twenty. Don't do it. Let me live! You're dear to me, Otto. Throw all your theories to hell. You're a handsome young man. Nobody told you that? Find yourself a woman, start a family. I'm talking to you! Why am I talking to you?! You almost ruined me, you always took advantage of my weaknesses ... touched my innermost secrets. Fine. Kill yourself. You always knew how to stick your nose inside the worst open wounds. The wounds are cured now! You hear? They're dry! Smooth skin. I'm not crying anymore. You came, you released your poison. Then, you sit there as if nothing happened. An innocent saint. A symbol of conscience and morality. You did your thing, though: you poisoned my life! How can I go on living with your sickness? I'll go on! I live! It's a fact! I'm fine! So, I'm not your ideal. I'm not the symbol of your values: morality, reason, beauty, truth! A perfect German, that's what you wanted? So, I'm not a perfect German! That's what you have, that's all. An imperfect German! OK? Wagner, or not, that's how I am, who I am! Despite your pathetic efforts — I love myself! As I am. A Jew, an Aryan, a Barbarian, whatever! Nothing will change this. I love myself! And I live! And how! Fight. Work. Gorge myself. Have sex. Sing. Dance. Come, dance with me, Otto! Come! (*The double and Otto dance a wild waltz. The double sings*)

> La la la, la la la. Fornicate and have fun!
> La la la, la la la. I live, I live!
> La la la, la la la. Yeh, yeh, yeh.

La la la, la la la. I fight and work!
La la la, la la la. I live and gorge.
La la la, la la la. Fornicate and have fun!
Bam, bam bam, bam bam bam, yeh, yeh, yeh!
La la la, la la la. Live, live, live!

(*They stop: they are dizzy and breathless*) You're warm? Let's take off these clothes. Just touch yourself. (*They slowly take off their shirts facing each other*) Such a young body. So warm. So virile. Remember the city. The river. The streets at night. The women. The men. They'll go on rushing about after you're gone. Sleep with each other. Spreading legs. Come. Come. Otto, come see the women with their round breasts bursting with desire. Otto, show your body! (*Their shirts are off. The double's breasts are naked against Otto's chest. Otto recoils, terrified. He raises the gun and shoots himself near the heart. Dark. There are knocks at the door*)

Enter Clara, Berger, Tietz, Leopold, Adelheid. They stand around Otto. Berger bends down, lifts his arm, checks his pulse.

LEOPOLD. He was a young man whose spirit found no peace in this world. Once he had delivered his soul's message, he could no longer remain among the living. He went to the place where one of the greatest men found his death, the Schwarzspanierhaus in Vienna, and there, with his own hands, destroyed his mortal body.

OTTO. I'm still alive!

ADELHEID. Otto! (*She rushes to him. They lift him up. She sits on the couch. They put him on her lap. His limp body reaches down from the couch to the floor*)

OTTO. (*To his father*) Yesterday I asked you to come with me to the bus station ...

LEOPOLD. I did!

OTTO. Six buses went by but I didn't leave.

LEOPOLD. Seven ...

OTTO. I told you where I was going to rent a room.

LEOPOLD. Yes ... Schwarzspanierstrasse 15!

OTTO. You saw me hesitate ... I didn't want to leave. You rushed me ...

LEOPOLD. It was cold outside.

OTTO. It was cold outside and it was cold inside. Berger?

BERGER. Yes ...

OTTO. Did I visit you these last days ...

BERGER. Yes, twice.

OTTO. Three times.

BERGER. Yes, the concierge told me ...

OTTO. That I waited a whole day ...

BERGER. Yes ...

OTTO. She gave you my notes?

BERGER. Yes.

OTTO. Three days in a row ... three days ...

BERGER. Yes: yesterday, the day before yesterday, and the day before that.

OTTO. And when you got home and she gave you my notes— did you try to find me?

BERGER. You wrote not to look for you ...

OTTO. Three days in a row ...

BERGER. Yes!

OTTO. I could have killed myself at once, one bullet in the head. And died instantly, not all night long. I shot myself near the heart. So I'm not only the executioner. A torturer as well. My own death torturer. Who was this Otto before this torture began? Who was this Otto, this man who had fifty more years to live? Otto after the torture, with only one hour to live, who doesn't remember, doesn't understand the other Otto. The one with the healthy skin ... no bullet near his heart. There is no I. There is no ego. There is no soul. There is no spirit. There is the body. Pain that separates from the world. And now when faith is most needed, there isn't any; there is only the body. I, the torturer and I, the tortured, know ... I'm telling you ... the torturer had an easy job ... simple ... nothing in the world stopped him. There was no force between the hangman and his victim. One thing alone could have stopped him ... someone ... to be wanted by someone ... to be wanted by someone ... Clara? How could I say that all a woman has in the world is the hope to be wanted by a man? What does a man have? Does he need anything else? Man too wants the same thing ... he too wants to know ... that somewhere a woman is waiting for him, wants him. (*An inner coldness overtakes him. He turns to his mother*) I'm cold. Cover me up. Wrap me up. Hold me, hold me tight. Stroke me. Good, that feels good, Mother. (*The lights dim slowly*)

nissim aloni

the
american
princess

TRANSLATED FROM THE HEBREW BY
RICHARD FLANTZ

characters

KING BONIFACIUS VICTOR FELIX of the House of Hohen-schwaden

FERDINAND: the Crown Prince, his son

AN ACTOR

voices

CAPITAN MIGUEL MEGERAS: police inspector

JEAN-PAUL KRUPNIK: film director

ELECTRICIAN

HERALD

act 1

SCENE ONE

The soft strains of a guitar are heard. Then this music is interrupted by a police siren, and the curtain rises. A strong spotlight falls on the face of Freddy, a young man of about twenty-five, who is seated on a stool on the right of the stage. He looks weary, but there is a strained, almost contorted smiled on his face. Over his clothes he wears a short scarlet cape, and in his hands he holds black gloves.

VOICE OF THE CAPITAN. Buenos dias, amigo. Here they call me Capitan, Capitan Miguel Megeras. That's a mighty big name in the police force — among the policemen and among the murderers too. So you'd better open up that big mouth of yours if you don't want us to start getting our hands dirty — entiendes? Go ahead and talk, amigo — we're listening.

FREDDY. (*Raising his head and looking up into the spotlight*) May I smoke, Miguel?

VOICE OF THE CAPITAN. (*Shouting*) No! . . . and wipe that filthy smile off your filthy face! Your father isn't even cold yet, Desalmado!

FREDDY. You don't have to sympathize with me, you know.

VOICE OF THE CAPITAN. Last night, between eight and ten o'clock, in the studio of Jean-Paul Krupnik on the Avenida Bolivar, you murdered your father with five bullets out of a thirty-eight caliber Browning revolver — so cut out the smiles, because all you've got coming to you is a filthy piece of rope, and you're not getting it to hang your dirty washing out on either, believe me. Sing your song, matador, and save your filthy soul. Get on with it!

FREDDY. Listen, Capitan — I don't mind you calling me a murderer. I bet it makes you feel good. But — (*Raising his head*) I want to see Senor Krupnik.

VOICE OF THE CAPITAN. No.

FREDDY. Why — no?

VOICE OF THE CAPITAN. Senor Krupnik, amigo, flew to New

York this morning.

FREDDY. (*Jumps up*) New York! (*Regains his self-control*) New York, eh? Salopard! Did he give evidence?

VOICE OF THE CAPITAN. Want to hear it?

FREDDY. Uh-uh.

KRUPNIK'S VOICE. I am shocked, amazed ... Fred! I had so many hopes for him—he is so photogenic ... I mean ... he has been nursing a ... a ... a blind passion, yes, passion, I think, how do you say ... to do something ... to define himself ... to ... he lost his sense of reality ...

FREDDY. That's enough. Thanks. (*To himself*) Lost his sense of reality. (*To the capitan*) It's OK, Capitan. You'll get your story. On one condition.

VOICE OF THE CAPITAN. No, amigo. No conditions.

FREDDY. Listen. Last night, between eight and ten o'clock, four people came to the studio in the Avenida Bolivar: three to kill and one to be killed. It was supposed to happen in a film, but it turned out to be in real life. Death. The camera stopped rolling and my father was still lying there—dead. (*Raises his head*) With a grin on his face. It's in the family. Want to know how it happened? Because of love. Yes. It happens. There was another character there among the four of us. Find her, Capitan. And bring her here. Quickly.

VOICE OF THE CAPITAN. Name.

FREDDY. (*Confused*) That's not so simple.

VOICE OF THE CAPITAN. So. She has no name.

FREDDY. She has. But it isn't her name.

VOICE OF THE CAPITAN. Give me the name!

FREDDY. Kokomakis.

VOICE OF THE CAPITAN. (*After a pause*) Kokomakis, eh?

FREDDY. Yes. Dolly. Dolly Kokomakis.

VOICE OF THE CAPITAN. From Shanghai.

FREDDY. No. New York. Calls herself the American Princess.

VOICE OF THE CAPITAN. The American Princess ... I've never heard of American princesses.

FREDDY. That's it. There aren't any.

VOICE OF THE CAPITAN. But you've got one?

FREDDY. Yes.

VOICE OF THE CAPITAN. Exactly what is this?

FREDDY. That's exactly what I don't know.

VOICE OF THE CAPITAN. Smart, eh? You know, amigo, it will give me great pleasure to wipe that smile off your face — and don't think I'm going to have to answer to God for it, because, you know something? God doesn't know you.

FREDDY. Three months ago, on Saturday, the 19th of May, around midnight, I was sitting in a bar, Café Vienna, on the Calle de la Mar, it was my birthday. Twenty-five. At midnight — yes it was midnight, I heard a clock striking somewhere — a man came in. He was tall, fat, bald and drunk — very drunk. He had a walking cane of cherry wood with an ivory handle, gold-rimmed eyeglasses and — no shoes. At first I thought he was a tourist looking for his shoes.

I was wrong. He was looking for me. In French. And blinking all the time. Then he bowed to me and fell down. Under the table. For a whole minute we exchanged blinks and grins. Very confusing. Finally he managed to say, in French, "L'americaine ... la princesse ..." He had left his shoes in the bar at the airfield. That was my birthday. May I stand up, Capitan? (*He stands up, picks up the chair and walks towards left front. Halfway he stops*) That was Jean-Paul Krupnik, the genius of the cinema ...

Some name, huh? He picked it himself. His real name is Ivan Krupnikov. Sad, isn't it? His father was a Russian chauffeur — ardent Bolshevik and all, but he blinked. The father doesn't fall far from the son. The revolution didn't approve of his blinking. They accused him of being cross-eyed. Lyrical types, those revolutionaries! He fled to Paris, married a Russian ballerina — from the Moulin Rouge — you know — and somehow, despite disappointments, despite the shortsightedness of the Fatherland, they brought Jean-Paul into the world — in the city of lights! (*He reaches the left front corner and raises his head*) May I smoke? (*Pause — silence*) Gracias.

VOICE OF THE CAPITAN. So one fine day Senor Krupnik appears from nowhere and whispers in your ear — "The American Princess"?

FREDDY. From under the table.

VOICE OF THE CAPITAN. And he had some news for you under the table, eh?

FREDDY. Exactly. He was here to make a film about my father's life.

VOICE OF THE CAPITAN. No me digas! A film about your father's life!

FREDDY. (*Raises his head to the capitan*) My father, Capitan, my late father, was a king.

VOICE OF THE CAPITAN. (*Exploding*) My late father, amigo, was Stalin.

FREDDY. Some democrat.

VOICE OF THE CAPITAN. That's enough. You expect me to swallow all this stuff about kings and princesses and the rest of the bull about filthy beatniks from the Calle de la Mar? (*Raises his voice*) I want the truth, amigo! You hear? (*Shouts*) The truth! The truth!

FREDDY. Look. (*The light falls on the throne where the king, in dressing gown and slippers, sits drowsing*)

FREDDY. (*Announcing, like a herald*) His Majesty King Bonifacius Victor Felix of the House of Hohenschwaden, King by the Grace of God over Great Bogomania, Prince of Upper Augusta and Marquis of the County of Pook. (*In his own voice*) Ex. (*The king sighs and turns over in his sleep*) Now, Felix van Schvank, teacher of French. (*Pause*) Ex. He's asleep. A long way below the equator. He's in exile. It's twenty years now. He had palaces, carriages, stables, petunia gardens, women. All he has left is the throne — and it's worn and shabby now. And the crown — he polishes it every day, to be prepared. Oh yes — and a book of poems, ex libris Bonifacius, bound in gold: Byron, Pushkin ... the lot. It's chained to the throne. And Freddy, what remains of the Crown Prince Ferdinand ... now plain Fred Vak. (*The king sighs, and Freddy echoes the sigh*) Yes, failures, failures ... but Papa never gave in. Even organized a league of exiled kings and appointed himself secretary of the South American branch. Then they spoke of revolutions and counter-revolutions, of the underground, of the degradations of democracy, of the new Middle Ages.

But the league disintegrated: no one paid their dues. And the few that did pay betrayed it in the end. They posed for photographs advertising mustard ... but not papa, no! He may have been dying — but he was proud! All sorts of scrawny fiery-eyed royalists made pilgrimages to him, fervently prophesying his return to the throne, in between mouthfuls. They would actually move him to tears, and then they would cut off locks of his hair for souvenirs. Now he's practically bald, and there isn't anyone to cut off his locks — hasn't been for years. Meanwhile Great Bogomania has grown a big black mane ... he started teaching French — (*Freddy suddenly pauses and turns towards the illuminated throne. The king, still sleeping, straightens up in his seat*)

KING. (*Shouting*) Schwank! Schwank! Schwank! (*The king immediately subsides again into his sleep*)

FREDDY. His civilian name obsessed him. Senor van Schwank! ... what a sound! ... he painted it on the door — in three different places, and again downstairs in the corridor, with an arrow pointing upwards. None of the tax-collectors ever made a mistake, not one ... but one day, about a year ago, a large heavy parcel arrived, with a huge Schwank scrawled in red letters over all six sides. U-S-A! There was a tape recorder inside, and a letter — signed: The American Princess. (*Light on the tape recorder*) That's how it began. A year and three months ago. Every month she sent five tapes, plus a thousand pesos, so that Papa wouldn't catch cold. And he recorded his memoirs. Not that he remembered anything — you understand, Capitan — Father remembered very little of the days of his reign, almost nothing. Nothing, in fact. (*To himself*) Maybe because he had tried so hard, for twenty years, not to forget the kingdom. It's like a man who pinches himself to keep awake till all he feels is the pain of the pinching. (*To the capitan*) But the letter from New York was addressed to His Majesty the King and signed with due respect and obeisance. Father even found a trace of a tear on it. The light broke through. He began filling tapes every day. He recorded them, put a stamp on them, and sent them back — express, registered airmail, to Dolly Kokomakis, Poste

Restante, New York 13. Charged to her. (*He urges his father to get on with his work*)

KING. (*Jumps up from the throne*) Oh Cecilia, Cecilia!

FREDDY. (*Almost ecstatically*) His Majesty never disappointed Dolly . . . (*Music. The king rises, a microphone in his hand*)

KING. Cecilia.

FREDDY. (*Returns to his corner*) The queen. My mother. She died giving birth to me.

KING. Oh Cecilia, my Cecilia, so soft, so white, with your auburn hair . . . do you remember the lake, Cecilia? And the canoe, and the pine grove, and the evening birds in the sky, and the glimmering lights in the pavilion that blushing spring. Oh, that silent whispering spring that will never, never return, Cecilia, oh Cecilia! (*Weeps*)

FREDDY. (*From his corner*) But life goes on . . . Bertha!

KING. (*Giggles*) Bertha! . . .

FREDDY. Bertha didn't give birth to me . . . she was the wife of a captain in the cavalry.

KING. (*Giggling mischievously*) Bertha, Bertha, little coy Bertha, with your sweet swanlike snow-white neck . . . the woods were full of blackberries then, and when suddenly the rain came pouring down and lightning bolts sent electric darts flashing through the wooden hut, through your startled eyes and your auburn hair . . . and then, by the fire, with burning logs crackling and smouldering . . . reindeer's horns on the wall . . . the bottle of madeira, your maddening gaze . . . that birth and death, oh Bertha . . . Bertha! (*The giggling turns into weeping*)

FREDDY. That capitan, Capitan, became one of the leaders of the revolution. But then they appointed him to the post of attaché in Oslo. That's where Bertha gave birth. (*Pathetically*) Oh, my brother, my brother!

KING. (*Pathetically*) Oh where, oh where are you, proud Matilda, restless Ludmilla, Olympian Greta. Oh Greta—how white was your gleaming forehead as your auburn hair streamed down upon it . . . and you, Olivia, so soft and pale, your skin the texture of the setting sun, and you, my delicate, fragile Lisetta, do you still remember our games of pinochle? Where, oh where? Where have you been strewn by the whirlwinds of fate, auburn-haired Dolores; Martha, my pale dewdrop; Sandy, mysterious Sandy—did you ever win that tennis championship? And you, Zelda, tootsie, did you make it to Palestine?

FREDDY. One of those tiny newly independent countries in Africa. Avid nationalists. Plenty of folklore.

KING. Today, the 19th May, is the twenty-fifth anniversary of the death of my beloved wife, Queen Cecilia. Today is the twenty-fifth birthday of my son, the Crown Prince Ferdinand. At night in this alien city, I see steam rising from the crevices of the earth. Oh Gods of the depths, will there be an end to this exile? I am alone, I have no one, save one poor lonely soul in the street of the moon—Marita ... at times, in my dreams, I see her in the image of my dead queen. Marita ... (*The light over the king goes out, leaving only a beam on Freddy in the left front corner*)

FREDDY. Marita ... she used to work on the Calle de la Luna, next to the railway station. You know her? Midnight shift, thirty pesos. Very religious girl, but the train whistles used to send shudders through her. Made her very popular. Some Saturdays I used to think the trains were there just for her! And people say religion is on the way out. Father and I weren't particularly religious, but we lived near the railway station, down by the port, in the Avenida del Puerto, and it's only natural that we went down to look at the trains. Not together, for sure. But in the same train. Around midnight—thirty pesos. Only ... father didn't know about our ... partnership ... he didn't know he wasn't as alone as he thought ... he could never have imagined, in his most auburn dreams, that ... I ... I? No, I wasn't crazy about Marita. Not at all. Pale. White. Covered with bruises, always ... but with Marita, I could sometimes feel that I was his son ...

VOICE OF THE CAPITAN. Desgraciado, pobre desgraciado!

FREDDY. (*Raises his head*) What is it, Capitan? My attitude not to your taste? Or do you think it's inconvenient to have the whole family in the same train? Not at all—until the American Princess cast her aura upon us there were no collisions. Father traveled twice a week. Tuesdays and

Saturdays, like he had a subscription ticket. I traveled all
the other days—if I had enough pesos. Marita, Capitan,
was always as formal as a conductor! There were times
when I had to pawn the crown, without Papa knowing, of
course ...

VOICE OF THE CAPITAN. You are nothing but a hunk of filth,
amigo!

FREDDY. You don't like me so much, eh, Capitan?

VOICE OF THE CAPITAN. (*In a whisper*) God has forsaken you.

FREDDY. And you're sure he yearns for you, eh? Could be,
could be ... anyway, as they say in the fairy tales, on the
19th of May Krupnik arrived—Jean-Paul Krupnik, the
genius of the cinema—to make a film about my father's
life. Father received the news with mixed feelings. (*Ship
sirens are heard*)

SCENE TWO

*The flat of the Hohenschwadens, in the Avenida del Puerto. In the
center, the throne. On the right, the tape recorder. The king, in
dressing gown and slippers, enters furiously, holding a bunch of
papers in his hand.*

KING. A film about my life! Of all the confounded impudence!
A film about my life! And you, my own flesh and blood—
you dare insist that I sign this contract giving this Kropotkin
or Kropochnikov—some name he's got!—the exclusive
right to turn me into a posturing king preserved in rolls of
celluloid, into a royal pudding cooked to the tastes of
spinster social workers?! You're generous, my boy. A true
son ... and if it isn't too much to ask, perhaps I may be
informed who and what this rare Krapnik is, this man
who takes on himself this heroic mission, this historic task,
of turning my life, my kingdom, into a conservatory, open
to the general public, with equal rates of entry for all?
(*Shouts*) I am not a museum! (*Enter Freddy holding a top hat
in his hands*)

FREDDY. Nice?

KING. A top hat!

FREDDY. Avenida Bolivar!

KING. Fantastic!

FREDDY. The gloves should arrive any minute.

KING. Gloves! Only a week ago the municipal tax-collector threatened to impound the throne, and now—gloves, top hat, caviar, asparagus—

FREDDY. You like asparagus!

KING. I don't like revolutions!!!

FREDDY. No one's killing you yet.

KING. And in your opinion, this contract guarantees me eternal life?

FREDDY. Death, life . . . this Jean-Paul's just a film director— when he says let there be light, out comes a film. That's all. He's making a film about your life because he's crazy about kings. Just imagine.

KING. Crazy about kings! Why doesn't he go and collect stamps?!

FREDDY. Too late. He's already made three films. All of them about kings. All of them failures, par excellence, but failures that opened an epoch.

KING. I can imagine the epoch.

FREDDY. He put Napoleon into a musical comedy.

KING. Napoleon was always funny!

FREDDY. Not on the screen. This was a musical comedy without a moral. Didn't bring in any money, but it did bring him a prize. Symbolic. And a name. In the trade journals they call him the King of Kings.

KING. (*Laughs*) Kropochnikov?!

FREDDY. (*Holding the contract*) What, you haven't signed yet? Tsk, tsk, tsk . . . Papa! Don't be naughty. Don't forget— Dolly sent him.

KING. Sent that charlatan?!

FREDDY. You think Jean-Paul could pay you that advance of one thousand pesos out of his own pocket?

KING. I have no intention of ferreting in M'sieu's pockets. All I know is that this Kropochnikov is not, has never been, and will never be the princess's emissary! It's absurd! You'll find out yet, son, that he isn't even Krupnik!

FREDDY. Well, you aren't exactly van Schwank.

KING. (*Hurt*) I am van Schwank, Ferdinand, because circumstances have forced Hohenschwaden to bow his head, until his hour comes. And that hour will not be long in coming, I swear to you, but till then Hohenschwaden must protect himself from every Krupnik, even if he isn't Krupnik.

FREDDY. Papa, Jean-Paul knows your memoirs by heart. You know who chirped them in his ear? Not the birdies. Those tapes, Papa, bearing all the glory of the House of Hohenschwaden, are in the sole possession of Madame. She can play with them, engrave them on the tables of her heart, or erase them.

KING. Erase them?

FREDDY. But no. Madame is gracious. Jean-Paul arrives in New York. The tapes are sent to him at his hotel. When he hears them, he wets his pants, believe it or not, drinks and drinks and drinks, throws crying fits. For nights. Loses shoes all over the place. Till Dolly chirps in his ear again and says "Go to him, make a film about his life. Money's no object." If not for Dolly, Papa, Jean-Paul would have come here from New York on foot.

KING. But it's incredible! Why, why a film?

FREDDY. Why not?

KING. The princess must know what price you and I will have to pay for these colored reels — the crown!

FREDDY. Which means what, Papa?

KING. *You're* asking me?

FREDDY. Why not I, Papa?

KING. You're the Crown Prince, Ferdinand.

FREDDY. Which means exactly what, Papa?

KING. Ferdinand ... you don't know what you're saying ... *we* give up the kingdom?! You, you, give up, yield, renounce the kingdom ... we'll never be able to go back, never ... we'll no longer be able to hope, to believe, to yearn for the kingdom ... we'll be condemning ourselves to eternal exile ...

FREDDY. Papa, the kingdom is lost.

KING. No! No! Never!

FREDDY. Lost, finis, foutu. It's twenty years now. You're asleep. Open your eyes. Read the papers. (*Goes out*)

KING. (*Calls after him*) I read the papers! I go to the city

library every day! Gray, gray, gray—that's what Great
Bogomania is today, with its democracy! Gray clothes,
gray houses, gray hearts. They're all hypochondriacs, all
those democrats! Neurotics! Suicides! A plane crash every
day! Small wonder they're all looking for their souls ...
Every day! I sit in the city library and envisage my return
(*To Freddy, who is approaching the stage*) with you, Ferdinand!
You will return—to be King! (*Enter Freddy, an untied tie
around his neck*)

FREDDY. Meanwhile fix my tie for me. (*Lowers his head*) Don't
waste my time, Papa, sign.

KING. And if I don't?

FREDDY. (*Walks away from him*) Look, if I suddenly have the
good fortune to be visited by a plump fairy with wings of
gold, then, Papa, I'm not the boy to say "Gracias, but my
father needs the crown for higher roles." (*The tie is tied*)
Gracias.

KING. Plump ... fairy?

FREDDY. Jean-Paul.

KING. Why fairy?

FREDDY. Don't you know? He's a well-known homosexual.
(*Goes out*)

KING. (*Shouts*) Ferdinand!!! (*Paces around the room*) Bon dieu
de bon dieu! That's all I needed! No, no, no. (*Shouts*)
Ferdinand! Come in here at once!

FREDDY. Is that the gloves?

KING. I must speak to you. Sit down.

FREDDY. Must it be now? Don't worry. I won't get pregnant.

KING. (*Shouts*) Sit down! (*Freddy sits down*) Oh, if your mother
were only alive! (*Paces around the room*) Ferdinand!

FREDDY. Yes, papa.

KING. You have to get married.

FREDDY. Not to Jean-Paul, Papa!

KING. Shhhhh! I don't like your brand of humour young sir!
You have to get married. Straight away. And don't give
me any excuses. I know: the choice isn't easy, and there
aren't many to choose from. And you know very well what
I think of those royal families ... miserable creatures! ...
but we must forgive and forget ... you have to get married.

Recently, by your leave, I have been thinking a great deal about young Pauline Schtumpf-Schattau ... the daughter of that ape who sells his family on television ... but ... forgive and forget ... her name, at least, doesn't appear in the gossip columns of the social register, thank God.

FREDDY. She's dead. Died in the flush of her youth. Fifteen years ago. Scarlet fever.

KING. Scarlet fever? In our times? Strange, strange ... she was so young ... fate! ... but you have to get married ... you remember Charlotte, I hope, Charlotte of Gindenburgen —

FREDDY. Papa! Charlotte's a nun! Been in a convent for ages! One fine day she discovered that Gindenburgen hasn't existed for six hundred years.

KING. There you are! The newspapers! ... you can't be sure of a thing! ... but you have to get married. There's still — God help us — Isabel ...

FREDDY. No. I can't get married.

KING. No?! Why?

FREDDY. I'm about to become a father.

KING. You're about to become a what?

FREDDY. A father.

KING. (*Paces around the room*) Bon dieu de bon dieu. How? When? Why? Why didn't you tell me?

FREDDY. It only happened today.

KING. What do you mean, it only happened today?

FREDDY. I got a part in Jean-Paul's film.

KING. A father?

FREDDY. A father.

KING. Whose father?

FREDDY. My father.

KING. Your father? You mean —

FREDDY. You.

KING. Me?

FREDDY. Bonifacius Victor Felix of the House of Hohenschwaden. In the days of his youth!

KING. You — me — in the film?

FREDDY. Just imagine. Jean-Paul says I was born for the part. (*A ring*) Ah! The gloves! At last! (*Goes out*)

KING. (*Calls after him, softly*) You were born for the part. You were born to be king. Not a king of shadows with a tin coronet and a cardboard scepter. I no longer have a son. (*Enter Fred, elegantly dressed, wearing a top hat, holding a cane in one hand and something hidden in the other*)

FREDDY. (*Opening his hand*) You see, Papa? Browning, thirty-eight caliber. A humble token from Jean-Paul. (*Looks at the pistol*) "Mes homages. Jean-Paul Krupnik. The fifth of June." (*Puts the pistol in his coat pocket*) Instead of a sword. (*A car horn is heard*)

FREDDY. Jean-Paul. (*Takes the contract*) Sign, Papa. It's a gift from the gods. And believe me, I'm not going to let this opportunity slip through my fingers even if Jean-Paul asks me to pose as a cube. (*Turns to go*) You aren't going out tonight? It's Saturday. The railway station ...

KING. Yes, it's Saturday ...

FREDDY. And don't forget. Asparagus. It's good for your health. Adios. (*Goes out*)

KING. (*Walks to the porch*) A king of shadows! (*Comes back into the room*) The kingdom is not lost! (*Takes the microphone, in firm determination. Music. The lights focus on him*) The lion hunt. Green, green, green — (*But his heart is not in it*) light green, dark green, rare, gleaming, greenish green, strange green, bright green, blazing green, pale, soft, sad green was the forest, the virgin forest of the wild lion, the forest kingdom of the proud lion, the prairie lion, the auburn lion ... (*Softly, helplessly*) green was the green forest, green and dark and only the death of its king was brown ... auburn ... it was winter in the forest, the last winter ... (*The music stops. He puts down the microphone, approaches the throne, sits down, opens the book lying there, and reads*)

"O wild west wind ...
Scatter, as from an unextinguished hearth
Ashes and sparks, my words among mankind!
Be through my lips to unawakened earth
The trumpet of a prophecy! O wind,
If Winter comes, can Spring be far behind?"

(*Closes the book, musing*) Oh Browning, Browning ...

SCENE THREE

A spotlight on Freddy.

FREDDY. The soiree at Krupnik's was private. Just the family
circle. And what a family! No less than a dozen Shake-
spearean character actors as footmen, heralds, soldiers, and
country girls from the County of Pook. Three philosophy
students from Paris who volunteered to portray the leader
of the Bogomanian liberation movement. A checkerboard
horse, of plywood — very heroic. And father's women, of
course, all of them. Bertha, Martha, Sandy ... straight
from the "Sexy" Night Club, Paris. Only Lisetta was
Turkish ... apart from that, everybody, without exception,
ate almonds. Some Indian fakir wrote a book saying almonds
are good. Since then in film circles they all eat almonds.
Me too. He was right, that fakir. They're not bad. Just
have to get used to them. Anyhow, in between almonds, I
discovered my family. No, not in the film. In real life. The
House of Hohenschwaden. Without the veil of the pine
groves. For Krupnik, Capitan, had no intention of filming
the pine groves, or the petunia gardens, or that silent
spring ... the script was all action. In one of the very first
scenes Father — me — appears in Venice, fighting a duel
with an Armenian chemist for the favors of a plump
prima donna called Batashova. He's passionate — Papa —
in the film. And they cut his name down a bit, too. Bonny!
Short and to the point. I guessed at once Papa wouldn't be
too keen on the script. Especially as because of that delay —
Venice — he turns up late for the opening of the winter
session of Parliament, drunk as a lord (*Smiles*) and makes
the Prime Minister sing a duet with him in front of the
whole assembly. I'm sure Krupnik must have meant something by that, but I doubt if Father could have grasped it;
actually — he was never very musical — at the most he'd go
to an opera now and then. It was a breezy script, Capitan,
full of fireworks, you know, the kind that burst in the sky
and stay stuck in your eyes ... the queen, my mother — I
mean my wife — (*Pause. Looks up at the capitan. Smiles*)

Krupnik brought her back to life. She no longer died
giving birth to me. During the whole film she paces up
and down on the roof, naked, alarming the capital with
prophetic cries. To the background of a Viennese waltz.
Or something like that. Krupnik must have meant something. I wanted to know what. I took the script, went
through the almonds, and got to Café Vienna. It was
almost morning when I finished reading, and then the
phone rang. Yes, Krupnik. (*Music. A sign descends:* Café
Vienna. *A table and a chair. The filmscript lies on the table. Fred
retreats to the table, sits down on it, the receiver in his hand*) Yes,
Jean-Paul. It's me. (*Lowers the receiver. To the capitan*) By his
voice I could tell he'd completely lost his shoes. (*Into the
phone*) Come out from under the table, Jean-Paul, you'll
feel freer . . . No, you don't have to call me "Your Highness",
it's already dawn . . . What? What are you blabbering
there? . . . No, I don't understand Russian . . . Not a
word . . . I don't speak it either . . . Yes, that's right, I've
never tried, right, because of the political situation . . .
(*Listens*) I know Shakespeare was a Russian, that's not
new, but be a little less lyrical, Jean-Paul, and tell me
what you want . . . OK, I'll call you Vanya . . . No, you
don't have to sing now, Vanya, it doesn't sound so good
on the phone, and there's birds already . . . Birds, the
things that fly, yes . . . Vanyusha . . . What? (*Looks around*)
No, there no one else here, there can't be anyone here, I'm
alone . . . Speak more clearly, Van — (*Stops talking and gets
off the table*) To break the contract? . . . To run away? . . .
Listen, Jean-Paul, take two aspirins, get into bed — (*Listens*)
Jean-Paul, I have a contract, you signed it yourself, stop
mumbling there, damn you. I have a contract, you hear?
A contract. Signed and sealed. And I'm not running away
anywhere, I'm going to ride that horse, plywood or not.
(*Appears to be getting angry*) Speak clearly, man! Why do I
have to run away? Who do I have to run away from?
What are you mumbling there, Krupnik? (*Listens and then
says at once*) Stop singing, damn you, stop singing. No, I
don't know Persephone, let Persephone go to hell, I spit on
Persephone . . . I didn't sign any contract with her, I —

(*Stops talking. Lowers the receiver*) Oh, no. No that. (*Picks up the receiver*) Stop crying, Jean-Paul ... Vanya, Vanyusha ... Vanyushka ... No, you're not filth ... you're not shit ... you're not a son of a bitch ... I know you're all alone ... Pain, pain, pain, right ... And illusion ... All right, the last one ... To you ... To the king ... Yes, we'll make a film, we'll make a king, buenas noches ... No, Ivan, this is not the time to recite Romeo, believe me ... (*Listens*) that sounds more like Juliet ... Yes, in Russian it's different, I'm sure, completely different, the other way round, in fact ... Jean-Paul! (*Listens*) Jean-Paul! (*Listens*) Vanyusha! (*Listens. No answer. Puts down the receiver*) Filth. (*To himself*) Persephone. (*To the capitan*) You know who Persephone is, Capitan? Never mind. I didn't know either. I never had a classical education. She was a goddess, that's all. The Greek press — of the time — crowned her Queen of Hades. Hell. You understand, Capitan, in Krupnik's script, the old king has to appear in the second half of the film. What happens then is simple: I stop being my father, and I become my father's son, and I spray five bullets into him. In the film. Krupnik must have meant something.

SCENE FOUR

Darkened stage. Only the voice of the electrician is heard and, in the background, chuckles of workers, pounding of hammers, footsteps, etc. It's the film studio.

VOICE OF THE ELECTRICIAN. Hey, Ernesto! Give us some light 'ere so's we can see somethin' in this dark. Gawd almighty! Is that the king's flag? What've we come to? Look at it, jus' look at it — you can see what kind of a king we got jus' by lookin' at the flag. Better turn off the light, Ernesto, so's we can't see it. (*Laughter*) You know, this Senor Krupnik may be a great man, but if you ask me, I says he ain't normal ... hey, put the light on again, Ernesto, let's 'ave a look at the flower. (*Light on the flower*) Christ! Jus' like me ol' woman's face! An' what's it for? This a king what eats sunflower seeds? (*Laughter*) 'E ain't normal, I tells you ...

listen — yesterday, when we's shootin' that scene in the forest, he suddenly grabs 'old o' me, jus' like that, and says, "Listen," 'e says to me, "you're a good electrician, so tell me — what's better: a bird in the bush or two in the hand?" What do you say, eh? Reckon that's normal? So 'elp me, man's a strange animal. Lives so many years and still, don't understand nothin'. Two birds in the hand or one up the bush! Up his ol' woman's bush! And then you gotta work your guts out for a bloke like that. Ah! 'Ere's another one. (*Enter the king*) A new actor every day.

KING. (*In a rage*) Senor Krupnik!

VOICE OF THE ELECTRICIAN. With a 'at like that 'e'll rule the roost 'ere.

KING. (*In the center of the stage, in the focus of the colored lights*) Please move these lights away, Senor Krupnik, I demand that you switch off these lights immediately. (*Tries to get out of the circle of lights*) You can't blind me with these lights, Senor, and if you're trying to be funny I don't think you can outdo the scurrilous script you've called "My life and loves" — but nothing can surprise me any more! Where is my son?

VOICE OF THE ELECTRICIAN. With 'is ol' woman, if you ask me.

KING. You think that's funny? Let me tell you, Senor Krupnik, there is a limit even to stupidity. And if your fertile imagination allows you to presume that you have before you a helpless man, one whose life is subject to your caprices, then allow me to inform you, categorically, that you are making a mistake, Senor, a mistake that is no less crude than your manners. You think you can work your whims on both the living and the dead, do you? Well, I won't allow it! (*White light on the king*) Cecilia in an isolated wing! (*Shouts, almost choking*) My queen! Who gave you the right to take the queen out of her grave and to portray her as a madwoman whom, I, I, with my own hands, imprisoned in an isolated wing of the palace?!!! Why? Why? Why?

VOICE OF THE ELECTRICIAN. Medra, a speech out o' Shakespeare! Don't understand.

KING. (*Waving the filmscript*) But this you do understand! Here you swim like a fish in this filthy puddle you so calmly call my life, my life? Venice! Could you be so kind, Senor Krupnik, as to give me a clue, a slight hint, as to how I happen to find myself, in the dead of night, in a dark canal in Venice, go on to fight a duel with some Armenian chemist for the favors of some prima donna from some state opera by the name of Batashova? Have you taken leave of your senses, Senor Krupnik?

VOICE OF THE ELECTRICIAN. Listen, I got a question to ask you—

KING. I have never been in Venice! Never! I despise Venice! And who is this tempestuous Armenian chemist? Where did he suddenly spring from? What is all this Armenian chemistry about, anyway? What purpose does it serve? What's it for? Why—

VOICE OF THE ELECTRICIAN. Listen, I got a question to ask you. Two birds in the hand or one—

KING. A Saturnalia! A fool king, half imbecile half villain, is crowned in a lavish ceremony, while the mad queen screams from the isolated wing of the palace, suffering from labor pains! I suppose, Senor Artiste, that the reference here is to my son, my real flesh and blood son; for in another part of your masterpiece—this, no doubt, being your famous sense of humor—you drop a hint that my late Aunt Flora gave birth to a calf!

VOICE OF THE ELECTRICIAN. As long as it ain't the other way round, what do you care?

KING. In the name of my family, Senor, in the name of a family that, true enough, is much reduced and impoverished, I express my resentment. And I shall not conceal from you, Senor Krupnik, that this morning I wrote a letter to New York.

VOICE OF THE ELECTRICIAN. You don't say!

KING. And I sincerely believe, Senor, that very soon an end will be put to this witches' dance.

VOICE OF THE ELECTRICIAN. Amen. As long as they pay the wages. And stick on a different beard. In red it looks like a carrot.

KING. I thank you deeply.

VOICE OF THE ELECTRICIAN. Thank my ol' woman. Now let's

see your profile.

KING. (*Suddenly*) How dare you, you Bolshevik!

VOICE OF THE ELECTRICIAN. Bol-sher-vuck yourself. We gotta shoot the next scene —

KING. You don't have to shoot anything! No more scenes! No more pictures! There isn't going to be a film! (*Music. The king stops talking. Freddy enters very slowly in a blue spotlight — very tall, wearing a long robe, a crown on his head, and holding a scepter. His face is frozen. He slowly walks towards the front of the stage*)

KING. (*Softly, not believing*) Ferdinand!

FREDDY. (*Slowly, a sort of smile on his face*) Bonifacius Victor Felix of the House of Hohenschwaden ...

KING. You ...

FREDDY. You!

KING. The king ... the crown ... the scepter ...

FREDDY. The palace ... the petunia gardens ... the pine groves ...

KING. You're radiant ... the aura of kingship is upon you ... so tall ..

FREDDY. It's the shoes. (*Raises the robe and shows him*) Very high heels. (*To the electrician*) Move the light away. That's enough. Buenos dias. Gracias. (*Normal stage light*) You see, Papa? Twenty kilowatts of electricity. What brings you here to us? You haven't signed yet. We're going to start shooting —

KING. I read the script. You left it at home.

FREDDY. (*Takes the script*) Yes. Enjoy it?

KING. Ferdinand, please, trust me. Believe me. I hear rumbles of laughter, but I can feel a dark hand, a threatening hand, and a malicious mind — Venice! I never set foot there! ... but the man who's reshowing my life managed to discover with that special sense of his that I detest the city, and stuck it under my belt along with some dubious prima donna called Batashova.

FREDDY. Papa — you have been in Venice.

KING. Me? You're joking?

FREDDY. But you have been there. In Venice.

KING. What do you mean? How do you know? When?

FREDDY. You told me.

KING. I told you?

FREDDY. The tales of my childhood. The bridge of sighs ... Verrocchio's Condotierre, on horseback ...

KING. I don't remember any horse or any condotierre!

FREDDY. (*Softly, as if trying to imitate his father*)

Dans Venise la Rouge
Pas un bateau qui bouge
Pas un ...

How did it go? The silent boats in blushing Venice, the ladies preparing for the Ball, putting black masks over their eyes, in front of the mirror ... Venise ... Venise ...

KING. Yes, that poem, Venise ... Venise ... but Venice ... I don't remember!

FREDDY. Try.

KING. Venice ... So many years ... (*Looks at his son*) Are you sure, Ferdinand?

FREDDY. I remember.

KING. Perhaps ... I can't remember ... at times I'm not sure ... so many things in a jumble ... like a whirlpool ... Venice ... I must have been very young ... I traveled a lot ... overseas, too ... to Sweden ... yes ... Sweden ... a strange country ... Venice ... I can't remember ... (*Approaches Freddy as if he were his last resort, says softly*) and yet, perhaps I have never been there ...

FREDDY. You have been there, Papa, and that isn't the only bit of fun that's slipped your memory.

KING. (*Starts, steps backwards. After a pause*) You don't believe—

FREDDY. Dolly Kokomakis, of New York, our princess, claims that mother was locked up in the palace in an isolated wing, from the day I was born till the day they kicked you out and blew up the palace. The funny thing is that they didn't find her among the ruins. Nor anywhere else. She disappeared. You don't remember anything like that, do you, Papa?

KING. No!

FREDDY. No, Papa?

KING. I say no!

FREDDY. No what, Papa?

KING. I say no film! There'll be no film!

FREDDY. Think so?

KING. (*Leaps up to his son's head, snatches the crown, holds it in his hand*) Yes!

FREDDY. Are you mad?

KING. Yes, I'm mad.

FREDDY. Father —

KING. Maybe I don't remember. But I know.

FREDDY. Listen. Give me the crown.

KING. You're spitting on the crown. You aren't a king.

FREDDY. We have to start shooting any minute. As soon as Jean-Paul turns up. Give me that crown.

KING. Never! I'm the king!

FREDDY. You're a child. (*Takes the crown*) A bit ridiculous, isn't it? You're losing your head. The crown's yours, don't worry. I'm only king on the screen. A reflection. And that's all I need.

KING. Ferdinand, for you to be king of these shadows your father must die.

FREDDY. When you calm down you'll see that isn't necessary. (*With Freddy off guard, the king leaps up and snatches the crown again*)

KING. It is necessary.

FREDDY. (*Approaches his father and takes his arm*) Listen, Papa, what we're making here is a film, but not about you. You've forgotten. Everything. Long ago. The film's about me. Yes, me. Here. Now give me that prop. We have to start shooting.

KING. You are not my son.

FREDDY. I want that crown on my head — now.

KING. (*In a loud voice, suddenly*) We, Bonifacius Victor Felix of the House of Hohenschwaden, King by the Grace of God —

FREDDY. (*In a whisper*) Father!

KING. Hereby publicly announce that he who was our son, the Crown Prince —

FREDDY. Father!!

KING. Ferdinand of the House of Hohenschwaden — (*On the rear curtain appears a huge shadow of a man carrying a cane and wearing glasses. They both shift their gaze to the rear curtain and then look up again at the man who is casting the shadow*)

KRUPNIK'S VOICE. I apologize, Your Majesty . . . please forgive me . . . I had no right . . . I'm terribly sorry . . .

FREDDY. (*Gently taking the crown from his father*) Senor Jean-Paul Krupnik—

KING. (*To Freddy*) Don't come to my house. (*Turns towards the light, looks for a long while at the unseen figure, and says quickly, waving his umbrella*) You people want to kill a king. (*Turns and goes out quickly*)

FREDDY. (*To Krupnik*) Papa. (*Lights out*)

SCENE FIVE

The scene is the same. In the dark a trumpet is heard and then the voice of the herald.

VOICE OF THE HERALD. Hear ye, hear ye! The Coronation Day of Bonifacius, the Great King, by the Grace of God, of Great Bogomania, Prince of Upper Augusta, Marquis of the County of Pook. Hear ye, hear ye!

Coronation music. Freddy, the young king, stands stooped on the coronation stage, to the right of the flag, holding three colored balloons. Suddenly the shrill scream of a woman is heard, and then repeated. Freddy jumps up, raises his hand, and with his left hand raises the balloons.

KING. Ladies, gentlemen, my people. The queen is bringing the crown prince into the world! (*Applause. He raises his hand to silence it*) Not yet! Not yet . . . (*Waves the balloons*) Ladies, gentlemen, my people. On this my coronation day, I have brought you three balloons. In colors. Not with symbolic intent, nor, God forbid, in irony, but because I am firmly resolved not to make a coronation speech. A few brief remarks, yes. I am sure that in these balloons you will find, each of you according to his understanding and world outlook, the entire text of the coronation speech. That's it. Applause, please. (*Silence. He looks around and then grins*) No? Such nice balloons? Such pretty colors? No?

Alas, alas, alas. I thought I'd find understanding. I even thought we'd sing some rounds together. (*Sings*) Papa loves Mambo ... mama loves Mam ... (*Silence*) No? By no means? We're starting off on the wrong foot. Tomorrow it'll be in all the papers. Banner headlines. "Rupture in Relations between King and People." (*Suddenly jumps up and runs in confusion to the sunflower*) Rupture? (*Picks some seeds out of the sunflower, and cracks their shells between his teeth as he speaks*) I know what you're thinking. I know what's buzzing through the red veins of your agitating brains! I have a sensitive skin. Yes? Pardon? What? (*Becomes quiet, then giggles*) You'll chop off my head? You? Uh uh. Good chance you won't. Passions today aren't what they used to be. They're getting soft. Democracy. Desires drop by fifty percent. Statistics! As for historical sense — nil, zero, zero. The head's safe. What next? (*Suddenly*) Exile? (*Leaves the sunflower and runs to the point of light under the sign: "Silence. Shooting in Progress."*) I haven't finished! (*Reaches the point of light*) Exile! A bad mistake! Tsk ... tsk ... tsk ... tsk. How? For I'll still be here with you, comrades, far away perhaps, but here, with you, in the city squares, in your innermost rooms ... what? You'll all give up smoking king-size cigarettes? You'll stop drinking Royal Beer? You won't ever go to the Rex Cinema? (*Softly*) And no one, ever again, will shout Ex-cel-si-or? No, comrades: not exile. (*Approaches as if telling them a secret*) You have to kill me. To kill me, to burn the body, the crown, the sceptre, the robe — every single thing ... not to leave a trace ... (*Straightens up*) And even now, at this very moment, the queen is giving birth to the crown prince, the king who will succeed me! You can hear the pains from here. (*Pause. Looks around*) You are silent. There's only the buzz of those agitating brains ... buzz ... buzz ... (*Like an adviser*) The king must be killed, comrades, I tell you the king must be killed — but who'll do it? Who? Who? (*Raises his head*) Him? Him? Won't be long now, he'll feel the pain ... stop! I heard something. (*Runs to the coronation stage and climbs onto it*) Him? Him? I can hear something. Yes. (*In the silence the scream of a woman is heard, and the young king straightens up and spreads out his arms*) Ladies, gentlemen, my people! The queen has given birth to the crown prince. (*Shouts*) Applause! (*Silence*) I thank all those who have congratulated me. I thank all the visitors. I thank all those who have thanked me. Out. (*Softly*) I shall remain with my son, the crown prince. (*Bows his head. Coronation music*)

KRUPNIK'S VOICE. Cut! Lights! (*The lights gradually drop. Freddy stands still, his head bowed*)

KRUPNIK'S VOICE. You're a great king, Fred, a great king, by the grace of the gods. (*Freddy takes off the crown, contorts his face. Lights dim into darkness*)

SCENE SIX

Guitar music in the distance. Misty light on the stage. On the right, a streetlamp. Downstage, a neon sign: Hotel Excelsior. The king enters from left, carrying a bunch of flowers. He stops, takes his watch out of his pocket, glances at it, and returns it to his pocket. Takes out a notebook, leafs through it.

KING. (*Repeating to himself*) Oh, Marita!

I am gone

Away from my own bosom: I have left
My strong identity, my real self,
Somewhere between the throne, and where I sit
Here on this spot of earth ...
            But cannot I create?
Cannot I form? Cannot I fashion forth
Another world, another universe.
To overbear and crumble this to nought?
Where is another chaos? Where?

(*He concludes with a theatrical gesture, and when he turns around sees Fred*)

KING. Is that you, Ferdinand? (*A train whistle blows. Freddy approaches his father slowly, hands in pockets*)

FREDDY. Yes, it's me. How are you?

KING. What are you doing here?

FREDDY. (*Takes a cigarette out of his pocket*) Banging around. (*Lights the cigarette*)

KING. Here? Such a long way from Avenida Bolivar?

FREDDY. I've got a car.

KING. A car ... you're quick. Seems to me it isn't a week since you left home ...

FREDDY. Yes. A week. About that.

KING. I didn't know you took an interest in the area around the railway station.

FREDDY. Yes ... yes ... And you?

KING. Me?

FREDDY. What are you doing here?

KING. I'm doing here what I'm doing here.

FREDDY. Reciting.

KING. Reciting!

FREDDY. I thought you only recited Tuesday and Saturday nights. Today's Monday.

KING. Today's Monday, that's right. Why should that upset you?

FREDDY. It doesn't upset me at all. I'd noticed that you had fixed habits. Now I notice a change. That's all.

KING. Am I supposed to understand that you've been spying on me?

FREDDY. You used to tell me yourself.

KING. That I go to the railway station!

FREDDY. To watch the trains.

KING. To watch the trains. You have no objections, I hope?

FREDDY. No.

KING. Well then, I'm *going* to the station. On Monday.

FREDDY. (*Gestures with his head*) With flowers?

KING. What?

FREDDY. (*Points to his hand*) What you're holding there, behind your back.

KING. (*Brings out the flowers*) With flowers!

FREDDY. You're going to watch the trains with flowers.

KING. I'm going to watch the trains with flowers.

FREDDY. I go without. (*A train whistle*)

FREDDY. A train.

KING. (*Takes out his watch*) Yes. Departing.

FREDDY. That station never rests.

KING. (*Was absorbed in his watch and did not hear*) What?

FREDDY. Nothing.

KING. (*Looks at his watch*) This fog ...

FREDDY. (*Looks at his watch*) Midnight. A little after.

KING. Thank you. Excuse me. I must go.

FREDDY. Father — (*The king turns*) I can give you a lift.

KING. (*Confused*) No ... no ... thank you ... I want to walk around a little while longer ... as far as the station .. I love walking around these streets ... alone ... to remember ... I remember ... I remember a lot. Too much ... it's all I have left now — my memory ... my fool memory ...

FREDDY. You haven't heard from — Dolly?

KING. No. I'm still waiting.

FREDDY. Both of you are always waiting to hear from her.

KING. Both of us?

FREDDY. You and Jean-Paul. But maybe she's gone away for a holiday. It's stifling in New York now, or maybe she's found something more interesting. Or again she might have forgotten all about the two of you. She isn't writing, the old Kokomakis.

KING. She'll write ... she'll write ...

FREDDY. Join me for coffee?

KING. Coffee? No, no, I have to go ... it's late ...

FREDDY. You know, for years I've been waiting for a chance to have coffee with you at Asphodel's.

KING. Asphodel's?

FREDDY. The café next to the station ... don't you always sit there, Tuesdays and Saturdays, before you go — to watch the trains?

KING. How do you know all this?

FREDDY. Simple. I went after you.

KING. What do you mean, went after me?

FREDDY. Your stories ... from the dawn of my youth I felt drawn to your trains. It's in the family, as they say.

KING. Then you followed me!

FREDDY. Only at first. Afterwards I found the way myself.

KING. The way to where?

FREDDY. To your trains.

KING. To the trains?! The trains ... why didn't you ask? You could have told me ... you could have asked ... to come along ... to have coffee together ... the station isn't so far ... and the view's so exhilarating ... a glimmering of distances ... the dust of long dark journeys ... the puffing of engines ... whistles ... trains arriving ... trains departing. You could have told me — (*A train whistle*)

FREDDY. Arriving.

KING. (*Takes out his watch*) Yes. (*To Freddy*) I've already had coffee ... just a few minutes ago ... excuse me ... it's late ... I really must go ... it's very late. You could have told me everything ... then ... goodnight. (*He turns and heads for the stage-right exit*)

FREDDY. (*Very gently*) Papa. (*The king halts, but does not turn around*)

FREDDY. To the right, Papa. (*The king turns and looks at him*)

FREDDY. To the right, then the first turn to the left, the third house from the corner. Hotel Excelsior.

KING. (*A stifled shout*) What do you want from me?

FREDDY. It's thirty pesos, and ten for the room. You pay more? She's having troubles lately. The income tax boys are on to that little pimp of hers, and if he doesn't butter up enough bread for a whole lot of hungry dogs, and quick, he's got it coming to him now for every little mark he's scratched. She hasn't told you? So you see, Papa, flowers aren't exactly what she needs now. Flowers aren't exactly what she needs at all. She has a heart of gold.

KING. (*Stamps towards him, stops in front of him, on the verge of tears*) What are you talking about? What are you talking about?

FREDDY. They call her Saint Marita, because with every train that comes in or goes out, she crosses herself. And Sunday, after mass, is the padre's day. Gratis. That's Latin, he says. And he calls her my daughter, just imagine. The holy father's probably fixed her up with a kiosk in heaven.

KING. You — don't —

FREDDY. No, I'm no saint. I pay. Every time.

KING. You haven't been with her?! You haven't —

FREDDY. I'm just coming back from her.

KING. (*Suddenly shouts*) I love her. (*Pause*)

FREDDY. Goodnight, Papa. Watch yourself. You're a rich man now. If you tell her about the advance, she'll return your love. Goodnight. (*But he does not leave*) Funny. For a second then I felt my heart go — click. Just like that. Click. My father plus Marita plus — my mother. Remember? And me inside the whole mess. Click. But I'm tired. And I feel sick. Maybe it's only this fog. Beunas noches, Padre. (*Goes, but halts at once*) You know, it's strange. Click — in the heart. Bet that's how you start seeing steam rising from the crevices of the earth. And kingdom, exile, love. And then, hoop-la, God and all the angels. Already I can only go it twice with Marita. Alas, the youth of Saint Ferdinand is passing. And it came to pass, that as he was alone in the bordello ... (*Goes*)

KING. (*After Freddy's exit. Calls after him*) Ferdinand! Ferdinand! (*But Freddy has already disappeared. The king stands still, under the streetlamp, and calls again in a low voice*) Ferdinand! (*Then he turns to go, to the right, towards the sign* Hotel Excelsior, *accompanied by drums and flutes. He stops halfway and returns to the streetlamp. Looks at the bunch of flowers. Then he turns and walks straight ahead, to go off the stage. Again he changes his mind, stops, straightens up, and goes slowly, with measured tread, toward the sign. The drums and flutes accompany him again, and the stage slowly darkens*)

SCENE SEVEN

A waltz blends into the drums and flutes.

VOICE OF THE HERALD. Hear ye, hear ye! The waltz of Bonifacius and Cecilia! Hear ye, hear ye! Their majesties the king and the queen!

Applause. The waltz is played. The stage is illuminated. On the smaller stage is the sunflower. The young king enters, dancing the waltz, holding a large dummy dressed in a long white robe, with a featureless face and black hair on which rests a coronet. The

*applause ceases. The young king dances around the circle of light.
Suddenly, after a quick turn, he halts. The music stops. Thin,
grating laughter echoes through the hall. A startled "Oh" is heard
from the unseen audience. The young king puts the dummy down on
the floor and kneels beside it. Silence.*

YOUNG KING. The queen has fallen down. (*Hostile murmurs from
the unseen audience. The young king looks around*) The Queen
has fallen down in the middle of the waltz. Just don't
panic, that's all. (*But the murmurs grow louder. The young king
lays his palm on the dummy's forehead*) The queen feels fine.
No fever. (*Takes her sleeve*) Her pulse is beating. I can feel
it. (*Looks at her from close up*) Her lips are moist. Her
nostrils are dilating. That's clear. (*The murmurs grow louder*)
It's perfectly in order to go on with the waltz. (*But the
murmurs continue. He gets up*) There is no cause for worry.
No grounds for fear. Please don't get alarmed. Please don't
get anxious. Don't lose self-control. Don't start a panic.
The family doctor will take care of the queen in a scientific
manner. This is a family matter. Entirely. Be quiet. Go on
dancing. (*Bends over the doll and picks her up in his arms*) Little
doll. Pretty doll. Pretty little crazy queen. (*The waltz plays
on. The young king dances off with the queen in his arms. As he
exits, the thin, grating laughter is heard again*)
KRUPNIK'S VOICE. Cut. Lights. (*Lights drop and only the circle of
light in the center remains*)
FREDDY. (*Entering*) You know, Jean-Paul, you could cut out at
least one of those laughs. (*He continues on his way out*)
KRUPNIK'S VOICE. Fred—
FREDDY. (*Tired*) Yes, Jean-Paul.
KRUPNIK'S VOICE. I have received a letter from New York.
FREDDY. (*Looks at him for a long while*) I can see you're up in
the clouds. (*Waltz music. Lights out*)

SCENE EIGHT

*Three high-pitched ship's sirens blend into the waltz. The light
comes up on the king and Freddy in the Hohenschwaden flat on the
Avenida del Puerto. Freddy reads from a letter.*

FREDDY. "My dear Jean-Paul. I have seen the rushes. They're wonderful. You're a genius. I can hardly wait to see the second part. Dolly" (*Slowly approaching his father*) P.S. (*Reads*) "The actor who is to play the old king will arrive in two days' time, but the film won't be complete if His Majesty himself doesn't appear in the final scene. I want that. Don't disappoint me. Full stop. Mon cher. Full stop. Dolly." (*Offers the letter to his father*) Congratulations, Papa. You're a film star. (*The king grabs the letter from his hand. Freddy moves away and walks towards the capitan*) I think he couldn't believe his eyes. Was this the same salt tear he had discovered in its premiere performance, when the tapes first arrived? Was this the light that had broken through then? He stood there a little man in pince-nez glasses, with a white goatee, trembling at the sight of Kokomakis's new face, and all of a sudden he didn't know left from right, up from down ... that's what they say, isn't it, Capitan? When Papa wasn't understood, he couldn't understand a thing. That kind of character ...

KING. (*Shouting*) Forgery!

FREDDY. (*To the capitan*) Too pathetic for a film star.

KING. (*Continues*) Forgery! All of it! From the beginning! Forgery! Forgery!

FREDDY. What can you do? Goats don't always understand bitches.

KING. (*Continues*) And all those letters? All this year? That light, from there? The hopes?

FREDDY. The hopes! That burnt him up ... they'd stolen all his hopes ...

KING. And I ... naive idiot ... tricked by every rustle from the leaves of a white poplar ... believing, believing ... doddering old fool ... (*Shouts loudly*) THEY'RE MAKING A PARODY!

FREDDY. Always lyrical, Papa ... with a fine spray of pathos ...

KING. (*In the same voice*) And the truth? Where's the truth? In Krupnik's kingdom of shadows?

FREDDY. That's what they're all like — these birds with their classical culture, with their principles in their drawers.

They get married to the truth. And when they suddenly find Madame in bed with a bird from another establishment, they don't overturn the bed — uh-uh — they try to overturn the world, with hymns and cembellos, claw out each other's eyes, tear out each other's feathers till you can't see a thing except down, down, down. Read, Capitan, read — there's a lot of paperbacks on the subject!

KING. A parody ... they're making a parody ... she, the princess (*Looks at his son, says softly*) She's turning my life into a farce ...

FREDDY. You ought to thank her. Most people's lives turn into a fizzle.

KING. I was a king!

FREDDY. (*Approaches him*) You were a king ... Papa, you were booted out of the palace, remember!? They booted you out, threw you to the dogs, they didn't need you any more. This is your life — here, now, in this God-forsaken hole below the equator ... forgotten! ... why, even all your royal families have long since crossed your name off their lists. That "treacherous ape" Schtumpf-Schattau, barely knows that you're still alive ... and Cindenburgen's mongrels have long forgotten what you smell like, so doesn't it warm your heart a bit, Papa, that Kokomakis alone retains allegiance to you, farce or no farce?

KING. No!

FREDDY. Don't you understand, Papa, that she and she alone has held your head above water, for a whole year, at a thousand pesos a month, and now the year's over she's given you a bonus, ten thousand, and put your only son on a horse, even though it's only of plywood?

KING. (*Shouts*) I WILL NOT BE A FILM STAR!

FREDDY. Then you'll die.

KING. (*Looks at his son. After a pause*) Yes, there are black poplars in your eyes ...

FREDDY. It's this climate. Papa. Too little air. And everybody wants to breathe it. Days it's hot. Night it's cold. And windstorms now and then, that fill your eyes with sand. Not much fun. The funny thing is that even in this climate, everyone's dependent on someone else. Like, for instance,

I'm dependent on you. And maybe vice versa. You know the multiplication table. Work it out.

KING. I'm not working anything out.

FREDDY. Good luck to you. (*Walks away*)

KING. (*Shouts after him*) I will not die!

FREDDY. (*Halts, turns around*) No? You have other plans?

KING. (*Suddenly*) I will live, Ferdinand, until a faithful heir is born to the throne of the House of Hohenschwaden.

FREDDY. (*Smiles*) A faithful heir, eh? That's a bit complicated, a faithful heir. Do you have a queen? (*The king does not reply*) You aren't by any chance thinking of all the suggestions you made me a few weeks ago ... somehow we always seem to be bumping into each other in the arena of love ... and I shouldn't need to remind you what a shortage of labor there is at present among the royal families ... well, Papa, who's going to be Mama?

KING. I'm redeeming her out of the night.

FREDDY. You're doing WHAT out of the night?

KING. Marita isn't going back to Hotel Excelsior.

FREDDY. Marita?

KING. I'm all alone ... I have nobody ... just one poor lonely soul, from the street of the moon ... Marita, my queen ...

FREDDY. (*Slowly*) You're redeeming her out of the night ... you've been speaking to the padre lately, eh? Redeeming! That's quite a word ... that'll work with the Lamb up in heaven, but not with the pimp in the Calle de la Mar.

KING. I'm redeeming her from him.

FREDDY. How?

KING. I gave her ten thousand pesos.

FREDDY. (*After a pause*) What did you do?

KING. I gave her ten thousand pesos. She's going to open a restaurant.

FREDDY. To open a restaurant ...

KING. Yes.

FREDDY. (*After a pause. Very quietly*) You know, Papa, right now I could kill you.

KING. (*A half-smile on his lips*) That's the amount I was paid for my life.

FREDDY. When did you give her the money?

KING. Yesterday.

FREDDY. In cash, of course.

KING. In cash.

FREDDY. Sure. No point in asking if you got a receipt.

KING. No receipt is necessary.

FREDDY. Sure. It's love.

KING. Yes, it's love. It was my money —

FREDDY. (*Groans*) No, it was not your money, it was never your money, you goat, you goat, you goat! And you know where it's gone, that money, that juicy money that came just when I'd begun to think no miracle like that could happen to me? Into a restaurant, sure — into Perez El Gatto's restaurant in the Calle de la Mar, where the whore's little energetic pimp sits every morning, stupido, and that's where the romance stops, the end, 'cause you won't get that money out of his teeth even if you knock them out one by one, and this very day, at midnight, when you're through reciting, it'll be her turn to recite, stupido, your queen with the weeping eyes, and she'll say "what could I do, Jesus Maria, what could I do, it was him, the pimp, the worm, madre mia, the reptile, the leech, he took it, simply took it, and if I open my mouth he'll smash my head in, the rat, el bruto, el suzio, and what'll I do now, got to work up to the norm again, 'cause he sits there every morning, the reptile, waiting, waiting, all the time, without a heart, without a heart." Papa ... Papa ...

KING. I am redeeming her out of the night.

FREDDY. I'd better get out of here. Fast. Believe me. I feel like I'm dangerous to you, Papa. (*Exits*)

KING. God help me. (*The stage darkens. Light on the left front corner. Freddy appears*)

FREDDY. (*To the capitan*) No, it's true. Even goats have a god. There's something like that in mythology. And the god of the goats helped him ... (*Laughs a loud coarse laugh*) A tragedy!

act 2

SCENE ONE

Spotlight on Freddy in the left front corner.

FREDDY. (*To the capitan*) Yes, it's true. God came to Papa's aid. By way of the income tax offices. You understand, Capitan — Marita, Saint Marita of the railway station, thirty pesos, just didn't give her pimp the money. Simple as that — ten thousand good pesos — she didn't give it to him! And the income tax boys invited him to come in for ten years. She, the rebellious sheep, caught on at once that what she needed now was new pastures — completely new, and far away. It's dangerous to pull a double cross on the Calle de la Mar ... there's still a pastoral idyll among the pimps. She found a new patron right away — His Majesty! Not in the union, of course, but still a patron. And the pasture? (*Gets up*) Great Bogomania ... the pavilion ... the pine groves ... the petunia gardens. Isn't it strange — the graftings of life? Papa, plus Marita, plus Hohen-schwaden ... he decided to return to the homeland — via the Champs Elysees ... Marita just had to see the Champs Elysees. During all these years, after mass, after the padre, she used to go to the art theatre. She was crazy about plays on the lives of Parisian prostitutes. And how she cried! Catharsis! Can't do without the classics, I suppose. And Father? He didn't go to Asphodel's any more, on Tuesdays and Saturdays ... the train parked at home ... he was floating on clouds! Even bought himself a new hat! He felt he was already there in the palace, incognito for the time being ... or perhaps he envisaged the two of them, in a little country church with a red-tiled roof, standing in front of the priest, with all the bells. M'sieur et Madame van Schwank ... and then, by the grace of God, a little van Schwank, new, auburn haired, the bearer of the flame of the House of Hohenschwaden ... the steam ... the true son ... the true heir. I wanted Marita.

Earlier, when we were fellow passengers on the same train, I'd thought that through her, I ... with him ... with Papa ... I'm getting lyrical. I wanted Marita, with the bags under her eyes, in the little room with the narrow window, the peeling walls, and the yellow lamp, Hotel Excelsior, thirty pesos, I had the pesos. But Marita didn't come back to the Calle de la Luna. Papa had redeemed her. From me. For ten thousand pesos. Lyrical as ever. He redeemed her and rejected me. Yet it was impossible to make a complete break ... that's how things work out ... that's how this worked out ... that was at the end of the first part of the film. My days as the young king were over. Now began my days as the young crown prince. I galloped to the pavilion on plywood, after a long period abroad ... (*Trumpets. The inner curtain rises, revealing Freddy sitting on the horse*) To the pavilion! To the palace! To the crown!

KRUPNIK'S VOICE. Be proud, mon cher, proud, in a voice the world has never heard, Fred—

FREDDY. To the pavilion! To the palace! To the crown!

KRUPNIK'S VOICE. No no no no no no! Vibrant, Fred, radiant, unique—

FREDDY. To the pavilion! To the palace! To the crown!

KRUPNIK'S VOICE. To the crown! To the crown! To the crown! To the crown! For God's sake, Fred!

FREDDY. To the pavilion! To the palace! To the crown!

KRUPNIK'S VOICE. Head high, Fred, daring, strong, proud, bright-eyed, broad-chested—

FREDDY. To the pavilion! To the palace! To the crown!

KRUPNIK'S VOICE. You're the crown prince, Fred, you're going to be the king, Fred, the king, the walls of cities fall, swords turn to rust, words die in books, and only the king, only the king ... give me a cor anglais, bon dieu, a cor anglais. (*A cor anglais is heard*) Do you hear, mon orgueilleux, mon cher, mon cher petit ... give me a piccolo, a piccolo (*A piccolo is heard*) You will be our legendary king, Fred— brave, golden, forgotten, the scent of secret caves that have filled up with earth, dust, a king, a king—

FREDDY. (*Shouts, suddenly*) Medra! Medra! Medra!

KRUPNIK'S VOICE. Lights! (*Lights rise on the horse and its rider.*

Freddy can now be seen clearly—dressed in his red robe. He is barefooted. The piccolo plays on)

FREDDY. (*Shouts*) That frigging piccolo! (*The piccolo is silenced. Freddy gets off the horse*) Thanks. (*Lights a cigarette*)

KRUPNIK'S VOICE. I'm sorry, Fred. You're a bit nervous, I know—

FREDDY. Look, Jean-Paul. I am not nervous. I've been riding this frigging horse since morning, but I am not nervous. I've repeated "To the pavilion. To the palace. To the crown" over three hundred times, but I am not nervous. Personally I think this scene and the whole film stink to high heaven, but OK, everything comes to an end. But, Jean-Paul, I can't stand your lyrical patter any more. I've had enough. If you want my head two degrees to the north you don't have to sell me the complete canon of Greek mythology. Just say two degrees to the north. I'll get the message. And shove that frigging piccolo in later, in the dubbing. The pleasure will be all yours. I'll go on galloping without a piccolo. As for my eyes, you'd better take them as they are, and if you think they lack that spark of majesty, add the spark in the laboratory. That's all. We're shooting, Jean-Paul. It's a movie. So let's leave the soul in the storeroom. When the time comes for the soul, the public relations boys will look after it. That's their job. That's all. Yes. I love you. I always love you. I can't live without you. Forever. Your turn.

KRUPNIK'S VOICE. I'm sorry, Fred, I'm sorry. (*Raises his voice*) Thank you very much, gentlemen, we've finished for the day— (*Enter the actor, dressed in the coronation robe on the same high-heeled shoes*)

ACTOR. Finished?! Finished?! Uh-uh! We're just starting! (*In the center of the stage*) Servus, Jean!

FREDDY. (*To Krupnik*) Who the hell is this scarecrow?

KRUPNIK'S VOICE. That's ... our new king!

ACTOR. Servus!

FREDDY. (*Looks at the actor*) I don't have much luck with fathers.

ACTOR. Excellent! It'll be a blood bath. Aha!

KRUPNIK'S VOICE. I see you're getting along fine together, so I'll leave you to yourselves. You'll have a chance to get to know each other. Au revoir.

FREDDY. You — my father?

ACTOR. Me, my son, Bonifacius Victor Felix of the House of Hohenschwaden. Servus!

FREDDY. Say ah.

ACTOR. Ah!

FREDDY. Lower your nose.

ACTOR. With pleasure. (*Bends over him*)

FREDDY. (*Pulls the nose*) Real!

ACTOR. Pull it, pull it, sir! As much as you like! Don't be frightened! No illusions! Plastic surgery! (*Freddy releases the nose*) Please, go ahead. Examine the ears, the chin, the nostrils, one by one, if you like to pick — not a single flaw, aha! Not a single flaw! A true Hohenschwaden!

FREDDY. Funny, but I also am, aha! a true Hohenschwaden!

ACTOR. But of course! I knew it at once! His Highness the prince! The eyes, the forehead, the profile. The moustache — is it yours?

FREDDY. As a rule.

ACTOR. (*Tests the moustache*) Excellent! But allow me a word of advice: moustaches and beards — always keep them in your kit bag! It's a rule! Allow me to introduce myself. Actor of the highest degree. International expert on elevated characters, hard, uncompromising types who come to tragic ends. Technicien par excellence. Please have a look — my diploma! (*Takes out of his back pocket, not a diploma, but a whiskey flask*) Drink?

FREDDY. No.

ACTOR. Excellent! To the death of the king! (*Drinks*) A great man, Your Highness, is a dead man — that's my motto! You wonder, I suppose, why I, I, do not have a name? Yes, Your Highness, that's how I am: no name, no individuality, no face, no ego! (*Whispers into Freddy's ear*) Just plastic surgery! Dozens of operations! And I feel superb! Never a bad mood! No depressions! Please allow me to remove these shoes before I burst.

FREDDY. Please do.

ACTOR. (*More lightly*) Operations come, operations go, and nothing remains of my buttocks! But nothing! Servus! Dedicated to the art of the cinema!

FREDDY. Get some from others. There's no lack of buttocks.

ACTOR. (*Shocked*) From others?!! But what are you saying, Your Highness?! Others! But it's a painful problem! Poor material, defective, falsch!! Others! They look after their faces all right, but the buttocks — absolute neglect, absolute, Your Highness! Sabotage on a worldwide scale! Allow me to remark, categorically: (*Pathetic*) Not every seat is meant to be sat on!

FREDDY. Sorry.

ACTOR. But this is the twentieth century: everyone sits! And they cultivate only their faces ... only their egos ... their individual biographies ... their personalities. (*Shouts*) Haberdashery! (*Pathetic*) Oh, wretched century!

FREDDY. It'll pass, it'll pass ... Servus!

ACTOR. Where is Your Highness going, if I may ask?

FREDDY. To eat.

ACTOR. To eat?!!!

FREDDY. I'm hungry.

ACTOR. But Your Highness is going to kill me, damn it all! Hungry!

FREDDY. In our family we only kill after dinner.

ACTOR. Believe me, Your Highness — you shouldn't joke about it. Dying is my specialité!

FREDDY. Spoilt.

ACTOR. You do kill me, don't you?

FREDDY. If it'll give you any pleasure.

ACTOR. Knife?

FREDDY. Revolver.

ACTOR. Pity. There's nothing like a knife. Cold. Smooth. I was Julius Ceasar — wonderful! Twelve knives ... (*Shudders at the delightful memory*) Brr ... (*Suddenly asks*) You don't feel a kind of shudder, a kind of mysterious thrill, a refined tremor ...

FREDDY. I'm not the one being killed, you know.

ACTOR. But you're the killer!

FREDDY. (*Slowly, after a pause*) I'll only be killing a plastic surgeon's handiwork.

ACTOR. Wrong! You'll be killing your father!

FREDDY. (*Approaches him*) Senor, you exaggerate.

ACTOR. Aha! You're angry! You're upset! Admit it, admit it:
you're pretending. You are not at all that innocent youth
you seem, with that apathetic face and those cold eyes. I
can see it: the murder is nestling in your fingertips. The
murder is glittering in your eyes. Admit it! And you're
waiting for it, for that shudder, that thrill ... for a long
time now you've been waiting ... you want to feel that
sense of communion ... you know what I'm talking
about ... between murderer and victim ... between father
and son ...

FREDDY. Who are you?

ACTOR. Me? (*Avoids the answer*) I am your father's double,
Your Highness! Drink?

FREDDY. (*Shouts*) No!

ACTOR. Excellent! (*Takes out the flask*) Oh, Alphonse — to the
memory of the sands of the Sahara! Alphonse Lieberman,
colonel in the Foreign Legion. A great drinker. Dead. I
played him two weeks after his death, but a great man is a
dead man. Does His Majesty your father still suffer from
rheumatism?

FREDDY. You know everything about him.

ACTOR. I know everything about him. (*Smiles*) Even the number
of teeth in his mouth. (*Approaches Freddy*) Would you like
to count? Two fillings.

FREDDY. Shut your mouth.

ACTOR. Sorry.

FREDDY. Yes. What's this, everything?

ACTOR. Everything! (*Avoids the issue*) The pine groves ... the
petunia gardens ... the pavilion ... the women ...

FREDDY. The women?

ACTOR. Agatha ... Ludmilla ... Bertha ... Martha ...
Cecilia! (*Pause*) A dozen ...

FREDDY. A dozen?

ACTOR. And one more — the last ...

FREDDY. The last —

ACTOR. (*Recites*) She returns, the thirteenth, and still she's the
first: The one and the only — or the moment alone? For
you, are you queen, are you first, are you last? And you,
are you king, only lover — or the last one?

FREDDY. You aren't so funny.

ACTOR. I'm the king.

FREDDY. (*Stops laughing*) Listen, fool. You are nothing but a prop stuck into Madame's payroll. So sit in your corner and keep quiet and just do your role. Don't start waving your plastic nose around whenever you see me in the neighborhood. And if I feel a kind of shudder, or thrill, in my fingertips, it'll only happen if you forget who you are again. So look out. I'll always know you.

ACTOR. Are you sure, Your Highness? (*He disappears behind the curtain*)

FREDDY. I'll always know you, Fool. (*The actor appears in front of the inner curtain*)

ACTOR. Like this too, Your Highness? (*He is wearing moustache, beard and wig*)

FREDDY. God.

ACTOR. (*Recites*) Green, green, green, green was the green forest, and only the death of its king—(*Walks quickly to Freddy, pulls off the beard, and continues*)—was brown.

FREDDY. I'll always know you, Fool.

ACTOR. Wait 'til twilight, Your Highness.

FREDDY. (*Falling on him and grabbing his robe*) Don't move. Don't move. Just do your role.

ACTOR. You're ruining the robe, Your Highness. We have some more shooting to do.

SCENE TWO

The sign Silence. Shooting in progress *is illuminated. Scene unchanged. The inner curtain opens like a gate. Trumpet blasts.*

VOICE OF THE HERALD. Hear ye, hear ye! His Majesty Old Bonny meets His Highness Young Freddy returning home after a period of studies abroad! Hear ye, Hear ye!

Enter the actor-king, in a long robe and high-heeled shoes, and stands on the inner stage with legs apart, next to his flag. He smokes a pipe. The scene is acted in the style of a Western.

ACTOR-KING. Abroad! Everyone that comes back from abroad thinks he's entitled to turn up late! When I wait an hour, I can barely be paternal, let alone sentimental! (*Music. Enter Freddy, on the horse*)

FREDDY. Hi there, Dad!

ACTOR-KING. At last. Dad! ... Get down, get down. Let's have a look at you, Fred. (*Freddy jumps off the horse and stands in front of his father*)

ACTOR-KING. Yes ... I thought you'd be taller.

FREDDY. That's the height abroad. Cigar?

ACTOR-KING. Not this round. When'd you start to smoke?

FREDDY. (*Lights his cigar*) Where there's smoke there's fire.

ACTOR-KING. Revolutionary ideas already. Good, I hope the family reunion is over. Are you going back abroad?

FREDDY. No, Dad. Why the colored balloons?

ACTOR-KING. Oh, really. Leave me alone. No one understands me anyway, so what does it matter if I tell you what they're for or if I don't tell you what they're for. Balloons! Once I used to be real serious, but they grew so suspicious of me that I became cynical. Did you bring any presents?

FREDDY. No, Dad. Where's Mother? Can't see her around.

ACTOR-KING. Mother? Why this sudden interest in Mother? You been studying psychology?

FREDDY. Abroad they say she's not well, Dad.

ACTOR-KING. She's perfectly well, Fred. Mad as a hatter.

FREDDY. Abroad they say she warns you all, from the rooftop.

ACTOR-KING. She sure warns us. What's she got to do all day?

FREDDY. Abroad they say that's not too good, Dad.

ACTOR-KING. Good, so it's not good. What do you want her to do, jump off the roof?

FREDDY. Abroad they say you ought to go on a pension. (*The king takes the pipe out of his mouth and makes a move toward Freddy, who jumps away, gracefully*) Uh-uh!

ACTOR-KING. (*Slowly*) Freddy-boy, you want war.

FREDDY. Sure I want war. I'm no Communist.

ACTOR-KING. Freddy-boy, you'll get war.

FREDDY. Sure I'll get war. That's why I'm here. (*Silence*)

ACTOR-KING. I can't say that you don't appeal to me, Freddy-boy.

FREDDY. Me too, Dad, I also can't actually say that you don't appeal to me, Dad.

ACTOR-KING. It's a good thing the father doesn't fall far from the son, Freddy-boy.

FREDDY. No comment, Dad.

ACTOR-KING. Damn it, I'm starting to get both paternal and sentimental. I waited for you a long time, you know.

FREDDY. Dad, if I hadn't been late you would've thought I hadn't been abroad.

ACTOR-KING. You're right. How are things abroad?

FREDDY. So so. Over there they say that abroad is here.

ACTOR-KING. You didn't bring any presents?

FREDDY. No.

ACTOR-KING. Souvenirs?

FREDDY. Uh-uh.

ACTOR-KING. So that's that.

FREDDY. That's that. I suggest first of all a duel. Swords. Before dawn.

ACTOR-KING. A duel. Swords. Before dawn.

FREDDY. A duel. Swords. Before dawn.

FREDDY. If that doesn't work, we'll think of something else.

ACTOR-KING. We'll think of something else.

FREDDY. So long, Dad.

ACTOR-KING. Freddy-boy ... (*Freddy stops*) you should have brought some kind of present ... (*Freddy climbs on the horse*)

FREDDY. Giddy-up! (*The horse is taken out. Music accompanies Freddy's exit*)

ACTOR-KING. Any old present ... no matter what ... (*The music rises in volume. Trumpet blasts*)

KRUPNIK'S VOICE. Cut. Lights. (*The lights go down, leaving only working light on the stage. Enter Freddy, without the red robe*) Fred —

FREDDY. You're still here. What are you doing there, Jean-Paul?

KRUPNIK'S VOICE. I'm ... setting up the final shooting.

FREDDY. The final shooting ... exit fool, enter king.

KRUPNIK'S VOICE. Yes. Enter the king.

FREDDY. (*Lights a cigarette*) Jean-Paul — actually why do you need the king that much? Why can't you make do with the plastic substitute?

KRUPNIK'S VOICE. But ... no, no ... don't you understand, Fred? We have to ... only the king .. the true king .. the exiled king ... (*A pause*) it has to be that way, Fred ... the princess wants it ...

FREDDY. She's capricious, our princess ...

KRUPNIK'S VOICE. Yes.

FREDDY. Jean-Paul, why does she want father dead?

KRUPNIK'S VOICE. Dead? But ... it's only in the film, Fred, you —

FREDDY. Why does she want him dead, Jean-Paul?

KRUPNIK'S VOICE. It's ... a fitting end ... for the film ... don't you think?

FREDDY. (*Coming forward*) A fitting end ... for the film. No, Senor Krupnik. He won't come. Senor Hohenschwaden won't be here. He's weighing anchor. In another few days he'll be walking around the pine groves arm-in-arm with his muchacha from the Calle de la Luna.

KRUPNIK'S VOICE. But ... that's impossible ... he has to ... has to ... without him we can't finish the film ...

FREDDY. (*Raises his voice*) He won't come, Jean-Paul. (*More to himself*) To bring him here you need a long line, with the muchacha on the hook at the other end, here, in the studio, Avenida Bolivar.

KRUPNIK'S VOICE. You ... aren't going to him, now?

FREDDY. (*Rapidly turning towards the voice*) No!

KRUPNIK'S VOICE. The final shooting is in another two days ... speak to him ... we need him ... only the king ... like an open wound ... an old pain, wearying, forgotten ... playing ... in the heart of the whirlpool of illusion ... the colored baubles ... the king ...

FREDDY. (*Shouts*) He won't come, damn you! (*Lowers his voice, says hotly*) And as for that pain, and all the lyrical rot that goes with it — sell it at the next festival in Venice. Not to me! Adios.

KRUPNIK'S VOICE. Fred — (*Freddy halts*) Sometimes you're like a little whore. A tough one.

FREDDY. (*After a pause, smiles*) That's all right. It doesn't come cheap.

KRUPNIK'S VOICE. Forgive me, Fred—

FREDDY. Adios.

KRUPNIK'S VOICE. Bring her here, that girl from the street of the moon, bring her here!

SCENE THREE

Distant ship's sirens blend in softly with the guitar music. Then they stop and the lights come up on the Hohenschwaden house in the Avenida del Puerto. Everything looks brighter now—a vase of flowers, embroidered cloths on the tape recorder and the throne, a huge poster displaying the curvaceous body of a woman and the words: Marita Trocadero. *Freddy sits on the throne, plays with the king's crown, and holds a bag of chestnuts. The king enters. The music stops. The king hurries to the tape recorder.*

FREDDY. (*Offering him the bag*) Chestnuts?

KING. (*Not moving*) No, thanks.

FREDDY. Straight off the fire.

KING. No, thanks.

FREDDY. In all the school text books it says you're crazy about chestnuts, 'cause they're auburn. (*Looks around him*) It also says you don't like revolutions.

KING. What do you want?

FREDDY. (*Walking around the room*) Flowers ... embroidery ... lights ... quite a revolution! (*Looks at the poster*) The Trocadero! (*To the king*) She's modest, Mama ... never told me about her days of glory at the Trocadero ... when do you sail?

KING. In three days.

FREDDY. So soon? Will you go to Venice?

KING. What do you want from me, Ferdinand?

FREDDY. And what if she leaves you flat, all of a sudden, along the way, near some out-of-the-way railway station, some-where between Venice and the Champs Elysees? Huh? Like she left her other pimp. What'll you do? You haven't even got a pension ... she, at least, has a collapsible shop. Just has to hang out the sign ... the sign's the same, in every language ... you teaching her French?

KING. Every day.

FREDDY. Not on Dolly's tape recorder? (*He approaches the tape recorder, but the king blocks his way*)

FREDDY. It's no joke. The Trocadero on the Kokomakis tape recorder ... sandwich ... you still sending the tapes to New York? No? (*The king doesn't answer*) Ugh, Papa ... you've already grown a paunch ... like a spinster social worker ... and what did old Kokomakis do to you, anyway? She only pulled out a breast for Krupnik to suck on as well. Don't you think it's overdoing it a bit to break off all relations — just because Madame gives of her bounty to one more passing beggar ...

KING. It was a mistake ... from the start ...

FREDDY. A mistake? But now you keep yourself nice and warm by the light of that mistake, eh? Say what you like, it was Kokomakis who gave you the Trocadero, when all's said and done ... even the price of the boat ticket, ridiculous as it may seem ... plus that scarf ... everything, in fact. (*Looks at the crown*) In the final analysis, you know, Papa, if not for Dolly, who knows — you might have had to sell this (*Waves the crown*) or this (*Points to the throne*)

KING. Yes. That's true. I don't deserve them. You're right.

FREDDY. And the pesos? You deserve *them*? Doesn't she ever ask you, that Trocadero, where it all came from — the ten thousand?

KING. I am a French teacher.

FREDDY. French teacher?! But you told her, didn't you, what your true profession is, your destiny, your —

KING. I am a French teacher.

FREDDY. (*Shouts*) But a French teacher of the House of Hohenschwaden, damn it all!

KING. My name is Felix van Schwank.

FREDDY. (*Not believing*) Papa —

KING. Felix van Schwank! Van Schwank! Van Schwank! (*Silence*)

FREDDY. (*Softly*) Just like that? So simple? No steam? No crevices, no depths?

KING. I am not a king.

FREDDY. (*Same voice, soft, unbelieving*) All this — for the sake of the Trocadero? One fine morning you get up and make her a present of the whole kingdom, of all the paraphernalia ... after twenty years of stubbornness ..

KING. I made a mistake. A king doesn't make a mistake.

FREDDY. (*After a pause*) Isn't it funny that at this very moment the American Princess insists on putting a crown on your head?

KING. A crown?

FREDDY. She sent me a memorandum. She wants you for the film.

KING. Complete with tail, peacock's feathers, and cockscomb, eh?

FREDDY. With public relations, receptions, press interviews. She'll give you back your name, Papa. She'll give you back your body, your face, your memory. She is bestowing her grace upon you, Papa. She's putting you back in the palace.

KING. (*Raises his voice*) In the chicken coop!

FREDDY. You aren't seeing it in the right light ...

KING. True ... true ... you're right ... I saw that old duck in the shape of a swan. (*Raises his voice*) But she's only a duck! A princess of ducks! A princess of Krupniks! (*Softly*) I was weary, weak, hungry — true ... I saw a few grains on the ground, and I didn't notice the net! I almost fell right into that chicken coop, into that buzzing pantheon of Mrs. Kokomakis's swarming with mannequins and prophets from the boxing ring or the movies. All she needed was a king! A torn, ragged king — for an appetizer ... a queer old rooster, with plucked feathers. She'd even let me crow all I liked, to liven things up ... a fool king, that's what was lacking in her collection ... the old duck ... I was a king, yes! A marquis! A prince! By the grace of God! But I'm not needed any more. I know. My palace is in ruins. My petunia gardens have been trampled down. My queen you people are portraying as a madwoman. Now nothing remains — except to turn my life into a parody ... a movie ... film ...

FREDDY. The end of the legend of the House of Hohenschwaden ...

KING. Yes. The end.

FREDDY. But there's still a glimmer. One, last, solitary, glimmer.

KING. A glimmer?

FREDDY. The crown prince, Ferdinand.

KING. You noticed those grains quick enough.

FREDDY. Look at me, Papa. I'm twenty-five. And three months. Middle-aged, almost. No? What've I got? Half a horse. With no legs. Perhaps not even very regal. But it's a good horse. I can feel it. And it's strong. I want to ride it. But it turns out you've got its legs. I need them. Give me them. End of the crown speech.

KING. I haven't got any legs of any horse.

FREDDY. The day after tomorrow is the final shooting, Papa. Avenida Bolivar. (*Turns to go*) Be there.

KING. No.

FREDDY. You'll be there, Papa. (*Approaches the tape recorder*) You'll be there. (*Looks at his father*) This the last French lesson? (*The king moves up to prevent him from turning on the tape recorder, but Freddy is quicker. A whistle is heard, and then the king's voice, singing an aria from an opera. Freddy, surprised, turns to his father*) You?!

KING. (*Erect, proud*) Me!

FREDDY. Love, eh?

KING. (*Loud, stifled voice, on verge of tears*) Love!

FREDDY. You're out of tune. Adios, Papa. The day after tomorrow. Avenida Bolivar. (*The voice of the king singing grows louder. Freddy goes out*)

SCENE FOUR

The sign Silence. Shooting in progress *descends. The voice of the king singing blends into the "William Tell" overture.*

VOICE OF THE HERALD. Hear ye, hear ye! The great duel between Old King Bonny and Young Prince Freddy! Hear ye, hear ye! The auburn prairie lion versus the black shadow rider! Alley-oop!

The duel is seen on the darkened stage — only the crowns, rubber swords and robes of the two combatants and the outlines of a horse are visible, illuminated by an ultraviolet lamp. At the end of the duel, when it is clear that neither of the two is victorious, the light falls on them and they voicelessly sing the duet of the father and daughter from Rigoletto. *At the end of the duel full lights come up on the two and the applause of the film crew is heard.*

FREDDY. (*Quickly takes his hat and coat*) Adieu.

ACTOR. (*After him*) Your Highness —

FREDDY. To the street of the moon! (*Freddy disappears. The applause continues*)

ACTOR. (*To the film crew*) I thank you. (*The applause continues*) I thank you! (*The applause ceases. He looks in the direction Fred had taken*) Thank you. Thank you. Thank you. From the bottom of my heart. Our profession, colleagues, our fatal profession, forces me to part from you and to fly to distant parts. To Australia! And so, if you allow me a couple of words, perhaps even three. Colleagues! The question which has been reverberating around the world in recent times, is: What is man? Admittedly, a pertinent question. What is man? And if you will allow me, colleagues, I will give you a pertinent answer: yes — plastic surgery! (*Applause*) An operation everyday, colleagues! A new face every morning! A fresh ego every evening, a clean biography, a personality in all the colors of the rainbow! (*To himself*) Otherwise, it's impossible. (*Raises his voice*) To the Golden Age, colleagues! Onward, to the light! (*Applause*) And allow me to tell you, fresh colleagues: you're making a great film! A great film! I can smell it! I only regret I can't stay till the end! Bravo, Jean-Paul! (*Applause*) And now — to Australia! It can't be avoided! A great man awaits me there. Captain Cook, James. A great man. And dead. Adieu. (*Applause*)

SCENE FIVE

Jazz background music. Light falls on sign, Café Vienna. *A table and two chairs at the front of the stage. Freddy, drunk, sits on one of the chairs, holding a telephone receiver.*

FREDDY. (*Humming his father's love aria in between words*) She isn't there, Krupnik ... she's gone ... the girl from the street of the moon ... thirty pesos ... Ex-cel-si-or! Gone. (*Sings*) And if it's the boys from the Calle de la Mar who've laid their hands on her, Jean-Paul, then you'll have no pain and no king˜ ... no final shooting ... no film ... 'cause Bonny of the House of Hohenschwaden, the auburn prairie lion just won't be there for the final shooting ... he won't be there ... the proud prairie lion ... (*Enter the Actor*)

FREDDY. (*Rising*) What, you?

ACTOR. (*Also appears quite drunk*) Yes, me ...

FREDDY. Aren't you supposed to be on your way — to Australia?

ACTOR. Australia? When I'm so depressed? Can't you see it? Can't you sense it? It's all disintegrating.... all the operations ... all this wonderful structure ... I'm myself again, Your Highness ... with an ego ... with a biography ... I'm all haberdashery, that's all, a nothing, I ... (*Approaches Freddy*) Take note, Your Highness, take note: I am not at all sure who I am ... at all ... I don't remember ... it was a long time ago ... such a long time ... in Bogomania ...

FREDDY. So you're from Bogomania too.

ACTOR. From the County of Pook.

FREDDY. A royalist?

ACTOR. A patriot. And you?

FREDDY. Ex.

ACTOR. I understand. Avant-garde. Not me. I'm a patriot. A loyal son of the homeland. On all my travels I dream the dream of beautiful Bogomania, with its hills and mountains, the cradle of my love, my only love. Listen well: when I see the flag I tingle all over. I admit it. And the marching songs of the homeland — ah, those marching songs! My love also went with them — to New York ...

FREDDY. New York?

ACTOR. New York, New York ... 13 ... Poste Restante ...

FREDDY. (*Sits down*) Kokomakis ...

ACTOR. (*Very close to Freddy's face*) My wife. (*Sits down*) Servus!

FREDDY. (*Pours two drinks from the bottle, sips quietly, and says*)

Here's to you.

ACTOR. Please wait. (*Takes the flask out of his pocket*) I brew this
whiskey myself ... can't trust anyone ... they sell poison.
(*Drinks, then points to the bottle on the table*) Go ahead, drink,
drink ... down with haberdashery. You love?

FREDDY. On time payment.

ACTOR. (*Raises his voice, pathetic*) I love, Your Highness! I love!
Her! Seven months she was with me, back there, in the
homeland ... she was gay ... singing softly throughout
the house ... used to go out at dawn to pick flowers and
came back all dewdrops. And I ... I was a great actor!
With a face! With a future! One morning she didn't come
back ... flew off, just like that, phttt ... with an American
coal king. (*Takes the flask out of his pocket*) Drink?

FREDDY. (*Pours from the bottle*) Only poison, thanks. (*Drinks*)
Coal, eh?

ACTOR. Coal! Why? What for? We don't understand women.
Believe me, I didn't know where to hide my face ... so I
had plastic surgery ... then another one. You get used to
it ... ego on top of ego ... one Chinese general ...
a dozen famous statesmen ... I've forgotten their
names ... Hannibal! Yes, yes ... Hannibal. And when
she returned — the princess — she always returns — can you
imagine the horror? I wasn't me any more ... nothing ...
no ego of my own ... no personality ... no face ...
nothing ... all plastic ... nothing of my own ... and she,
she, can you imagine? She wouldn't look at me ... I cried,
I threatened, I shouted ... no use ... she'd changed. The
coal! Her hands are cold, Your Highness ... the touch of
death ...

FREDDY. (*Leering*) So she did touch you, all the same?

ACTOR. (*Stands up and shouts*) She turned me into a courier!
(*Softly*) Over the phone ...

FREDDY. An errand boy ...

ACTOR. Of plastic ...

FREDDY. To the grocers.

ACTOR. (*Raises his voice*) To her lovers. Your Highness, errands
of love ...

FREDDY. (*Stands up*) His Majesty, Old Bonifacius?

ACTOR. She loves him ... my wife ... she loves him. The king with the face ... since back in Bogomania ... since the pomp ... when he pranced on his horse, in the parade ... and the marching songs ... in the golden boulevard ... and the king ... on his horse ... in the capital ... my wife. (*Also stands up*) And me, Your Highness? What about me? What about me?

FREDDY. (*Leers*) You have no character, Fool.

ACTOR. Ah! You're wrong there, You Highness! You're wrong! Wrong!

FREDDY. Rags and patches ... haberdashery ...

ACTOR. Ego! Ego! Ego! (*Approaches Freddy*) You're looking all over for the girl from the street of the moon —

FREDDY. (*Turns quickly and grabs him by the shirt*) I'm looking for her.

ACTOR. You're wasting your time! She's flown ... gone ...

FREDDY. (*Shaking him*) Where is she?

ACTOR. Up in the sky ... first class ...

FREDDY. (*Giggles*) I'll kill you, Fool! I'll kill you!

ACTOR. Direct to the Champs Elysees ... no stops in transit ... I put on the beard, and the wig, and the moustache. (*Laughs*) She didn't know the difference ... couldn't distinguish the king from the fool ...

FREDDY. (*Releases him*) That's how it is, when love fills the heart. (*Leers*)

ACTOR. Yes, Your Highness. His Majesty will not come for the final shooting!

FREDDY. He won't come ... you're right ... he's all alone ... he can allow himself that luxury ... not to appear. He'll run around the rooms a bit. Maybe he'll wonder how she suddenly vanished into thin air ... but he's a bit dumb, whatever way you look at it. Love! And the girl from the street of the moon will finally open up her restaurant near the Champs Elysees. So long, Dad. (*Turns to go*)

ACTOR. Wait! Please wait, Your Highness! Wait!

FREDDY. I have to deliver the news to Krupnik.

ACTOR. Please, wait ... listen. (*In his drunkenness he climbs onto the chairs and table, turns them over, falls down, and reaches Freddy in almost a crawling position, and there he kneels*) I ...

FREDDY. You what?

ACTOR. I, I ... please listen ... no one'll know the difference ... no one'll notice, believe me. Do me this favor ... let me play the king in the final shooting! Let me die in the final scene! Believe me, dying is my specialité. Please let me ... she won't know — the princess ... she won't know ...

FREDDY. Your ego's swelling up to the heavens.

ACTOR. Allow me ... please allow me, Your Highness ...

FREDDY. Be there tomorrow.

ACTOR. She won't notice ... she won't notice ... (*And it is not clear if he is crying or laughing*)

SCENE SIX

Nine strokes of a clock. Beams of light on the shooting-stage in Avenida Bolivar. The sign Silence. Shooting in progress *lowers. Freddy, dressed in black, smoking, walks nervously about the stage.*

KRUPNIK'S VOICE. It's nine ... he won't come ...

FREDDY. He'll come. He'll come.

KRUPNIK'S VOICE. Fred, listen, this is it, the hour ... the moment. Believe me, Fred, please ... you may never have another chance like this ... another moment like this ... all your life. Run, Fred ... run away ... don't be afraid of being a coward ... of being weak. Break the contract, now, fast ... run — don't look back ...

FREDDY. (*Abrupt, commanding*) Quit it! (*Toward Krupnik*) You swine ... for three whole months, eight hours a day, day in day out, with the aid of all your Franco-Russian equipment, you've been frying me omelets from eggs laid by all kinds of mythological hens, just because you thought that'd add a spark of majesty to my pretty eyes, because you thought I'd finally see that it's written in the stars that I've got to kill my father. And now, when it comes to eating the omelet, you suddenly get a gutache. So look, Ivan, get this into your head. This is just a film. A film. A real live film. Just mythology. For God's sake, this is no time to start squawking!

KRUPNIK'S VOICE. You don't know ... you don't know, Fred ...

FREDDY. (*Shouts*) I do know! (*Softly, to himself*) You should've gone on eating potatoes a lot longer, Ivan. (*Raises his voice*) You hear, Krupnik? Don't be scared, and don't start hoping. The crown prince won't hand you the old exiled king's head on a platter.

KRUPNIK'S VOICE. Fred, Fred—

FREDDY. (*Shouts*) Cut out these shivers, damn you! (*Softly*) If you'd only left someone else here who can handle the camera tonight, believe me, I'd climb up there right now and throw you to the devil. With these royal hands. But you wanted your final shooting quiet, when you still wanted it. Quiet. A cult of quiet. In the family. All right. You'll get your cult of quiet. Up to the ears. Just sit there and keep quiet yourself. Till the end. Shoot. That's all. Till the end.

KRUPNIK'S VOICE. The orchard walls are high and hard to climb ...

FREDDY. Krupnik!

KRUPNIK'S VOICE. And the place death, considering who thou art ...

FREDDY. Krupnik!

KRUPNIK'S VOICE. If any of my kinsmen find thee here ... (*Squealing of brakes outside*) And the place death ...

FREDDY. He's here. Quiet. We're shooting. (*Raises his voice*) Turn down the lights, Krupnik! Turn down the lights! (*The stage darkens*) Music, music! (*Trumpet blasts*)

VOICE OF THE HERALD. Hear ye, hear ye! The death of Great Bonifacius, formerly King of Great Bogomania, Prince of Upper Augusta, Marquis of The County of Pook. Hear ye, hear ye!

Coronation music. Light comes up and breaks through a colored pane on which are painted the figures of the old king and the young crown prince. Freddy stands to the front of the stage, in his red cloak, with the crown on his head. Enter the king, in an old, shabby coat with gold epaulettes. On his head is a crown. He holds the Trocadero poster rolled under his arm.

KING. (*All smiles and smirks*) It's you, Ferdinand ...

FREDDY. Drunk ...

KING. Is that you, Ferdinand?

FREDDY. It's me, Your Majesty.

KING. I can't see a thing ... I lost my pince-nez, on the way. It's dark here ... where do I go? ... ah, here. Shall I come up, Ferdinand?

FREDDY. Come up.

KING. Do I look all right?

FREDDY. Excellent, Your Majesty.

KING. My profile ... you know ... isn't of the best ... not photogenic ... en face, please, en face ... I come out good en face ... but I can't sing, nor dance ... just a bit ... a tango perhaps, if it's necessary. Do I have to dance?

FREDDY. You don't have to dance, Your Majesty.

KING. No ... well then, it's not so bad. And when you shoot, I just fall down, eh?

FREDDY. You just fall down.

KING. Will there be music? An orchestra perhaps?

FREDDY. Records.

KING. That's all right. I don't have to shout? To make some noise? No?

FREDDY. You don't have to shout.

KING. Of course. Perhaps "Ohhh." No?

FREDDY. If that's how you want your kingdom to come to an end.

KING. Yes. Yes. "Ohhh" is good.

FREDDY. (*Gradually changing the tone of his voice*) Do you have any last requests, Your Majesty?

KING. Last requests? Me? No ... I hope my costume's satisfactory ... just the pince-nez ... I lost it ... on the way. But the crown's shining ... I polished it ...

FREDDY. Your kingdom is approaching its end.

KING. I know, I know ...

FREDDY. The palace is surrounded. Paratroop units have set up their headquarters in the pavilion in the pine grove. Two battalions have taken up positions in the petunia gardens. The artillery corps have dug in by the lakeside.

Guards have been posted at all the gates. Tomorrow morning a parade will take place in the palace square. We shall release white doves, to the tune of an artillery volley. Tomorrow morning I shall command the soldiers to destroy the kingdom.

KING. As you please, as you please. I understand.

FREDDY. We shall destroy all the churches, all the schools, all the entertainment centers —

KING. Naturally —

FREDDY. We shall get rid of all the educational programs, we shall punch holes in all the traditions, we shall rip up all your works of art —

KING. Wonderful!

FREDDY. We shall light a slow fire and roast all the philosophers, teachers, educators — everyone who ever pretended to teach, to instruct, to educate, to train, et cetera —

KING. Et cetera —

FREDDY. We shall castrate all the artists —

KING. A grandiose plan!

FREDDY. And you will die.

KING. In the morning?

FREDDY. Now.

KING. Pity ... I would've liked to have seen you at work, in the morning ... but, of course ... immediately. And with that I conclude my role?

FREDDY. No.

KING. As you please, as you please. Anything. Just tell me.

FREDDY. We have come to liberate the queen.

KING. The queen?

FREDDY. Where is the queen, Your Majesty?

KING. (*Laughs*) The queen! The queen! Here ... here ... I brought her with me. (*Unrolls the poster*) Here you are. Please photograph her. Here she is! The queen! Please, go ahead, photograph!

FREDDY. (*Quickly turns his head towards Krupnik*) The queen!

KING. That isn't the queen?

FREDDY. (*Turns back to the king*) Drunken fool!

KING. I'm not playing my part properly?

FREDDY. No, Your Majesty.

KING. What can you do now, Ferdinand?

FREDDY. I shall kill you.

KING. But that's why you called me here ... why you brought me here ... isn't it? You people want to kill a king ... a king. That's what you've all gathered here for ... all the killers of the king. That's what this battlefield is for ... these cameras ... these stained glass windows. But (*Bursts out laughing*) I'm not a king ... not a king ... I'm a French teacher, or I was ... my name is Felix van Schwank ... Van Schwank, former French teacher. And you, Ferdinand, Crown Prince Ferdinand, what else can you steal from me? Not a crown ... just a woman ... a poor, lonely woman ... from the street of the moon ... where is she, Ferdinand?

FREDDY. You are not entitled to make a speech before your death.

KING. Of course, of course ... give me back the woman, Ferdinand—

FREDDY. In the name of the killers of the king—

KING. Give me back the woman—(*Freddy shoots. A cry of surprise bursts through the king's lips*) Eh? (*He falls. Freddy shoots another four bullets into him*)

FREDDY. (*To Krupnik*) Cut. Lights. (*Shouts*) Lights, Krupnik! Lights! (*The lights come up*) It's over. (*Approaches the king. Softly*) Get up and get out of here before they find out who you are, Fool. (*Walks away*) Papa, Papa, you've filled your role. It's over. (*But the king does not move. Freddy approaches him*) Get up. (*Bends over him*) Your specialité, Fool. (*He raises his head and pulls the beard. Looks at his hands. Gets up*) Blood. (*Bends down*) He's dead.

KRUPNIK'S VOICE. Dead, dead, dead! The king is dead! The king is dead! The king is dead! (*Coronation music*)

FREDDY. Father.

KRUPNIK'S VOICE. Welcome, colleague. (*Dark. The coronation music plays on until the light comes up again on the left front corner. Freddy is sitting on a stool*)

FREDDY. It was supposed to happen in the film. But it turned out to be in real life. Death. The camera stopped rolling, and my father was still lying there, dead. (*Grins*) In real

life. That's what they say, isn't it, Capitan? Really dead.
(*Grins*) Next to the girl from the street of the moon. Like
in all the fairy tales.

VOICE OF THE CAPITAN. Desalmado, desalmado ... and that's
what you people in the Calle de la Mar call—defining
yourself? Go and pray amigo, go and pray, if you get the
chance (*Laughs in a low voice*) Ha! Caporal! Bring him in!
(*Enter the actor*) Know each other? Take it off, take off the
beard, And the rest of it. That's right. Now you're pretty.
(*Roars*) Cante, artista. (*Freddy stands up*)

ACTOR. (*Smiles*) You imagine, Your Highness, that I wanted
to die as a king ... young, so young ... no, your highness,
not to die, to kill ... to kill the king she loved ... that's
what I wanted. And you? (*Approaches Freddy*) Admit it,
admit it ... I could see it on your forehead, your highness
... the murder nestling in your fingertips ... and—phttt—
nothing comes out. You shot, you didn't kill—Krupnik
thought. And I, yes, Your Highness, I put the live bullets
in your revolver ... and that same evening I went to the
old king ... I told him where he could find the girl from
the street of the moon. (*Laughs*) In the Studio ... Avenida
Bolivar ... with you ... his son. He came, the king, and
we killed him ... each of us a little ... a third each, more
or less. Forgive me for laughing ...

FREDDY. Only it's all so stupid, Fool, all so stupid, that he's
simply—dead ... not a third, more or less ... but
dead ... so stupid, it's even funny. (*Also laughs*)

ACTOR. Stupid and funny ...

FREDDY. Stupid and funny. (*Turns to the capitan*) And the
princess, Capitan? Kokomakis? Dolly Kokomakis?

VOICE OF THE CAPITAN. No one's ever heard of anything like
that. (*Laughs*) The earth has swallowed her. (*His laughter
grows*) The earth has swallowed her ...

FREDDY. Once upon a time there was a princess ...

ACTOR. Once upon a time there was a king ... (*Drums and
flutes*)

a. b. yehoshua

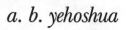

possessions

TRANSLATED FROM THE HEBREW

BY MICHAEL CARASIK

characters

EZRA SAPORTA

ROCHELLE: Ezra's mother

AUNT TILLY: Rochelle's sister

EVA: Ezra's sister

ODED: Eva's husband

SHIRA: Ezra's wife

NADJA: Rochelle's maid

DANIELLA

act 1

Six o'clock in the evening. An old apartment in Jerusalem, part of it orderly and part heaped with possessions, open boxes, piles of objects, household utensils, cleaning equipment, cups and plates, jars of cooking oil, and so on. The mother, Rochelle, is wandering about the house by herself, from time to time moving something from one place to another. She has several lists in her hand. Her activities are centered around two closets; she is taking things out of them and putting things into them. A few seconds pass in silence. She takes out a large, gaudy umbrella, opens it, and puts it back. All this can be done while the house lights are still on. The light goes out while she is looking at one of the objects. And when it comes back on we see Ezra, suitcase and briefcase at his side, kissing her lightly on both cheeks. There is a fundamental tiredness about him.

MOTHER. What happened? You said you'd be here at four and here it's six-thirty.

EZRA. I warned you not to wait.

MOTHER. What do you mean you warned me not to wait? You said you'd be here at four.

EZRA. I said maybe. I said maybe. (*He's already moving about restlessly, looking for something. He goes into the study at stage right and leaves the suitcase there*)

MOTHER. You didn't say maybe. You said you'd leave at two and get here at four.

EZRA. (*Not looking at her*) Maybe. We thought we could but we didn't make it.

MOTHER. You took a nap at noon again. You said today you wouldn't do that.

EZRA. What are you talking about? We didn't nap.

MOTHER. So why didn't you leave at two like you said you would?

EZRA. I'm telling you, we just couldn't get organized. Shira's class wasn't over till after one and I had a meeting at the university.

MOTHER. But it's vacation time now.

EZRA. Not from meetings.

MOTHER. Then you didn't sleep at all, at noon?

EZRA. We rested for maybe half a minute so I'd have the strength to drive without getting into an accident. But what's your hurry? I could have said I'd be here at six and I'd be here now.

MOTHER. You could have, but you said you'd be here at four.

EZRA. But you know I've got a key. I didn't ask you to wait.

MOTHER. But I waited ...

EZRA. That's your business ... your nervousness.

MOTHER. What are you looking for?

EZRA. I'm just looking for the radio. Where did you put the radio? There was some wonderful music on while we were driving, I want to catch the composer's name.

MOTHER. Now it's music, that's what you came for.

EZRA. (*Looking at her for the first time*) Okay ... that's not important ...

MOTHER. We have so many things to do. I'm moving in two weeks, the place is still full of his things. It's a terrible job and I can't handle it. I'm going to be stuck here ...

EZRA. You won't be stuck ... you're exaggerating terribly ... I've moved plenty of times; we can finish it one-two-three.

MOTHER. Not from a house you've lived in for fifty years, not at my age ... I just said help me for a few days and then I'll move and you'll be done with me.

EZRA. No problem ... no problem ...

MOTHER. And there's still your father's clothes, his books and papers ...

EZRA. I'll see that everything's taken care of. Before I forget, here are those copies of the death certificate you asked for, I made five copies at the university ... so you'll have them whenever you need one.

MOTHER. Oy, five, what am I going to do with so many?

EZRA. Just so you'll have them.

MOTHER. You don't want to keep one?

EZRA. What for?

MOTHER. All right, thanks. Let's get started. Do you want to eat something first, or shall we get started with the things so you can decide. Maybe we ought to wait for supper, till

Shira gets here . . .

EZRA. No, she'll eat at her conference; she'll be home late. I warned you on the phone she wouldn't be eating here.

MOTHER. All right, so eat now and be done with it.

EZRA. I'm not hungry.

MOTHER. Don't start with me now, everything's ready . . . there's not much food.

EZRA. (*Wavering*) I'm not hungry . . . (*Moves toward the bathroom*)

MOTHER. All right, at least have some coffee.

EZRA. All right, just coffee. (*Goes into the bathroom*)

Ezra's mother unplugs the telephone in the study and hides it in the closet, then goes to the kitchen to make coffee. Ezra comes out of the bathroom, finds the radio but the music is over. She brings the coffee. He takes it into the study and looks for the telephone.

EZRA. Mama, where's the phone? What happened to the phone . . .

MOTHER. Don't start with those long calls of yours. You came to help me, don't start with those long conversations with your Jerusalem friends.

EZRA. I just have to make one quick call.

MOTHER. (*Desperately*) Not now, later. You're late enough already. You didn't come to help me at all, you just came for Shira's conference.

EZRA. Where's the phone, Mama? I swear, I'll make sure everything gets done. What's there to sort out? Most of it's got to be thrown out anyway.

MOTHER. I'm not giving it to you now — later.

EZRA. (*Continuing to look the whole time*) Fine, I'll go to a pay phone. What do you think? I'm going to just forget it if I have to make a phone call? (*Finds it in the closet, since he's been looking skillfully and efficiently. Dials*) Two minutes . . . Meir? Ezra . . . Yes, we just got in . . . No, Shira went straight to the conference . . . On Nietzsche . . . There's a conference on Nietzsche going on. Haven't you heard? . . . I might drop in tomorrow . . . Sure, got to . . . I'm free in the evening, I haven't got anything to do . . . No, not here, the place is a mess . . . Yeah . . . She decided she's moving there. It's . . . Yes, we've heard good things about it

too ... I don't know what her hurry was, but she wants
to ... My sister grabbed a place that happened to open
up ... You know how that kind of thing opens up ...
Yes, a quick decision ... Maybe you'll manage to persuade
your father, too ... Ha, ha, ha, how's he doing? Listen,
did you happen to see my article? ... In *Literature* ...
(*During the conversation, the mother has gone back to her sorting*)
Have a look at it if you can ... You know I might be
coming up for review ... The dean said he might speak
with you ... He hasn't said yet ... I also wanted to talk
with you about the mini-conference the department wants
to organize for the Kafka centenary ... Just one day, six
lectures ... So it will be concentrated, over by evening ...
Specifically on autobiographical elements in his work, so
suddenly I feel it's important to get to work on biography ...
The connections ... If you happen to see my article you'll
understand what I'm talking about ... *Metamorphosis*,
maybe even *The Verdict* ... Think about something yourself ... It would be wonderful if you could come, the dean
could meet with you too ... We'll talk ... We'll talk ...
Another hour and a half ... I'll be in touch ... All right,
the pressure's starting here. I'll either drop by or call you
in a couple of hours ... (*Hangs up. His mother is standing
next to him, silently angry*) I'm ready. (*The phone rings*)

MOTHER. You see ... it's not over ... I'll kill myself ... I
waited for you and you promised ... (*He picks up the
receiver*)

EZRA. It's for you, anyway. Some woman.

MOTHER. Who is it?

EZRA. I don't know ...

MOTHER. (*Speaking listlessly*) Yes ... Oh, it's you ... Yes ...
Not now ... Same old thing ... Two hours ... Okay ...
I've got my usual troubles ... My son and his wife just
came up specially from Beersheba, I haven't got time ...
Maybe the day after tomorrow ... Bye ... (*Tries to end the
call*) Bye ... Bye ... (*Hangs up in the middle of a sentence*)

EZRA. Who was that?

MOTHER. It was that scum, Judge Meyuhas's widow.

EZRA. Why did you speak so impatiently with her? You'll end

up without friends.

MOTHER. Don't you teach me manners.

EZRA. You actually hung up the phone right in her face.

MOTHER. I didn't hang up ... she promised to send someone to buy the washing machine and nothing came of it.

EZRA. You're selling things to her? God Almighty!

MOTHER. What of it? There's lots of good things here. Someone's coming tomorrow to take the big curtains, a schoolmate of yours. She knows you.

EZRA. Who's that?

MOTHER. Someone named Daniella. She said she knows you very well.

EZRA. Daniella?

MOTHER. You'll see her tomorrow if you want. She knows you quite well. And yesterday I sold the TV to Professor Schirmann's sister.

EZRA. You got rid of the TV already? Are you crazy? What was the hurry? Won't you need it when you get there?

MOTHER. I don't want a TV any more ... it doesn't interest me. Since your father went to the hospital I haven't turned it on.

EZRA. But ... but ... wait ... what are you ...?

MOTHER. Enough, stop wandering around and let's get started. We don't have time. Somebody else will call you in a minute. Shall we start first with the papers or the things?

EZRA. What papers?

MOTHER. Sit down. You're making my head spin, you're so restless. There are some papers here that I don't understand. Now, what's this?

EZRA. This ... this is from the bank. Your dollar account.

MOTHER. So what do they want?

EZRA. They don't want anything. They're just reporting on the principal and the interest.

MOTHER. And this?

EZRA. This is salary ... this is the pension ...

MOTHER. I know, but what are all these numbers here? I can't figure them out.

EZRA. You don't need to figure them out. You just look in this place here. The amount written here is the only thing that should interest you.

MOTHER. And this?

EZRA. This is an invitation to Papa for some conference the city's having.

MOTHER. Write them that he passed away and they should stop sending invitations. It clogs up the mailboxes.

EZRA. I'm not writing them anything. Let the invitations come and just throw them away. What's so hard about that?

MOTHER. How about this?

EZRA. (*Taking out his glasses*) This, this is that same dollar account except from last month. It should be torn up. (*Tears it up*)

MOTHER. (*Alarmed*) Hold on . . .

EZRA. I'm telling you it's the same thing . . . it should be torn up.

MOTHER. How about this?

EZRA. This? What's this? This is something old.

MOTHER. What's this 820 here? Is it dollars?

EZRA. Hold on . . . no . . . it's something old . . . where did you find this?

MOTHER. In your father's papers.

EZRA. This is from the seventies. (*There's a kind of music in his voice*) It's not even in shekels, it's in liras . . . it's in liras. How in the world did this get here? It's only liras. (*Wads it into a ball and throws it in the trash*)

MOTHER. Hey, don't throw it away.

EZRA. Why not?

MOTHER. Just don't throw it away, what business is it of yours? (*Takes the paper from the trash and smooths it out*)

EZRA. Mama, it's eight shekels . . .

MOTHER. All right, I know . . . now, this is the last paper; it came yesterday. What's this signature here?

EZRA. It's a condolence note.

MOTHER. I know, but from whom?

EZRA. Stern.

MOTHER. Ah, now I remember him . . . your father hated him.

EZRA. Wait, I want to read it.

MOTHER. Not now . . . we don't have the time . . . I'm afraid you're going to run out on me all of a sudden. Sit down a

minute, on the chair here. You're making me terribly
nervous. Sit down a minute, you promised. I want you to
decide now what you're taking and what you aren't ...

EZRA. I'm not taking anything, Mama, I told you already. We
don't have any room and I don't need anything.

MOTHER. Sit down ... sit down ... (*He sits*) Just have a look
and decide. I've got everything ready ... whatever you
want, take, and don't do me any favors.

EZRA. Just don't argue with me.

MOTHER. All right ... have a look and decide. Want this?
(*Shows him a big pot with a lid that doesn't match*)

EZRA. What is it?

MOTHER. It's practically a brand-new pot.

EZRA. Don't want it.

MOTHER. You didn't even look.

EZRA. I saw it. I recognize it and I don't want it. (*He starts
looking at the newspaper*)

MOTHER. It's a wonderful pot.

EZRA. You see.

MOTHER. Well, what am I going to do with it?

EZRA. Throw it away ... throw it away ...

MOTHER. I've already thrown away a million things ...

EZRA. So throw away some more. Learn to throw out.

MOTHER. Maybe Eva will want it.

EZRA. Let her have it.

MOTHER. And this pot ... (*Shows him a little pot, a different kind
with no lid*) it's little, it's brand-new, a Teflon pot from
England. The handle wiggles a little but it can be tightened.

EZRA. No.

MOTHER. You're not even looking. (*The whole time he's been
reading the old newspaper in which one of the objects was wrapped*)

EZRA. I recognize it.

MOTHER. You can't possibly recognize it.

EZRA. It's a fact, I do recognize it, from the kitchen. I spent
enough years in this house, don't forget.

MOTHER. (*Laughs*) What are you talking about? This pot is
practically new. I never even used it ... I don't know
what pot you were thinking about.

EZRA. This pot.

MOTHER. You've never seen it, it's completely new ... it was for Passover.

EZRA. All right, it doesn't matter. I don't want it.

MOTHER. (*Pleading*) It's new ... take it ... you'll get lots of use from it.

EZRA. I don't need that kind of pot.

MOTHER. I wonder which pot you were thinking about.

EZRA. (*Gets up and points emphatically at the pot*) This one! You think I don't recognize this pot with the stain right here? You thought if you cleaned it ...?

MOTHER. What have you got against this pot?

EZRA. I don't have anything against it. I just don't want it.

MOTHER. So what am I going to do?

EZRA. Throw it out, the world won't come to an end.

MOTHER. (*Puts it aside*) Now just look a minute, get up. (*Takes a towel off a pile of dishes*) Get up. Look at this set of dishes; it's wonderful, genuine porcelain, from Czechoslovakia. This is practically a complete set, maybe three saucers were broken but you can use the cake plates instead ... in case you ever have a lot of people over. Let's say you have a party when you get your promotion. People will go crazy over these dishes ... this style is what's considered modern now.

EZRA. Well ... so ...

MOTHER. You don't understand these things ... I'll talk it over with Shira.

EZRA. (*Standing by the dishes, looking at the plates, picking them up and looking them over*) I remember these ...

MOTHER. So take them.

EZRA. Mama, we don't have any room.

MOTHER. How much room could it take?

EZRA. It takes. We're already up to our ears in dishes from the two sets we got at our wedding.

MOTHER. But you don't have one like this.

EZRA. (*Considering*) It's not that ...

MOTHER. I'll maybe talk with Shira ... we'll leave it in the meantime.

EZRA. Shira's not much of a housewife. She just buys things and brings them home and I have to find a place to put them.

MOTHER. I'll talk with Shira. (*She covers them. Ezra sits down, already tired*) Now, do you want these pliers?

EZRA. Let's see. All right.

MOTHER. I'll put them in this box for you. And do you want this screwdriver? It's a little bent. (*Shows him a large, crooked screwdriver*)

EZRA. (*Taking off his glasses as he looks*) All right, I'll take it.

MOTHER. It's bent, if you don't want it I'll throw it out.

EZRA. No, it's all right, I'll take it.

MOTHER. Now take this jar of oil, I've got three of them here. I'll give one to Eva, but you take the big one.

EZRA. Why are you giving away this oil, aren't you going to need it? They have a kitchenette there, where you can cook for yourself. Why are you getting rid of everything?

MOTHER. I have enough. Take the jar.

EZRA. How'd you manage to hoard so much oil?

MOTHER. I don't know ... I just stocked up ... because of the wars ...

EZRA. What war is it from? Yom Kippur is already ten years ago; it's spoiled for sure.

MOTHER. It's good oil, I promise you. It's not ten years, it's a lot less — since Sadat came ...

EZRA. (*Laughing*) Why in the world did you buy oil then?

MOTHER. There was a panic, someone said there was going to be a war. Fine, we'll put this aside, out of the way. If you want, you can take the little jar too. If Aunt Tilly doesn't take it.

EZRA. Let her take it. Give it to her.

MOTHER. Now what did you decide about the vacuum cleaner?

EZRA. Haven't thought about it.

MOTHER. You said you would.

EZRA. (*Sighing*) I don't know ... is it any good?

MOTHER. It's in perfect shape. I could sell it; it would sell, no problem.

EZRA. All right, I'll take it. I don't know where I'm going to put all this.

MOTHER. I told you, you need a good storeroom. If you'd enclose your kitchen balcony, you could put lots of things there.

EZRA. Why would we want to enclose it?

MOTHER. All right, now here's a frying pan.

EZRA. Don't want it.

MOTHER. It's clean and polished. You throw in the meat without a drop of oil.

EZRA. No.

MOTHER. Take it, take. (*She puts it in the box*)

EZRA. No, I'm not taking it.

MOTHER. Do me a favor.

EZRA. What does this have to do with favors?

MOTHER. I can't stay here with it any more.

EZRA. You don't have to stay with it. Toss it out.

MOTHER. I've already thrown everything out. The maid took home a basketful.

EZRA. So give her this too.

MOTHER. I can't give her such a good pan. I'm begging you, take it.

EZRA. (*Getting angry*) No! You listen to me, if you start up I'm not taking a thing. Take it out of there.

MOTHER. You're just obstinate. It doesn't matter. Now look at these binoculars. We bought them in Rome when we visited you. Opera glasses — unused, of course; it was impossible to drag your father out of the house to the theater, no matter how I tried.

EZRA. (*Picks them up and looks into them*) I don't get it ... I can't see a thing ...

MOTHER. Sure you can. I've used them. Give them to Ayil to play with. I've got better ones.

EZRA. Where are they?

MOTHER. I'll find them in a minute. (*Puts them in his box*) Now have a look at these dishes.

EZRA. I'm getting tired. Why don't we take a break? (*Goes over to the phone*)

MOTHER. We just started. You promised you'd spend a whole day on it with me. Now you're tired after five minutes. There's a lot of things here.

EZRA. Hold on a minute, just a short call.

MOTHER. I'm going to end up cutting the phone cord.

EZRA. Just to the kids.

MOTHER. To the kids, okay. (*Looks at the clock*)

EZRA. Maybe after seven ...

MOTHER. No, call if you're worried.

EZRA. It doesn't matter ... let's go on.

MOTHER. Here are the plates ... these are the soup bowls ...

EZRA. I'm not touching those plates, they disgust me.

MOTHER. So what am I going to do with them?

EZRA. (*Furiously*) Arrgh ...

MOTHER. All right, all right. Now have a look at something special ... something wonderful ... a little chair that folds up into a stick. You go out walking with it and when you want to rest you open it up and you have a little chair to sit on. (*Demonstrates*)

EZRA. (*Amused*) Where did you get a thing like that?

MOTHER. I bought it in Cambridge when we came to visit you. The English use them at the horse races.

EZRA. Why in the world did you buy one?

MOTHER. I thought for when I'm older ... if I get sick ...

EZRA. So keep it.

MOTHER. No, it's too heavy; it's more for an Englishman at the races.

EZRA. So what do you want me to do with it?

MOTHER. For you it's not too heavy. Go on a hike and when you want to rest ...

EZRA. Don't want it. I'm not filling up my house with all these shmatehs. I'm starting to understand why my poor father kept losing his temper with these things you kept buying all the time ...

MOTHER. Stop it ... I could have died too ... he never wanted to buy anything.

EZRA. All right, that's enough, let's go on. I'm not taking this.

MOTHER. Why should I go on if you keep insisting you're not going to take anything. You want me stuck here with everything. (*Silence*) Now this you'll take; it's really yours, it's the vase you brought us back from America.

EZRA. What do you mean ...?

MOTHER. It's yours ... you brought it, so you take it back ... I told you not to bring me any presents.

EZRA. All right.

MOTHER. Now have a look at these bathroom rugs I never used, brand-new, you don't believe me?

EZRA. They're okay, but they're the wrong color.

MOTHER. Why? These are the newest colors.

EZRA. Maybe, but it doesn't match our bathroom.

MOTHER. What color is it?

EZRA. Some kind of blue.

MOTHER. So, this matches ... we'll talk about it with Shira.

EZRA. That won't help you.

MOTHER. She'll take it, I'm sure.

EZRA. She won't take anything I don't agree to take.

MOTHER. It's not necessary. I can sell it to that friend of yours, that girl you went to school with; you'll live to regret it.

EZRA. Sell it, humiliate us all. We'll put up a sign here, "Old Clothes." Everyone will say, "Dr. Saporta's mother is selling rags."

MOTHER. They're not rags. All right, all right, you don't want to help me. There'll be others who will, if that's what bothers you. Enough. Now tell me what you decided about this wardrobe ... you measured your wall space?

EZRA. I measured. There's no room.

MOTHER. You're making a big mistake.

EZRA. What do you want me, to knock down a wall for this wardrobe?

MOTHER. You don't have to knock down a wall. You could arrange the whole deal with your carpenter.

EZRA. No. N-O. No.

MOTHER. Think a little more about it.

EZRA. I'm through thinking about it, don't make me lose my temper.

MOTHER. (*Thinks before speaking*) You want to take this knife? The handle's a bit broken, but the knife is all right.

EZRA. Okay.

MOTHER. (*Observing him*) And this little knife too.

EZRA. (*Examining it*) You're sure you don't need it.

MOTHER. No.

EZRA. Okay.

MOTHER. Now take this thermometer so you'll have a spare,

the kids always break them ...

EZRA. (*Taking it and looking it over*) I don't understand how you have no room there for a thermometer. Why don't you take it?

MOTHER. I have two others. It's all right.

EZRA. Take it, you can always use it. It doesn't take up any room.

MOTHER. No, I don't need it, I have enough. It was your father's, it's not for me. We bought it specially for him at the drugstore, with clear numbers; he never could read the numbers on the Health Service ones.

EZRA. (*Handing it back*) Actually, no, I don't want it.

MOTHER. But why? It doesn't take up any room. Because it was your father's? What's with you? It's completely clean; I disinfected it a thousand times. You think I'd give you an unsanitary thermometer?

EZRA. (*Still holding the thermometer, undecided, playing with it*) You know, I've had fever in the evenings lately ...

MOTHER. (*Not showing concern*) So see a doctor, don't ignore it. Now look at this fruit bowl. (*Taps it. The phone rings and Ezra hurries to it*)

EZRA. Yes, darling, it's Daddy ... How are you doing? Yes, Grandma's fine ... Mommy's still at her lectures ... What am I doing? Nothing, just helping Grandma get some things done. Put Michal on ... Michal, what's new? Everything's fine. You remember what I told you about the heating element in the bathroom? Don't forget, and turn off the gas. Tonight, yes. The rice is in the fridge. Heat it up on low, you hear? And lock up the doors. The shutters too. Now sweetie, you have to. With the bolt. Mommy's at a conference. And don't stay up too late watching TV. Make sure he eats. You look after him. All right, dear. Yes, I know, but do it for me. Just feed him this once. All right? For me. A special request. (*Kisses into phone and hangs up. Meanwhile Rochelle has taken an umbrella out of the closet and when he finishes she opens it in front of him*)

MOTHER. Take a look at this umbrella.

EZRA. It's broken.

MOTHER. That's nothing; you just fix this part and it's like new.

EZRA. Don't want it.

MOTHER. You're deliberately being stubborn.

EZRA. I'm not being stubborn.

MOTHER. Think about it.

EZRA. I don't want to think about it at all.

MOTHER. So what about the chair?

EZRA. What chair?

MOTHER. The one you're sitting on. You don't want to take it?

EZRA. (*Gets up and looks at it. Sits down again*) What do you mean? You're not taking it?

MOTHER. I have a couch, I don't have any more room. Who's going to sit on it, anyway?

EZRA. You're exaggerating how little room you'll have.

MOTHER. There's no room there. A little roomette. So what do you say about the chair?

EZRA. (*Gets up again, looks at it, touches it, even smells it*) All right, I'll think about it.

MOTHER. Think about it fast and tell me. If you don't want it, I can sell it easily. Now in this case there's a brand-new shoe brush. Take it. (*As if he was refusing*) Take it. (*Puts it in his box*) And there's two cans of cleanser here. Take one and I'll give one to Eva.

EZRA. You're sure you don't need it.

MOTHER. No, no, I've got more. Why don't you put everything in the car? Get it out of the house, so I can have a little air in here. Now are you ready to eat or do you want to take a quick look at your father's clothes?

EZRA. (*Astounded*) At what?

MOTHER. (*Opening a second wardrobe*) There are brand-new shoes here. He never put them on even once. Look.

EZRA. But he was a ten and I'm a nine-and-a-half.

MOTHER. It makes no difference. You can put those inserts in and make them small enough to fit — try it.

EZRA. (*Very angry*) How can you think in any way, shape, or form that I'm miserly enough to wear shoes that are too big for me. Tell me, what's gotten into you?

MOTHER. Miserly nothing, they're brand-new shoes. All right, don't get mad, don't take them. I didn't say anything. (*He lapses into a gloomy silence. She is a bit surprised*) What's the matter, don't you feel well?

EZRA. I told you I've been getting this fever. It comes and goes.

MOTHER. Maybe you should take your temperature now.

EZRA. Not now.

MOTHER. So go to the doctor. What do you want from me?

EZRA. I don't want anything from you. Just give me a bit of peace ...

MOTHER. What am I doing to you? God Almighty, what am I doing to you? I'm just showing you a few things. What's going on? You come here after not being home for three weeks and I show you a few things ...

EZRA. All right, that's enough. Don't start up again.

MOTHER. Now what about this belt of your father's? It's brand-new.

EZRA. Don't need it. I have belts.

MOTHER. So take one more. Put it on.

EZRA. (*Extinguished*) No ...

MOTHER. How could a belt like this bother you?

EZRA. No ...

MOTHER. You're cruel ... it's a brand-new belt; he never had a chance to put it on. We bought it a few days before we got the results of the tests. He'd be happy if he knew you were wearing it ...

EZRA. Don't talk that way ...

MOTHER. I'll put it in. If you find it ... you won't regret it. (*He sits down. Suddenly feeling weak, picks up the thermometer, examines it, and puts it in his mouth*)

EZRA. Let's take a break for a minute.

MOTHER. Just a minute ... now look at this purse for Shira. (*She holds up an enormous colored purse*)

EZRA. No ... no ...

MOTHER. What do you know?

EZRA. No ... no ... next.

MOTHER. And this is a game which your kids left here once ... it's yours.

EZRA. Mine ... very good. (*Gets up with the thermometer in his mouth, takes it and tears the game apart in a furious rage*)

MOTHER. What's the excitement? I could have given it to the maid's boy. Now have a look at this mixer, not electric, kind of a hand mixer. (*Ezra doesn't answer. With the thermometer in his mouth, as if he is producing the fever himself, he looks at her gloomily*) And this is for lighting the gas.

EZRA. I have one.

MOTHER. (*She is annoyed by the gloom and lethargy that have come over him*) What's the matter with you?

EZRA. Nothing, I've had it ... give it to Eva.

MOTHER. She doesn't want anything; she's worse than you. (*Hesitating and undecided*) Now just look at this kettle. (*Ezra doesn't look*) You're not looking.

EZRA. You're crazy ...

MOTHER. What a thing to say ... This kettle's in perfect shape.

EZRA. (*Looks at thermometer*) Mama, stop ... I have a fever again.

MOTHER. What's your temperature?

EZRA. Almost a hundred ...

MOTHER. What is this fever of yours?

EZRA. I don't know ...

MOTHER. What does it feel like?

EZRA. Nothing. (*He gets up and begins to walk restlessly about the house*)

MOTHER. So go to the doctor ... what do you want from me?

EZRA. Okay ... let's take a break ... This is enough ... a little rest now ...

MOTHER. Just so you know that we've hardly even started.

EZRA. I'm staying here till tomorrow afternoon.

MOTHER. But you'll run off with your friends, just like the last time. I know we won't get anything done.

EZRA. Between one thing and another you can see I don't want to take anything. I'm not going to be your garbage dump.

MOTHER. You're not a garbage dump. These are all good things I'm giving you. What am I going to do with them?

EZRA. Throw them out. Learn to throw things away. There's nothing valuable here.

MOTHER. (*In a rage*) I threw things away ... I throw things

away all the time ... I throw things away at night ...
I'm alone here ... I've handed out to the neighbors, I've
given to the maid, but there are certain things I can't
throw out. Certain things are just impossible to throw
out ...

EZRA. Everything's possible.

MOTHER. At least you have to look ... I'm asking you ... it's
a month since you promised you would come ... and look
...

EZRA. Mama, please, I have a fever, give me a little peace.
(*Goes to the study and lies down on the bed*)

MOTHER. (*To herself*) Really, your fever is the last thing we
need ... suddenly you're feverish? You finally get
here ... so take an aspirin. What do you want me to do?
You won't die from it. You want to rest? Go ahead and
rest. But don't start with those endless phone calls of
yours. Just say that for once you came to Jerusalem on my
account ... here, let me fix it for you. (*Straightens the
bed while he is stretched out on it*) Here, let me give you a
pillow ... you might actually want this one ... take
it ... remind me to ask Shira about it ...

He turns out the light. Blackout.

EZRA. (*Lying down, talking on the phone*) Yes, I hear you,
Ze'ev ... Okay ... Yes, of course we'll pay travel expenses
and a little honorarium too. But you know according to
the university pay system it can't be much ... Sure, sure,
we'll make it four hours instead of two. Certainly ... I'm
lecturing too ... On Kafka's *Metamorphosis* ... Maybe
you saw the article I published? There's a little innovation
in it, an innovation, as Dov Sadan says ... The description
of the cockroach ... An explanation of the cockroach ...
Yes ... I've read a lot ... There's no end of interpret-
ations ... But to me it's not a symbol, not an allegory, but
a real description ... Not now, it's something shocking
but in my opinion also terribly sad ... Read it if you
can ... Then it's settled; the secretary will send you the
invitation ... I'm here getting things done ... I'm going
out of my mind ... My father? Not six months yet ...

What a rotten year ... All right ... Yes ... Okay ... I meant to ask you ... Have you got a minute ...? Our dean said he would talk with you about my review for promotion ... There was a thought that maybe it's time for it already ... I know ... I told him to speak with you ... I've been sitting at this rank for a long time now ... They might ask you to be on my committee, I'm not sure ... No, I'm not pressuring them ... It was the dean's idea ... So maybe he'll talk with you ... When are you leaving ...? All right, obviously only if it works out ... Good-bye ... (*The whole time his mother has been walking back and forth outside the door, half listening, half immersed in organizing things. Blackout*)

Mother is standing with Aunt Tilly, who is much older than she, a tall, bony old woman, always in sunglasses, a big basket in her hand. Mother wishes to press more things on her. Now they're fighting over the stick-seat.

TILLY. Why don't you take it yourself? You'll need it.

MOTHER. No, no, take it.

TILLY. The children might want it.

MOTHER. I asked Ezra but he has no room.

TILLY. What about Eva? Maybe Eva.

MOTHER. Eva? Eva doesn't want to touch a thing. She's just not in the mood for this right now.

TILLY. But I don't have any room either.

MOTHER. Yes, you do. I'll show you — in the bedroom ... take it, take it. Do me a favor.

TILLY. What will I do with it?

MOTHER. It's something the English use ...

TILLY. (*Laughs*) But I'm not English.

MOTHER. Not, it's for everyone ... you're out walking and when you want to sit down and rest. (*Demonstrates*)

TILLY. It's really nice. So why don't you take it yourself?

MOTHER. I don't have any room. I'm moving into a hole, a box, a closet ... otherwise I'd take it myself.

TILLY. But it's heavy.

MOTHER. Ezra will take you in his car. He promised me.

TILLY. But he's got a temperature.

MOTHER. What can we do? He'll take the bottle of Lysol for you too.

TILLY. And where's Shira?

MOTHER. Shira's at some kind of conference, she'll be here later tonight. She's always studying and he takes care of them all. Such a good husband. Let's see if he's all right. He might have woken up. (*Opens the door to the study and turns on the light*) Ezra, come say hello to Aunt Tilly.

EZRA. (*Gets up, kisses her warmly*) How are you?

TILLY. All right ... all right. How are the children?

EZRA. All right.

TILLY. How old is Michal now?

EZRA. She's seventeen.

TILLY. We're all getting older. What's this fever your mother's been telling me about? Don't neglect it.

EZRA. No, it'll be okay.

TILLY. Your Uncle Saul had a fever like that. That doctor gave him some pills and that took care of it.

EZRA. When was that?

TILLY. About a year before he died.

MOTHER. No, no, don't give him ideas. He has plenty already, Ezra, I told Aunt Tilly you would give her a ride home.

EZRA. All right.

TILLY. Your mother's always giving me things. She forces me to take them.

EZRA. Take them, take them. It's nothing ...

TILLY. What am I going to do with this bottle of Lysol and this stick that's like a chair?

EZRA. So you'll have them, it can't hurt. Come on, I'll take you home. Here, let me ... I'm going to drop in on someone afterwards.

MOTHER. But don't run off on me now, you haven't even eaten.

TILLY. Maybe he can eat at my house, Rochelle?

MOTHER. No, why on earth? There's plenty of food here. Eva might come too.

EZRA. Eva?

MOTHER. She just called. She's in Jerusalem. She was looking for Shira. They're at the ... lawyer's ...

TILLY. What happened?

MOTHER. Nothing. More troubles.

EZRA. She's getting divorced, Aunt Tilly.

TILLY. Divorced?

MOTHER. (*Winking crookedly at Ezra*) Not exactly.

TILLY. I always thought they didn't suit each other, but it lasted ... he looks old enough to be her father. But what happened now?

MOTHER. They're arguing about something.

EZRA. They're beyond arguing.

MOTHER. (*Extremely annoyed*) They're not exactly divorcing ...

EZRA. They're sort of divorcing ... well, let's go ... (*He takes Tilly's things and they exit. Mother resumes her arranging. Blackout*)

Eva is sitting in the armchair. She's a refined woman of about forty. Her mother is hovering around her.

EVA. I brought you three copies of the death certificate, just as you asked.

MOTHER. You too? Ezra already brought me some. What am I going to do with so many copies?

EVA. (*Irritated*) But you asked me ...

MOTHER. All right ... all right ... maybe you need one. In case you're ever asked for his death certificate.

EVA. What in the world for?

MOTHER. All right, it doesn't matter. You've got a little time?

EVA. Well ...

MOTHER. Tell me, what's this? (*Shows her a paper from the bank*)

EVA. I've told you a thousand times, that's yours and Papa's dollar account.

MOTHER. And this?

EVA. That's the pension check.

MOTHER. For which month?

EVA. For ... it doesn't say.

MOTHER. Ezra said it was for March.

EVA. So why are you asking me?

MOTHER. I wanted to be sure.

EVA. I don't see where he found March here.

MOTHER. All right, it doesn't matter. What about this?

EVA. This ... what's this? This is something terribly old ...

it's in liras. (*Wads it up and is about to tear it*)

MOTHER. No, don't tear it . . . it's money.

EVA. This is money? Mother . . . it's not worth the paper it's printed on.

MOTHER. It doesn't matter . . . maybe . . . (*Smooths out the paper and puts it in her pocket*) Don't tear it up. All right, it doesn't matter. Now, Eva, just have a look at this frying pan.

EVA. I've seen it.

MOTHER. Take it.

EVA. No.

MOTHER. Then what am I going to do with it?

EVA. Throw it out.

MOTHER. Are you crazy? This is a wonderful pan.

EVA. Straight in the trash.

MOTHER. There's no way on earth I'm throwing a pan like this in the trash.

EVA. Why not? I can't understand why you've held onto it all these years.

MOTHER. I'm not throwing it out, Ezra will take it.

EVA. He'll never take it.

MOTHER. He's good. He takes things from me. You're no help at all.

EVA. What kind of situation am I in, to take things? I'm also breaking up a household and now I'm supposed to throw in an extra frying pan on top of everything.

MOTHER. No one's asking you to break up your household. You know what I think about this divorce — it's completely unnecessary. What's the big hurry?

EVA. I can't wait any longer. All of a sudden he seems so old to me. How could I have lived with him all these years? Now that Papa's dead . . .

MOTHER. What does it have to do with Papa?

EVA. I didn't want to upset him.

MOTHER. And me you don't care if you upset?

EVA. Please understand, there are inner pressures forcing me to do this. He's dead as far as I'm concerned.

MOTHER. And what do I . . . (*Momentary pause. Eva looks at her as if seeing her for the first time*)

EVA. For you at least, when all's said and done, things worked out easy.

MOTHER. Easy? What? (*Shaking all over*)

EVA. No, Mama, don't start. I don't have the strength, let's go on.

MOTHER. Easy?

EVA. Let's go on, Mama. (*Momentary pause*)

MOTHER. So tell me what you finally decided about the carpet sweeper.

EVA. What carpet sweeper?

MOTHER. This one, the yellow one.

EVA. Don't want it.

MOTHER. That's final? You'll regret it.

EVA. All right. I'll regret it.

MOTHER. Then Ezra will take it.

EVA. Let him.

MOTHER. Now you see this pot? Just look a minute.

EVA. I'm not looking. God, I'm going to take pots now?

MOTHER. You're making another mistake.

EVA. All right.

MOTHER. This whole divorce of yours is a big mistake. You'll live to regret it.

EVA. All right, I'll regret it.

MOTHER. Now you see this purse . . . (*Shows her the same colored purse she offered Ezra*)

EVA. (*Astonished*) What is this?

MOTHER. It's a brand-new purse. I never used it.

EVA. How did you get it?

MOTHER. I bought it but I never got around to using it.

EVA. What a monstrosity.

MOTHER. What?

EVA. What awful colors.

MOTHER. These happen to be the colors that are going to be modern.

EVA. When?

MOTHER. Soon, you'll see. (*Eva laughs*) If you don't want it, give it to your maid.

EVA. My maid isn't crazy enough to take something like this.

MOTHER. But I haven't got any room . . .

EVA. Learn how to throw things away.

MOTHER. I'm not throwing it away ... I've been throwing things away all my life ... I'll find someone ... do you want this jar of oil?

EVA. Sure. I'll take it.

MOTHER. Don't do me any favors.

EVA. All right, I'll take it.

MOTHER. Take the little one, I already gave the big one to Ezra.

EVA. Okay, okay. (*All the while looking at her watch*) So what time are they going to be home?

MOTHER. What about that armchair you're sitting in?

EVA. What about it?

MOTHER. Don't you want it?

EVA. The armchair? Aren't you taking it with you?

MOTHER. What do I need it for? Who's going to sit in it?

EVA. What do you mean who'll sit in it?

MOTHER. Who'll come and visit me there on the weekends?

EVA. What are you trying to say? What's your game now?

MOTHER. No, seriously, who'll visit me? I don't even want them to visit me. I'm going to die, you'll be rid of me there.

EVA. You think we want to get rid of you?

MOTHER. I'm not saying you want to, but you will, and just because I ask you to help me a bit you don't want to ...

EVA. We're not the ones who told you to go there ... you decided! You said you couldn't stay in the house forever. You're making a mistake.

MOTHER. You wanted me to stay here?

EVA. I'm not saying anything. I gave up trying to talk to you a long time ago. I'm just arranging what you want. I was lucky to find a place there, a place opening up soon ...

MOTHER. What do you mean soon? Isn't it ready?

EVA. It's all right, there's a room ... it's lucky I grabbed it ... you're lucky, you really are very lucky.

MOTHER. I'm lucky? Are you crazy? What are you talking about?

EVA. Things could have turned out a lot worse.

MOTHER. How could they have been worse? What could have been more horrible than what I went through in the hospital ... that dreadful illness. How dare you say a thing like that?

EVA. It could have lingered ... you'd still be going from hospital to hospital. They'd have sent him back here with all those tubes. You'd have had to take care of him here ... months, years ...

MOTHER. (*Screaming*) I took care of him here!

EVA. For a short time ... very short ... it could have been a lot worse. Be thankful that he died on you quickly. You don't know how it can drag on sometimes ... exactly the same kind of case. David's mother, for example ... four years.

MOTHER. Don't tell me about anyone else, I'm not interested.

EVA. Give thanks ... give thanks. We should all give thanks. It was cheap, too, dirt cheap.

MOTHER. I'm not giving thanks ... what do I have to give thanks for? Why should I give thanks. Who should I thank? You two maybe ...?

EVA. I didn't say that.

MOTHER. Each day in the hospital, you barely dropped in and you were gone.

EVA. What did you want us to do? Leave our houses and come live with you?

MOTHER. I was alone here. He didn't want to get out of bed. He could barely sit up ... he'd just ring that bell that you left ... every minute to the bathroom ... he relieved himself on me. Thanks for what?

EVA. It was a short time. There are families that go on for years like that, it was an easy death.

MOTHER. (*Screaming*) For you! (*Ezra comes in, opening the door with his key, surprising them*)

EZRA. What are you two screaming about? I could hear you all the way downstairs.

EVA. Where's Shira? Didn't you bring her?

EZRA. No, she's still at her conference on Mt. Scopus. She'll be home late.

MOTHER. (*Shaken*) You'll be the death of me ...

EZRA. What's happened now?

EVA. I just told her that Papa's illness didn't last long, that it could have been a lot worse ...

EZRA. (*Reflectively, in a gloomy but quiet mood, almost abstractedly*) That's true.

MOTHER. You too? You too? How could it have been worse? You didn't do a thing ...

EZRA. Don't say that.

MOTHER. I'll say it. Why not? You didn't do a thing ... you came to the hospital a couple of times.

EZRA. How many times? Every other day. From Beersheba.

MOTHER. Only if you had an errand to do here. Even your father said, "He doesn't come for me, he comes to advance his career."

EZRA. What? He couldn't have said that ...

MOTHER. He did.

EZRA. I came to see him every two days. How can you say a thing like that?

EVA. Why do you say such things?

MOTHER. Stop it! What do you want from me? Everything could be worse, but this was bad enough ... he gave up, he wanted to die already.

EZRA. And you answered, "So go on and die ..."

MOTHER. I didn't say a word. What could I have said? What makes you think I had the strength to tell him anything? Alone ... really alone ... alone now, too ... I'm dying ... and if you really want to be rid of me, just help me move out of here. Take a few things, take some of these things, help me and I'll give you peace and quiet ...

EVA. Just throw them out. Why don't you understand how to throw things out?

MOTHER. You ... you ... you ... (*Sobs*)

EZRA. Leave her alone, Eva, what are we fighting for? (*Absentmindedly puts the thermometer in his mouth*)

EVA. This is crazy.

EZRA. Please ... please ...

EVA. Why are you taking your temperature?

EZRA. I've been running a fever in the evenings recently.

EVA. For no reason?

EZRA. For no reason.

EVA. So go to the doctor.

EZRA.   Maybe I will. I hope it's nothing. Shira says it's nothing.

EVA.   No, go to the doctor, get a checkup ... you've got to.

EZRA.   We'll see.

EVA.   No, promise me. So I shouldn't wait for Shira?

EZRA.   I think it'll be quite late.

EVA.   I'd wait. I don't mind, but he'll be here to pick me up soon.

EZRA.   He's here?

EVA.   Yes, we were together at the lawyer's ... it could be over within a month ... I'll have a divorce.

EZRA.   You've decided?

EVA.   I've decided.

EZRA.   (*The thermometer is in his mouth all this time, but he speaks gently and quietly*) Well, all right ... (*Their mother has been looking at them the whole time, expectantly*)

EVA.   I'm giving up a lot, but the main thing is to be free of him ... I shiver every time he walks in the house ... I'm so scared of him ...

EZRA.   Scared? That's something new.

EVA.   Maybe, yes, it's new ... scared ... I don't know. It's as if some silent phantom entered the house ... I want so much to talk with Shira. What time will she be here tomorrow? We'll be here tomorrow, too. We have another meeting with the lawyer.

EZRA.   Why a Jerusalem lawyer? Who is it, anyway?

EVA.   Friedman, a guy I went to high school with ... the only one I trust ... all the lawyers in Tel Aviv are friends of his. Are you staying all day tomorrow?

EZRA.   Not all day ... (*All the while he has been talking with the thermometer in his mouth, taking it out from time to time to check. Now he is finished taking his temperature*)

MOTHER.   Well, are you two finished?

EVA.   Do you have a temperature?

EZRA.   Yeah ... it doesn't matter ...

EVA.   What is it?

EZRA.   99.8.

EVA.   And you don't feel anything?

EZRA.   How do I know what I feel?

EVA.   Strange ... (*Meanwhile their mother has picked up a large bowl and come up to them quietly.*)

MOTHER. Do you want this bowl?

EVA. Are you starting again, Mama? No.

MOTHER. So you take it.

EZRA. What in the world ...?

MOTHER. Take it, it's wonderful. Don't listen to her. (*Ezra hesitates*)

EVA. Leave him alone.

MOTHER. What business is it of yours? What do you care? Take it, try it.

EZRA. (*Gently*) I don't have any room, Mama, really.

MOTHER. How much room does it take ...?

EVA. Leave him alone.

MOTHER. Leave me alone. Take it, it's good ... you won't regret it ... your father really loved it. He used to eat his cereal out of it ... (*Holds it out to him, thrusting it at him*)

EVA. What does that have to do with it?

MOTHER. (*Ignoring her, trying to get him to take the dish*) Your father loved it.

EZRA. I warned you before, we're not turning Papa into a saint. It's not ...

MOTHER. Try it, I beg you. (*Pushes it at him. He holds out his hand hesitantly; the bowl falls and breaks*)

EVA. You see ... you see ...

The mother, white with rage, goes to get the dustpan and broom. At the door, which is slightly ajar, Oded stands tall and bald, very well dressed; he is in a relaxed posture, whistling softly.

EVA. You're here already ... (*He doesn't answer*) What a shame I didn't take my own car; tomorrow we'll take both cars. (*Oded smiles at Rochelle, who is sweeping up the pieces, and at Ezra, who is standing gloomily in the corner*)

ODED. (*To Ezra*) Hello.

EZRA. Hello.

ODED. (*To Rochelle*) Hello.

MOTHER. Hello, Oded.

ODED. What's new?

MOTHER. You can see, I've got troubles.

ODED. Why?

MOTHER. I'm stuck here with all this stuff and they don't want to take a thing. (*Oded smiles*) What's going to happen? And you, why do you have to make trouble for her just when I'm moving? Couldn't you have waited a little?

ODED. Me? Ask her ... this came out of the blue for me too. "You're too old for me, you frighten me." All of a sudden I frighten her, all of a sudden I'm too old for her ... did you ever hear of such a thing? But if she wants to ... I only do what she wants, you know me.

EVA. (*In a venomous whisper*) You bastard ...

ODED. (*Ignoring her. To Ezra*) And how about you?

EZRA. I'm okay.

ODED. Shira and the kids?

EZRA. Getting along ...

ODED. Great. You're going back to Beersheba tonight?

EZRA. No.

MOTHER. Oded, can I offer you something to drink?

ODED. No thanks.

MOTHER. Perhaps you'll take something from here ...

ODED. What?

EVA. Mother ...

MOTHER. Maybe this padlock. (*Pulls a big, rusty padlock out of one of the cartons*)

ODED. No, thank you.

MOTHER. Maybe you'd like these opera glasses.

EVA. Mother, I'm surprised at you. Leave him alone.

ODED. Opera glasses ... (*A spark of interest is lit and he takes them*)

MOTHER. It's perfect for the theater.

EVA. Really, Mother, he's never gone to the theatre in his life. (*Oded looks at them through the opera glasses*)

MOTHER. Those are wonderful, you'll enjoy them.

EVA. Mother? Stop ingratiating yourself with him.

MOTHER. They don't take up any room, either. (*Oded hands them back*) Aren't they any good?

ODED. They work fine.

MOTHER. So don't you want them?

ODED. No thanks.

MOTHER. Why not?

ODED. I don't look at the theatre through opera glasses. (*Motions to Eva with his little finger*) Come on ... so long, hang in there. (*Exits*)

EVA. (*Leaving her mother with a kiss, taking the jar of oil*) So I'll call Shira in the morning and make arrangements for tomorrow. (*Exits. Ezra gets up and goes to the study*)

MOTHER. Where are you going?

EZRA. I have to rest, I've got a fever, it's for real. (*He lies down on the bed, picks up the phone, starts to dial but stops in the middle and turns out the light*)

Late at night. Rochelle is in a nightgown. Shira sits, in a boyish jacket, eating at the table. Ezra and his mother are serving her.

EZRA. But I still don't understand why you were so late.

SHIRA. By the time it was over ... by the time I got a ride here ...

EZRA. How were the lectures?

SHIRA. The whole afternoon was pretty mediocre, but the last one of the evening was outstanding.

EZRA. What was it about?

SHIRA. The moral question.

MOTHER. Eat something.

SHIRA. I already ate supper over there; I'm really not hungry.

MOTHER. Eat just a little zucchini salad. I made it special for you, just the way you like it.

SHIRA. You didn't have to ...

MOTHER. I ran around all day yesterday to find some zucchini and I made it for you, just the way you told me you like it.

SHIRA. Thanks very much, it's wonderful.

MOTHER. Do you want anything to drink?

SHIRA. Coffee, but I'll make it myself in a minute ...

EZRA. Coffee at this hour? We're just about to go to sleep.

SHIRA. Don't worry, I'll fall asleep.

MOTHER. Maybe you'd like that plate.

SHIRA. Which one?

MOTHER. That one. That one you're eating from, with that painting.

SHIRA. (*Not understanding*) What?

EZRA. She wants to get rid of it. Please, Mama, not now. It's almost midnight.

SHIRA. Why are you giving it away? It's such a lovely plate.

MOTHER. It's beautiful ...

SHIRA. So keep it for yourself, really.

MOTHER. I haven't got any room for it.

SHIRA. You'll have room for it. Put it on the buffet, you could even hang it on the wall. It's beautiful ... I'll find you a place there specially for this.

MOTHER. Is the salad good?

SHIRA. Marvelous.

EZRA. Would you like a piece of bread?

SHIRA. I'll get it for myself.

EZRA. I don't mind ... where's the knife?

MOTHER. Here, give her some of this bread, it's fresher. (*She pulls out the knife and cuts it herself*)

SHIRA. It doesn't matter ... just a little slice ... don't trouble yourself.

MOTHER. I'm dying ...

SHIRA. Go on and rest. You have to rest.

MOTHER. Do you want some olives? I put them up myself.

SHIRA. I don't mind ... thanks. (*Tastes them*) Marvelous olives ... wonderful ... teach me how to make them?

EZRA. Not now, Shira, not now. I called your mother ... I talked with the kids ...

SHIRA. Great.

MOTHER. (*Bringing her the bathroom rugs which she had shown Ezra*) Have a look at these.

EZRA. No, Mom, not now, it's already practically the middle of the night.

MOTHER. They're brand-new.

SHIRA. Yes ... yes ... very pretty.

EZRA. (*Yells*) Mother!

SHIRA. What are you yelling for?

EZRA. Enough! Not now. She spent all evening killing me with these things of hers ...

SHIRA. Maybe we'll think about it tomorrow, after all. They really are pretty.

MOTHER. Sleep on it and tell me in the morning.

SHIRA. Okay.

MOTHER. I'm ready to give up hope. There were so many things here, and I just kept collecting them. "What are you buying this for? Why?" he used to ask me. Now I apologize to him.

EZRA. Apologize? Finally?

SHIRA. It's not so bad, we'll help you get everything taken care of.

MOTHER. But you never have any time.

SHIRA. We'll find time.

MOTHER. But how? After all, you don't ...

SHIRA. We'll find it. Come on now, let's clear the table and wash the dishes.

MOTHER. No, you'll never find your way around in this mess. You go to sleep, you're tired too. (*Pause*)

The two of them are in the study. Ezra closes the door. She begins to undress. He looks at her, walks around her, trying to touch her.

EZRA. My darling ... my wife ...

SHIRA. You go to pieces when you're here alone with her. Why didn't you get out? Why didn't you come to the conference with me?

EZRA. Oh, all these possessions of hers ... now she apologizes to him ... oh, if he could only rise from the grave for a minute to hear her. Oh, God Almighty ... I had a fever again. (*Meanwhile Shira has been undressing, putting on her nightgown and getting ready for bed*)

SHIRA. When?

EZRA. This evening.

SHIRA. What was your temperature?

EZRA. Almost a hundred. I'm awfully worried ... it's a bad sign.

SHIRA. It's nothing ... take it again now.

EZRA. I don't have the strength now.

SHIRA. Take it, take it ... why did you take your temperature in the first place? I told you to stop.

EZRA. She gave me Papa's thermometer.

SHIRA. Where is it? Just take your temperature now. Where is it? (*Finds it in his pocket and puts it in his mouth*) When exactly is she moving?

EZRA. Two more weeks. A space opened up, someone passed away ... we have to be ready at any moment ...

SHIRA. Don't even talk about it. Take your temperature. (*He puts the thermometer back in*)

EZRA. What went on at the conference?

SHIRA. In the afternoon I got there just for the end of the lecture and they said it was boring. But the evening was wonderful; a young professor from Tel Aviv has made a new edition of *Thus Spake Zarathustra*, with lots of footnotes, very stimulating. I didn't know there were such strong passages in it, on voluntary death, it would have really interested you. It's a shame you didn't come with. Death at the proper time; "Thus Taught Zarathustra" ... (*He listens abstractedly, takes the thermometer out of his mouth and puts it in his pocket*) So what is it?

EZRA. It's not very much this time.

SHIRA. How much exactly?

EZRA. 98.6 ...

SHIRA. You see ...

EZRA. It's a shame we didn't have time at noon. I'd be more relaxed now. (*Starts to undress*)

SHIRA. (*Already lying in bed, reading the conference program*) It's not so bad, tomorrow at noon ...

EZRA. But you have a lecture.

SHIRA. It doesn't matter. Pick me up at one. We'll eat something in town and come back here. We'll have time.

EZRA. No, we won't. You have another lecture at two-thirty. (*There is noise of objects falling in the living room. Ezra's mother is still arranging things*)

SHIRA. We'll manage. Your mother's still wandering around out there; she can't get to sleep.

EZRA. Like some awful lioness ...

SHIRA. You're still afraid of her.

EZRA. Don't be silly ... The way she begged his forgiveness ... oh, if only he could hear it ... if only he could rise from the grave just to hear it ...

SHIRA. He was no angel either ...

EZRA. Of course not. But to hear her ask forgiveness ... all those things she bought, that incredible purse. Wait and

see. That crazy purse with those colors, it'll drive you nuts
... (*In shorts and undershirt, full of emotion, he kneels by the bed,
throws back the covers, and begins kissing her legs*)

SHIRA. Well, you're feeling better.

EZRA. My beloved ... my darling ... half a day without you
here and I'm lost. (*Rochelle comes into the room holding a
tablecloth*)

MOTHER. Excuse me ...

EZRA. (*Gets up in a rush*) Now what?

MOTHER. I just wanted to remind Shira about this tablecloth
we talked about on the phone, so I don't forget tomorrow.

EZRA. You won't forget.

MOTHER. This is the tablecloth I was talking about, brand-
new embroidery.

EZRA. Mother!

SHIRA. (*Climbing out of bed to look*) It's beautiful! You really
don't need it ...?

MOTHER. No, no. It's for you.

EZRA. (*Looking in the suitcase for his pajamas*) Where are my
pajamas, Shira? Where'd you put them?

SHIRA. You said you were going to pack them.

EZRA. Oh, God.

MOTHER. You forgot your pajamas? No problem, I'll give you
some.

EZRA. (*Putting his shirt back on*) It doesn't matter.

MOTHER. I've got some of your father's pajamas.

EZRA. No, I don't need them.

MOTHER. (*Going right to the closet by the bed and getting the pajamas*)
He didn't wear them once while he was sick, I swear.

EZRA. It's not that. How could I have forgotten? It's never
happened to me before.

MOTHER. Here, take them. Try them on.

SHIRA. Go on, take them.

EZRA. They're too big for me.

MOTHER. What are you talking about? Take them, it gets cold
at night.

SHIRA. Take them.

EZRA. (*Hesitating*) All right, just the tops.

MOTHER. Put on the bottoms too.

EZRA. I don't want to.

MOTHER. They're clean.

EZRA. I know, I know.

SHIRA. Put them on, they're actually rather nice. (*Laughs. Ezra puts on the pajama top*)

MOTHER. Put on the bottoms too ...

EZRA. Mother, please, you don't have to interfere in everything.

MOTHER. All right ... goodnight ... I'll turn out the light for you.

SHIRA. Put on the bottoms, too. What do you care ...?

EZRA. I don't want to, I'm not cold. (*Gets into bed, puts out the light on the nightstand. Blackout*)

The stage is dark. Just a little nightlight is on by the kitchen. Ezra, silhouetted in his underwear, goes into the bathroom. The door is ajar; the splashing of the stream of his urine is heard. His mother gets up in the dark in her white nightgown.

MOTHER. Ezra? (*On purpose, he does not answer*) Ezra? Is that you? (*She turns on a tiny light; she is rumpled, disheveled*) Who is it? (*Her voice is trembling*) Who is it? Ezra? (*But she doesn't dare to get any closer to the bathroom. He finishes, passes her*) Is that you? Why don't you answer?

EZRA. What is it?

MOTHER. You frightened me terribly.

EZRA. Why? What did you think it was?

MOTHER. Why didn't you answer?

EZRA. Who did you think it was?

MOTHER. Nothing ... can't you sleep? Why don't you have a little cognac? I have the bottle I want to give you anyway.

EZRA. No, I don't need it ... goodnight.

MOTHER. I miss your father terribly.

EZRA. Now ... do you feel sorry?

MOTHER. For what? What did I do? For what?

EZRA. It doesn't matter. Let's not start, I want to go to sleep. Goodnight ... I've got to get some sleep ...

act 2

A sun-drenched morning. Shira, in a change of clothing, sits eating breakfast. Ezra's mother is hovering over her. A young Arab maid is washing the floor.

MOTHER. You're not eating anything.

SHIRA. I'm eating too much.

MOTHER. Are you ready for an omelet? I can make you an omelet in a second.

SHIRA. No, Rochelle, really, don't. Usually I only drink coffee in the morning and here all I do is eat.

MOTHER. You don't want an omelet? What a shame. It would give you energy for your conference. All right, I'll make coffee. The water's boiling.

SHIRA. I'll make it myself, don't get up.

MOTHER. No, you don't know how ... it's done already. Meanwhile just have a quick look and tell me what's in this letter. They won't explain it to me. (*She takes the tattered piece of paper and gives it to Shira. She goes to fix the coffee and stops next to the maid*) Clean under the table, too. And it's time to change the water. (*She goes to get the coffee. Shira is still engrossed in the letter. Mother looks at her, goes to the closet and takes out the purse, setting it aside*) Well, what does it say? Have you figured it out?

SHIRA. It seems to be from some bank. But it doesn't say here which.

MOTHER. Barclay's.

SHIRA. Barclay's? Oh, right. Here it is.

MOTHER. But what do they want?

SHIRA. They don't want anything from you. It has something to do with Aaron. It's a notification that he has 820 ... liras? They must have made a mistake, it should be shekels.

MOTHER. But what's the date on it? It could be from '71.

SHIRA. Yes, exactly, how did you know? This is very old but it's worth something all the same.

MOTHER. But it's not shekels, it's liras.

SHIRA. Maybe they made a mistake. Ask Ezra whether they

already had shekels back then.

MOTHER. (*Taking it from her and putting it away, looking at her lovingly*) All right, it doesn't matter, don't let your coffee get cold. You're so quiet. Don't you ever get angry?

SHIRA. At what?

MOTHER. At everything, at life. Before you go, let me show you a beautiful purse I wanted to give you — very practical. (*She shows her. Shira looks at it quietly*) I bought this purse when we visited you in Rome. It's a little big, but it's comfortable.

SHIRA. So why don't you keep it for yourself?

MOTHER. Father didn't like it, he couldn't stand it.

SHIRA. All right, maybe when I come back, after lunch, I'll sit down with you.

MOTHER. He won't let you, he'll want to go home right away. Believe me, I was up all night, I didn't even close my eyes. I won't get any rest until I get everything out of here and move. I can't stay in this house any more. I've really begun to hate it.

SHIRA. But why? You never hated it before.

MOTHER. I've hated it ever since he got sick. It's lost all the charm it had for me.

SHIRA. But you're moving soon. You'll meet new people there.

MOTHER. But how can I move when I have these endless heaps of possessions? I feel as if they're inside me. And none of you want to help.

SHIRA. What? Ezra came here just for that, and Eva's coming back today. They'll help you.

MOTHER. What'll they help me do? Throw everything out. You'll throw everything out. That I could do myself. That's not what I call help, that's just destruction. But to take something from here, so everything is not destroyed ... and he doesn't understand a thing about what I'm giving him. He's just stubborn. Take this tea service, for example. (*She removes a towel covering the pile of dishes*) What's wrong with it? Why doesn't he want to take it? What's there to be ashamed of? So what should I do? Just take them and break them all?

SHIRA. It really is a nice set.

MOTHER. It's lovely. Why shouldn't you enjoy it and take it out of here?

SHIRA. You're sure you don't want it.

MOTHER. No! No!

SHIRA. If you don't need it I'll be happy to take it.

MOTHER. Wonderful! There's just one little thing wrong with it. See, the handle of one of the cups came off, but you can glue it back. I'll glue it back for you, you won't even notice.

SHIRA. I can do without that one cup.

MOTHER. Maybe—since there's a saucer missing, too. But I'll glue it for you. If you don't want it, you don't have to use it. (*All this time, the maid has been listening to them, hardly doing any work*)

SHIRA. Okay ... oh, I'm late, I've got to run. I guess I'd better wake him up before I go. I don't know what's happened to him this morning.

MOTHER. No, don't wake him, let him sleep. He was up during the night too. So I'll put this in your box, you can take it today.

SHIRA. All right, thanks.

MOTHER. (*Kissing her warmly*) Thank you. I'm practically dead, just because I'm not crying, doesn't mean anything. I haven't cried since he got sick, I haven't been able to.

SHIRA. It's not good for you ... not to cry.

MOTHER. I know, it's good to cry: Happy are those who cry— I don't cry. I can't cry. What am I supposed to do? I'm still ...

SHIRA. You're still in shock.

MOTHER. Exactly. God bless you. I am shocked. Sometimes it seems like he's still around the house. I open the door to his room and I think he's still lying there just the way he did after they brought him back from the hospital ... when they insisted on sending him home in that awful condition ... that bastard of a doctor sent him here and then left me alone with him ... when I thought that any minute he might disintegrate. He was so thin ... like a matchstick, and I was afraid to touch him for fear that his hand would come off in mine. They shouldn't have allowed it—as if this were some kind of hospital. As if it could possibly be. Careful you don't slip there. (*Walks her to the door. She turns angrily to the maid*) Come on, take the bucket over there and keep going. They gave him this little bell and left, and he'd ring it all day and all night.

SHIRA. (*At the door, putting on her coat*) They thought if you made the effort at home, so you wouldn't have to run to the hospital all the time, it would be a little easier on both of you.

MOTHER. They shouldn't have put me to the test like that if they weren't prepared to sit here day and night and take care of him themselves. They shouldn't have put me to the test with such an awful thing. (*In a whisper*) He couldn't control himself. Here, she'll tell you herself, right, Nadja? You saw the man who was here the day you came.

NADJA. Yes.

MOTHER. Well?

NADJA. We had to change him all the time.

MOTHER. You hear?

SHIRA. But how long was that, a week?

MOTHER. Longer, two weeks. Almost two weeks—from Thursday until the next Monday.

SHIRA. Well, then we all realized it wouldn't work and he went back to the hospital.

MOTHER. Yes, but you've been mad at me ever since.

SHIRA. We are not mad!

MOTHER. Yes, you are. They're all mad at me, I can tell. That's why they don't want to take anything from the house—deliberately. They're punishing me by leaving all his possessions here on top of me.

SHIRA. No, they aren't—what an idea! If they're mad, maybe it's just at themselves. You did what you could.

MOTHER. They always think I can do more than I really can. (*To the maid*) Why are you just standing there?

NADJA. The door is closed.

SHIRA. Maybe we should wake him.

MOTHER. No need to, let him sleep a little longer. Go up and clean the window. What can we do?

NADJA. But how?

SHIRA. Listen, I've got to run, I'm really late. Tell him I took the car and I'll be back after lunch.

MOTHER. You're eating lunch here!

SHIRA. No, we're eating at the conference. It's already arranged.

MOTHER. Absolutely not. You come back here. I've already prepared it. What's this conference about?

SHIRA. It's a philosophy conference. Nietzsche.

MOTHER. Aren't you tired of studying? (*Shira smiles, kisses her and leaves*) Well, what are you standing and looking at?

NADJA. I don't have a rag for the window.

MOTHER. Well, forget the window. Come on and finish his room. (*Opens the door carefully*)

EZRA. Yeah?

MOTHER. If you'll get up, the maid is here to clean your room.

EZRA. (*Looking at his watch*) I don't know what happened to me. Where's Shira?

MOTHER. She already left. She took the car.

EZRA. She already left? Why didn't you wake me up? (*Jumps up*)

MOTHER. You didn't ask us to. Well, wash up and she'll finish cleaning your room right away.

NADJA. (*Coming inside*) Hello, sir.

EZRA. Hello—just a minute, just a minute. (*Puts on his pajama bottoms*)

MOTHER. Oh, come on, what's the big deal, just go out and let her do your room. She's been standing around all morning with no work to do. Come on, I'll fix you some coffee. (*He goes to the bathroom*) Hurry, clean under the bed, too. (*He comes back into the living room*) All right, sit down meanwhile, she'll finish right up. The woman who knows you is coming this morning to take the curtains.

EZRA. I still can't figure out who she is. What's her name?

MOTHER. Daniella.

EZRA. Daniella what?

MOTHER. I don't remember. But she knows you well.

EZRA. What?

MOTHER. All right, don't get mad. You don't take sugar?

EZRA. No.

MOTHER. I have saccharin.

EZRA. No.

MOTHER. You can't drink it this way.

EZRA. Who says?

There is a brief silence. They have nothing to talk about. Mother, gathering her energy, gets up to go back to work on the heaps of possessions.

MOTHER. All right, first of all I'm giving you two boxes of sugar packets — imported.

EZRA. But why? Keep them for yourself. I suppose you won't need any sugar there?

MOTHER. No, I don't want it. I have enough.

EZRA. Then maybe I'll just take one.

MOTHER. No, take two. Here, I'll put them in your box. I have some for Eva, too.

EZRA. Okay.

MOTHER. And these are candies for decorating cakes. Little candy coins, all different colors.

EZRA. You're not going to bake any more?

MOTHER. No, who's there to bake for? I haven't got any room. I've baked enough in my life. Take it.

EZRA. But you know Shira doesn't know how to bake. (*Takes the candies, examining them with interest*)

MOTHER. It makes no difference. Michal will when she grows up. They stick on, as many as you want. (*Ezra tries to taste one*) It's not for eating, it's for decoration, don't start eating them now instead of breakfast.

EZRA. Okay.

MOTHER. (*Puts on her glasses; she works from a list*) Now there's a jar of olives here.

EZRA. Olives?

MOTHER. Olives I put up myself. They're excellent, take them. Ayil likes olives.

EZRA. Okay. (*All the while he eats voraciously*)

MOTHER. Now look at this new kind of thing with wheels. You can attach them to a cupboard or something heavy if you want to move it.

EZRA. (*Laughing*) What? Am I moving my cupboards all of a sudden?

MOTHER. One day you might have to. What's the matter? It takes up so much room?

EZRA. You're driving me crazy. Why did you have to go buy these wheels in the first place?

MOTHER. I thought one day I might need them.

EZRA. What for?

MOTHER. I thought for your father's bed or mine if we were sick ... if they had to clean underneath them. Take it, take it; one day you'll find it and thank me. Now look here, there's some electrical things, wires and sockets, all kinds of things. Take the whole box and check through it when you get home. (*He tries to protest*) Listen a minute — leave what's good and throw the rest away.

EZRA. First thing in the morning and you're already getting on my nerves.

MOTHER. Take it, don't be stubborn. What you don't want you can throw out. (*Ezra is silent*) So I'll put them here.

EZRA. Fine.

MOTHER. (*Stiffly goes into the corner of the room, to the side cupboard, takes out a big paintbrush. Its bristles are white with black threads like a man's head of hair, but stiff and frozen. Shows it to him from a distance*) Now look at this brush.

EZRA. I actually happen to need a brush.

MOTHER. So take this one. I'll put it in.

EZRA. Let's see. (*Goes over and takes the brush*)

MOTHER. (*Hesitantly*) It's a little ...

EZRA. What do you mean it's a little? It's useless, it's completely stiff. The bristles are completely shot. Why are you giving me this junk? What goes through your mind?

MOTHER. It can be made like new. Put it in paraffin for a few days ...

EZRA. A paintbrush that's completely shot and you want to palm it off on me. The bristles are completely stiff!

MOTHER. Don't shout, don't shout, if you don't want it don't take it, but just don't shout at me.

EZRA. What went through your mind about this brush? You knew it was useless.

MOTHER. What useless? What useless? This is a wonderful brush. When you were a little boy you whitewashed the whole roof with it. If you don't want it don't take it. I'll find someone who will.

EZRA. Give it to me a minute.

MOTHER. No, no ...

EZRA. Give it to me. (*Takes it by force*)

MOTHER. Not in front of the maid. Go get dressed.

EZRA. I have to throw this away myself ... it's just impossible. (*Goes to the kitchen and puts it in the trash. The maid has been watching them the whole time*)

MOTHER. Throw it out ... throw everything out ... instead of helping, you just make trouble like always. Go get dressed. (*Turns to the maid*) And you—that's enough. You're finished. Get dressed, I'll fix you an egg. (*Ezra goes into the bathroom. Blackout*)

The maid, dressed in a short coat, stands with a large basket next to an open suitcase.

MOTHER. So you want this bag of salt after all?

NADJA. Okay.

MOTHER. I'm also giving you this jacket for your husband, and this chair.

NADJA. Just the jacket.

MOTHER. Take the chair. So you'll have a chair! It's not heavy, it folds up. (*Folds it and throws it into the suitcase*) But bring the suitcase back next week. I might need it, I'll give you some more things.

NADJA. All right.

MOTHER. (*Testing her*) Come here, I've got something else to give you—a teapot. Take this teapot, it's excellent. (*Gives it to her*) And here's a hat. Give it to your husband.

NADJA. No husband.

MOTHER. What do you mean no husband? You had a husband last time.

NADJA. Left me.

MOTHER. So here, give it back. (*Takes it*) Don't you have a father?

NADJA. I have a father.

MOTHER. So give it to your father. (*Nadja begins to close the suitcase*) Hold on. (*Goes and gets the brush out of the trashcan*)

What the heck, take this too. He doesn't understand a thing. It's a good brush. He's full of imagination. You know what imagination is? (*Offers her the brush but Nadja won't take it saying something in Arabic*) What? Take it. (*Nadja refuses, her whole body trembling*) What's the matter with you? Take it. (*Nadja still refuses, again saying something in Arabic at great speed. Ezra enters, fully dressed*) All right, all right. (*Hides the brush*) Enough, so you'll be here next Tuesday — with the suitcase. Don't run off on me, I'm going to need it eventually. And I have a lot more things to give you. Don't run off on me.

NADJA. It's all right, it'll be all right. Good-bye, sir. (*Leaves*)

EZRA. That's it, I'm going too.

MOTHER. You're going now?

EZRA. Why not? Haven't I been here long enough?

MOTHER. But we haven't finished a thing.

EZRA. I'm not taking another thing from here. Not a crumb. Not even a thread.

MOTHER. You're punishing me because of the brush. Why are you so afraid of it?

EZRA. Afraid?

MOTHER. But there's your father's books and papers, too.

EZRA. That's at lunchtime. That's just me. You won't have anything to do with that.

MOTHER. When are you coming back? At noon? You'll never finish. You'll just be in a hurry to get home.

EZRA. I'll finish, I promise.

MOTHER. I just wanted to dash over to the store for something. I don't have any meat for lunch.

EZRA. Who's stopping you?

MOTHER. But that woman, that Daniella is supposed to come this morning to pick up the curtains she bought and she didn't tell me when. What time will you be back?

EZRA. Around noon.

MOTHER. Such a nuisance. What an incredible nudnik, that woman. I ask her, "What time exactly are you coming?" and she can't promise. What am I going to do now? I can't leave the house. And you too. You have no pity.

EZRA. What makes you say that?

MOTHER. Because you don't. Since your father got sick you haven't had any pity on me.

EZRA. How long will it take you at the store?

MOTHER. A quarter of an hour, at most twenty minutes. I don't have a lot to buy; I just need to get the meat that Shira likes.

EZRA. No need. We'll eat the chicken.

MOTHER. No, I have to. Shira doesn't eat this kind of chicken.

EZRA. You know what? Hurry up and go right now and I'll wait here. If she comes I'll let her in.

MOTHER. Excellent. I promise I'll only take a second. Tell her to wait.

EZRA. Okay, okay.

MOTHER. Oh, you're a lifesaver.

EZRA. But hurry up, I want to go. I'm suffocating here. (*Picks up an old newspaper and begins to read*)

MOTHER. Right away. (*Hurriedly begins to get dressed right in front of him*) Meanwhile, if you have the time, look at these toys. They're yours — the children's.

EZRA. You're starting up again.

MOTHER. They're all yours. Take what's good, I'll throw out the rest. Here, this is the gun you used to play with, that you liked so much.

EZRA. All right, all right, you'd better get going.

MOTHER. I'm on my way. (*Puts on her coat, hurriedly taking her shopping basket*) Don't budge till I get back.

Ezra is silent. As soon as she leaves he turns on the radio. Music comes on. The music at once makes him attentive and uneasy. He's not so much conducting the music as moving with it. As he does so, he picks through the things, opens the cabinets, pulls out the parasol and looks at it but doesn't open it. Blackout. A light tapping at the door. Ezra doesn't hear it at first. The door opens slightly and he goes over to it. A woman of about forty enters, smiles, her movements slow.

EZRA. You're here for the curtains?

DANIELLA. (*Speaking with great calm*) Exactly, I'm here for the curtains.

EZRA. My mother went out for a minute but —

DANIELLA. That's okay, that's okay, I know I'm a bit early. Hello, Ezra Saporta ... nice to see you. How have you been? Your mother told me you were coming ... she was really looking forward to seeing you. How's your wife, how's Shira? There's some kind of conference here, a philosophical conference ... it must be the Nietzsche conference. I thought she might want to participate in that.

EZRA. (*Amused*) Excuse me, but what's your name?

DANIELLA. You won't remember me. I told your mother, "He won't remember me, but I remember him very well from school." My name's Daniella Rivlin but my maiden name was Daniella Sasson. I was four years behind you. I had a big brother Dubi Sasson, maybe him you remember? (*Silently he gestures with his head — it's impossible to tell whether he means yes or no*) And I'm his little sister. But maybe you've forgotten.

EZRA. Yes, it's a little hard to remember ... and I'm not sure why you remember me. You told my mother you knew me so well — I was beginning to get worried.

DANIELLA. Worried? But why? (*Ezra tries to answer*) No, I told her I knew your father well. She must have gotten the two of you mixed up.

EZRA. My father, of all people?

DANIELLA. He used to come to my library during the last year.

EZRA. What library is that?

DANIELLA. I'm sure you don't know it, there's sort of a little library that opened up at the end of Prophets Street in an old building that belongs to the city, in the basement.

EZRA. What kind of library?

DANIELLA. Just a library — all kinds of books. And when your father retired he started to hang around there ... not that he exactly had a whole lot to do in our basement, but he hung around. And he always used to talk to me about you and your sister and your mother. So I'm kind of up-to-date on all of you.

EZRA. Yes, he loved to kibitz.

DANIELLA. It seemed it was easy for him to make friends. He was always looking for someone to make friends with. He was a bit lonely once he retired and it was hard for him to sit at home with your mother all day. And you and your sister, I gather, couldn't make it to Jerusalem very often. So he became friends with me.

EZRA. Complaining all the time.

DANIELLA. A little bit. About you, but always with good humor.

EZRA. Yes, at least he had a sense of humor.

DANIELLA. Right. My husband knew him too and really liked him. My husband, though he's Ashkenazi and even comes from one of the old settler families, really likes these old Sephardim ... and we brought your father home with us once, we wanted him to eat with us and maybe even rest a bit but he ended up running off. He was afraid your mother would get mad at him.

EZRA. How did he complain about me? For example.

DANIELLA. Nothing special, he just complained.

EZRA. That I grew away from him because I'm busy all the time.

DANIELLA. Yes, something like that. More often he took pity on you because you were the one who took care of the house and kids while your wife studied all the time.

EZRA. That's ridiculous.

DANIELLA. It's not true?

EZRA. Of course not.

DANIELLA. That just seemed to be the impression I got.

EZRA. What else did he say?

DANIELLA. He used to accuse you sometimes of maybe being a snob — I don't know, it doesn't matter. All in all he really loved you and was proud of you and it hurt him terribly that you hadn't gotten your professorship yet.

EZRA. (*Becoming very cold*) Well, fine. What would you like? You have to wait for my mother. Would you like to sit down?

DANIELLA. No, in fact, I already paid your mother for the curtains. All we have to do is take them down.

EZRA. Would you like me to take them down for you?

DANIELLA. It would be great if you could. I'm in a bit of a hurry.

EZRA. (*Moves the table underneath the curtains, puts a chair on top of it and climbs up*) I don't understand how you came to get these curtains.

DANIELLA. I didn't exactly. It's more like they came to get me. When I found out that your father had passed away, which was already very late, because I noticed he hadn't come to the library for a couple of months and I decided to find out if something was wrong, and I called here and your mother told me, and the funeral and even the memorial service were already over, and I talked with her and she told me she'd decided to move and asked me if I was interested in buying anything, and that got me curious enough to come and have a look, and I saw these curtains, which are perfect for our bathroom, which we just redid . . . we'll shorten them.

EZRA. I see. (*Ezra has already begun to take down the curtains which are hung in two large, separate pieces*)

DANIELLA. It happened so fast.

EZRA. Yes, it was quick. They discovered it in the summer, around Shavuot, and he died in the autumn, just after Sukkot. Three or four months.

DANIELLA. In the hospital?

EZRA. Yes, he was in the hospital almost the whole time.

DANIELLA. We had the same thing a year ago with my husband's father, but we insisted on keeping him at home. (*Now Ezra is up above, slowly taking down the curtains, and she is below*)

EZRA. It depends on conditions.

DANIELLA. What do you mean?

EZRA. The physical conditions.

DANIELLA. No, that has nothing to do with it. My husband's father was in terrible shape, but we still brought him to our house and arranged for him to die at home. We thought it was important.

EZRA. (*Becoming increasingly tense*) It all depends. Every case is different. Some people prefer to die in the hospital.

DANIELLA. When they feel insecure. But we made him feel secure, and he cooperated with us to the end.

EZRA. It depends . . . it depends. There are different cases.

DANIELLA. It was so nice at the end, such a special time — somehow exciting. We talked with him a lot. The kids too, they were drawn to him. I used to ask them to play in his room and do their homework there, to distract him.

EZRA. From what?

DANIELLA. Death. We put the television near him so he'd always have people nearby, so he wouldn't sink into some terrible depression. We sang to him, and he used to sing too. It was exciting and wonderful. Of course, he knew he was going to die and he mourned with us. He helped us mourn. Death moved in and became part of the family. We touched it and it touched us. Everything took on a new dimension for us. What's important and what's not important, matter itself seemed to become softer — believe me, there was light in the house. To this day, when I stop and think, I can see that light, rich and pure, soft and summery. We got up from the seven days of mourning in some way light and joyful, filled with the memory of a profound experience. I have a little boy, he was five then, and he used to climb into the dying man's bed without fear, even with that little bag there, you know what I mean. When he lost consciousness the boy was with him, keeping him warm.

EZRA. (*Listening tensely all the while. He has stopped taking down the curtains for a moment*) How long did it take?

DANIELLA. Three or four months. He had what your father had. I told your mother.

EZRA. Well, it depends. Everyone's story is different. Where was his wife?

DANIELLA. We left her at their place, we couldn't have burdened her with caring for him. It wouldn't have been fair.

EZRA. It depends . . . it depends. You were here.

DANIELLA. Now that I think of it, your father even came by and saw him once while he was sick. Because whenever we had guests we always used to bring them into his room to see him and say hello.

EZRA. Maybe that's why my father didn't want to stay, as you mentioned to me.

DANIELLA. Maybe. Not everyone could take it. Apparently your father ran off, but everyone who could tolerate it used to come back.

EZRA. Interesting . . . here, this is the first half.

DANIELLA. (*She has been collecting the cloth in her arms as he lets it drop*) I had no idea it would be so heavy.

EZRA. Don't you have a car?

DANIELLA. Not here. I figured I would take them straight to the laundry, which isn't far from here. Maybe I should come back for the other part after lunch. You'll be here. Wait for me.

EZRA. So I shouldn't take it down.

DANIELLA. No, it's better not to roll it up on the floor here where it can get dirty.

EZRA. Okay. (*Gets down*)

DANIELLA. Excuse me, would you mind helping me fold it a minute? (*They fold it, touching each other as they do so*) I have some string, I brought some string. (*Takes some red string from her purse. The curtain is yellowish-white*)

EZRA. I see you're well organized.

DANIELLA. I try to be.

EZRA. So ... that's it. (*Hands in his pockets*)

DANIELLA. I hope you weren't hurt.

EZRA. Hurt? By what?

DANIELLA. I don't know. By what I told you—

EZRA. (*Blurting out*) About what?

DANIELLA. I don't know. You seem hurt.

EZRA. Why should I be hurt? What my father said about me? We had a very good relationship.

DANIELLA. I'm sure you did. I never said otherwise.

EZRA. And I happen to love my wife.

DANIELLA. (*Turning crimson*) I don't understand why you had to tell me that.

EZRA. I don't know, I just did.

DANIELLA. I hope you didn't misunderstand me. I simply made friends with your father. There, in our basement.

EZRA. Yes, I understand.

DANIELLA. (*Looking aside*) That's a picture of him when he was young. A good-looking man. (*Ezra's mother enters with her shopping baskets*)

MOTHER. Oh, great, you're here, I had my son stay on purpose, in case you came. So you're taking the curtains today.

EZRA. We took half down already.

MOTHER. Oh, how did you know how to take it down?

EZRA. I know how—see for yourself.

MOTHER. And what about the other part?

DANIELLA. I'll come for it after lunch.

MOTHER. Why not take the whole thing now?

DANIELLA. It's heavy and I haven't got my car here. I'm taking it straight to the laundry and I'm in kind of a rush after that.

MOTHER. Why don't you help her take it to the laundry? We'll take the whole thing down and be done with it.

DANIELLA. No, it's not worth bothering him.

MOTHER. It's no bother. He'll be glad to.

EZRA. I haven't got the time now, Mama. I'm in a rush myself.

DANIELLA. That's all right, I'll come back after lunch. Bye . . . maybe I'll see you again.

EZRA. No, we'll be on our way. (*Daniella leaves. Ezra turns angrily to his mother*) I don't understand why I'm supposed to drag her curtains around for her. What am I, her slave? What gives you the right to volunteer for me? (*A slight stutter begins to creep into his speech*)

MOTHER. I simply thought we could be done with it and not have to have her come back after lunch and be in our way. What a nudnik! She keeps talking and talking and asking and asking . . . again with the illness, and again with the illness . . .

EZRA. Where did Papa know her from? Did he ever mention her?

MOTHER. Never. Not a word. Wherever she came from, she nearly took the life out of me before she decided to buy the curtains. She came and measured them, and then she measured them again, and every time she came I had to be hospitable . . .

EZRA. (*Bursting in with a strangled groan*) Please, please, please! I can't take it. You're going to drive me crazy.

MOTHER. What's wrong? What did I do to you?

EZRA. Please, please . . . I'm sorry I came here at all.

MOTHER. Why don't you go out for a while? You can go out for a while now.

EZRA. I will. Right away. I'm just waiting for a phone call ... the hell with it. (*Goes to the door, then thinks better of it and comes back. He goes into the study, slams the door, and lies down on his back for a smoke. There is an empty silence in the apartment. Rochelle puts away her groceries. It is quiet for a while. She opens the door carefully*)

MOTHER. Do you want potatoes for lunch or don't you mind eating the rice I cooked yesterday?

EZRA. I don't want anything.

MOTHER. What happened? How did she get on your nerves so badly?

EZRA. Nothing.

MOTHER. Does she really know you, like she said?

EZRA. It wasn't me she knew, it was Papa. You got it mixed up.

MOTHER. No, besides your father, she said she knew you. She reads your articles.

EZRA. Nonsense. (*Sticks the thermometer into his mouth, but continues to smoke*)

MOTHER. Again with the thermometer? I'm beginning to regret I gave it to you. Here's an ashtray, go on and take it. Put it in your briefcase. (*The phone rings and he grabs it. The stage lights begin to dim*)

EZRA. Yes ... Yes ... All right, too bad, no, it doesn't matter, no, we've got to be home this evening ... It's not so terrible, I'll be here again in a week or two when my mother moves ... It's not so terrible ... if you're busy ... You have to finish what article? All right, it doesn't matter ... Yes, yes, no, no, I'm not putting any pressure on for the promotion ... I'll get it in the end I'm sure, I hope ... But if you can just read that article I published ... On Kafka's *Metamorphosis* ... I think there's something new in it ... In terms of the cockroach in particular ... You'll see when you read it. I don't take it as a metaphor or a simile or an allegory but literally ... (*All this while his mother is busy with her things, dropping them noisily*) In what sense? Read it ... Read it ... In a terrible sense, terrifying and shocking but in my opinion also terribly sad and even moral ... Read it and decide for yourself whether it's there in the text ... What a shame we can't get together ... (*Blackout*)

A few hours later. The remains of lunch are on the table. Rochelle is in the kitchen washing dishes. Shira and Ezra are in the study. He is trying to undress her, kissing her, kneeling; she is half resisting and half cooperating.

SHIRA. We haven't got time, Ezra.

EZRA. We have time, we'll make it.

SHIRA. We won't make it. It's not going to work. I have to get back soon, I don't want to miss the concluding session. I need time to get aroused. You relax by yourself again.

EZRA. No, you'll see, it'll be okay. (*Kisses her all over her body trying to arouse her*)

SHIRA. But the door's not even closed. Your mother ...

EZRA. The key's broken, I'll just block it. (*Moves furniture to block the door*)

SHIRA. Shh ... shh ...

EZRA. It's okay. (*Tries to lay her down on the bed*)

SHIRA. For God's sake, Ezra ... this evening, I promise, when we get home ... what's the big rush you have to do it here? We'll be home in a few hours.

EZRA. You'll be tired ... and the kids ... I've got to relax now or I'll go crazy, she's driving me completely crazy ...

SHIRA. So why didn't you go out this morning? (*All the while he keeps trying to undress her. It's hard to tell whether she's resisting or ready*)

EZRA. I don't know, you took the car and I thought I'd meet Ze'ev and he ended up canceling. He made some excuse ... come on, darling, come on, sweetheart ... honey ... let's hurry and do it.

SHIRA. It won't work, Ezra. (*Meanwhile Rochelle is at the door trying to open it*)

EZRA. Hold on ... what is it, Mama? Hold on ... I'm getting dressed.

MOTHER. Do you want to sleep now?

EZRA. We're trying to rest a bit. What's the matter? Is something the matter?

MOTHER. No, doesn't Shira have to go back to her conference

now? (*Shira begins to put her clothes back on*)

EZRA. It's okay. You've got to worry about that too? We know very well what time it is, I just wanted to rest a little bit. I've still got a two-hour drive ahead of me today.

MOTHER. All right, all right. I didn't say anything. I don't know, I thought maybe I'd show something to Shira in case I forget later.

EZRA. Oh, Mother, in the name of God!

SHIRA. Just a minute, Rochelle, just a minute.

EZRA. Oh, God. She'll never give me any rest.

SHIRA. (*Kissing him*) Come here a minute and move this stuff ... it's not nice to treat her this way. (*He frees the door, moving the desk and chair that were blocking it*)

MOTHER. Why did you move the desk like that?

EZRA. I was just looking for something.

SHIRA. What's wrong, Rochelle?

MOTHER. I'm shaking all over, I didn't sleep all night. There's no peace for me.

SHIRA. You're getting nervous about nothing. Everything'll be okay.

MOTHER. I can't get any rest. All these endless possessions ... as if they were sitting inside me, filling me up. I'll never get rid of them.

SHIRA. Yes you will, don't worry. You can even give them away, you can always find someone willing to take them off your hands.

MOTHER. No, there's no one like that.

SHIRA. We'll find someone, we'll take the things and give them to him.

MOTHER I wanted to show you something and I've forgotten what. I'm tired. Tired and upset.

SHIRA. Go to sleep for a bit, take a little nap.

MOTHER. No, if I sleep during the day I can't sleep at night.

SHIRA. You'll sleep. You can't fight fatigue. Get some rest.

EZRA. Yes, go on, go to sleep.

MOTHER. If I sleep a single minute during the day I won't close my eyes all night.

SHIRA. So sleep a little less at night, at least you won't collapse.

MOTHER. (*They lead her to bed*) I wanted to talk with you.

EZRA. But we want to rest too. I've got to drive two hours this afternoon.

MOTHER. Two hours. Two hours. Suddenly that frightens you. When you were in America you used to brag that you drove ten hours in one day. All right, all right, I'll rest a bit. So what time will you be back?

SHIRA. Soon. Four-thirty.

MOTHER. I have something to give you. (*Shira takes Rochelle into a small room at stage left and comes back*)

EZRA. (*Gently*) Come on, please.

SHIRA. No, Ezra.

EZRA. I'm begging you.

SHIRA. I don't feel like I could finish and I want to, too. This evening. This evening, I promise. (*Kisses him, caresses him. Ezra is disappointed. He takes the thermometer out of his pocket*) What, again? Do you feel something? Tell me.

EZRA. This low fever all the time. It scares me.

SHIRA. Why don't you take an aspirin?

EZRA. It's not an aspirin kind of fever.

SHIRA. Do you have some strange desire to be a little sick?

EZRA. No.

SHIRA. So don't be.

EZRA. But I've got this fever.

SHIRA. It's nothing. (*Ezra puts the thermometer back in his pocket*) Why are you putting it away? Go ahead, take your temperature. You've got a fantasy fever.

EZRA. Could be.

SHIRA. Don't start identifying with him.

EZRA. With whom?

SHIRA. With your dead father.

EZRA. All right. (*Kisses her*)

SHIRA. And go wash up.

EZRA. (*Insulted*) What for?

SHIRA. Brush you teeth, you smell funny.

EZRA. What do you mean? What are you jabbering about?

SHIRA. An unpleasant smell.

EZRA. What do you mean?

SHIRA. Go out for a while, go for a walk. You can go crazy with all these things here.

EZRA. You should've seen what she tried to press on me this morning, some sort of crappy brush with awful bristles full of white paint. I can't understand her any more. I've never seen her fall apart like this. This compulsion to throw everything out.

SHIRA. But what is she throwing out? Him? Herself?

EZRA. It's as if she swallowed him inside her and now she's chucking him out and herself too, the whole house, I don't know. Anyway go on, you're late.

SHIRA. (*Noticing the missing half-curtain*) What's this? You got rid of the curtain, too?

EZRA. Some woman came to take it, someone who went to school with me, who claims she knew my father and told me all kinds of stories. A real pest. You remember we saw a movie in England once about that old black guy in Boston ... they filmed him and his family all through his sickness until he died at home ... we saw it and we cried? (*Shira doesn't recall it*) All right, it doesn't matter. I'll tell you later, you'll remember. Come on, move it. You'll be late — and don't hang around there, we're going straight home.

SHIRA. Absolutely.

EZRA. And be careful, it was raining at lunchtime. Don't drive too fast.

SHIRA. I never drive fast.

EZRA. Is it starting okay?

SHIRA. Fine. But there's a light that goes on, on the dashboard sometimes.

EZRA. What light? A red light? And you kept driving?

SHIRA. Not a red light, a yellow light.

EZRA. You're sure.

SHIRA. Absolutely.

EZRA. It's the choke, I told you to close it all the way.

SHIRA. Okay.

EZRA. You're sure it was a yellow light.

SHIRA. A hundred percent sure, believe me.

EZRA. Let me check anyhow.

They exit. The lights stay on. The stage stays empty for a while, let's say half a minute. Then we begin to hear the indistinct stir, a rustling whisper which is Ezra's stream of thought. The words aren't clear yet. This sound should be slightly altered electronically in order to change and distort the voice. Ezra comes into the apartment, goes to the bathroom, leaves the door open, and begins to urinate. His back is to the audience. Then the stream of consciousness starts to become distinct.

EZRA. Why did I back down? I should have insisted ... she'd have given in, the pleasure's always more intense away from home ... you're hot, buddy ... my dear friend ... get smaller ... you'll have it tomorrow, I promise ... almost as good as screwing ... dark ... very yellow ... this morning too ... what is it? Maybe something to do with the fever ... have to take a urine specimen ... only not me, now ... I haven't got the strength to start with me, too. (*Flushes the toilet, goes to the sink and washes his hands, opens his mouth exhaling and smelling himself*) There's something ... the smell of lead ... everything's spiritual until ... spiritual death ... so what? Ah, ah ... (*Turns on the faucet, looks at the flowing stream of water, sticks a finger into it and raises his eyebrows*) That's how it starts ... feeble signs ... now there's no one left in between ... there was a story of Updike's ... what's it called? ... running to the hospital. As long as the father keeps struggling with death, the son is safe ... love of my life, my only support ... you'll fall apart ... just the arrangements and the papers at the bank, a little something wrong with the car. A yellow light, damn it! How many times have I told you and begged you ... half a day with the choke open. (*Meanwhile he goes to the kitchen, opens the refrigerator and yellow light spills out. He takes a bottle of milk and starts to drink*) It was yellow then on Saturday morning ... a yellow aura hovering over a yellow father in the hospital ... the movement of death is halted at night. For three days his hand was moving and searching (*He acts it out*) the nurse understood and explained it. When Death walks into the room we run to the corner, but there are people who talk with it, who know it, who understand the language. The same

with the woman we hired to be there at night ... a human
being ... she didn't blame me for being late that morning
... he struggled all night ... she just said ... you should
have been near him the whole time. How could I have?
What for? Free death ... Trampled Dirt, A Dying Cat, A
Used Car, that's the name, at the end of the anthology.
Quiet Realism. I taught it once. (*He goes into his mother's
bedroom, comes back and goes out, looking at all the things. He
opens the cupboard, takes out the parasol, doesn't open it, puts it
back*) She fell ... consuming herself ... what is this?
Where's it from? It's crazy, all these worthless things ...
afterwards she asks forgiveness ... you have to die to
deserve forgiveness ... Papa ... Papa ... (*He begins to
wander around near the curtain, looking at the remaining half,
which is moving slightly in some uncertain breeze*) There'll always
be complaints ... they'll always say you could do
more ... get into the dead man's bed and hug him ...
she was really a character ... where did she come
from? ... how did she get here? ... what tactlessness to
come and say he criticized you. What does she know?
Him, too, he used to like to kibitz everywhere in order to
be liked. What was she really trying to say! What does she
know? It's a good thing I didn't lose my temper ...
bragging about dying at home ... they played with the
dying man a little ... who knows what he really felt ...
dependent on their kindness. Sometimes it's perverted needs
in the guise of kind humanism ... the guests to see their
dying father ... thanks very much ... go to hell ...
practically a whore anyway ... I swear ... nice guy. Like
you? She didn't say. (*He begins to move the table, takes off his
shoes, climbs up and starts to take down the other part of the
curtain*) But the boy who got into his grandpa's bed ...
awful ... crazy ... that's the height of humanism ... not
to be disgusted by man ... how is it she couldn't remember
that movie about the old black guy in Boston ... I'll
remind her when she comes back ... the best things the
English do are their documentaries ... of all things ...
it's greater than art ... I cried ... everyone who dies gets
what he's got coming to him ... he wouldn't have been

able to stand it. Three months without a moment's peace, a single smile. Humor dies first. Anyone who has no patience for life has no patience for death either. (*The curtain comes down bit by bit*) What a character ... delicate cruelty ... she made friends with him. He knew how to kibitz with women. Just let her come and take it and scram. Here's your damn curtain. When they brought a partition in the evening and left it on the side, it was a relief. By then even I was in a hurry. (*The telephone rings. He comes down, shoeless. The curtain remains hanging by a single hook, forming a white drape which falls to the side. Loudly*) Yes? ... No ... Sorry ... What number were you trying to call ...? No, you have the wrong number ... You have the wrong number, sir ... (*Hangs up. He does not get up on the table again. Instead he starts wandering restlessly around the house. He turns on the radio and soft music begins playing, Schumann's* Spring Symphony. *He looks at the box that's been set aside for him and takes out the brush*) You didn't give up. What's behind it ... these bristles, like human hair, even when I was whitewashing the roof for two liras I used to imagine a little woman running ahead of me. Herself? Bits and pieces. The unconscious strikes forcefully, bursts forth like these possessions into reality. Impossible. (*The brush drops listlessly from his hand*) My explanation's correct. The Samsa family. The cockroach wandering around their possessions. The creeping unconscious is a sad thing among members of a family. What's happening to us? (*Again he begins to walk about uneasily, shoeless, making odd gestures*) I identify with him. I don't grieve for him. I think about what was uprooted from me. I don't think about him as he was. The bright yellowish light of the morning ... The noise of the bedpans and the carts and the old people groaning. We ran with a kind of relief ... at long last death came ... oh God, oh great God the loneliness. (*He looks up at the curtain, starts tugging from below in order to get down the last hook*) That little nursing student who came along and she didn't know he was dying and lifted him up for a cup of tea ... she didn't put him back down until we screamed at her. (*The curtain is now completely down. He pulls it as he goes along. From now on, whatever he does, he pulls the curtain along with him*) We didn't want him to die at home, we weren't being stubborn. What for? Who's going to warm his feet? Who's going to hold his skinny brown feet like that little black kid? Little black kids ... a smile from under the blankets, talking to him all the time, up to the last minute ... to distract him. Why? In fact, why not alone? A person's alone a little bit ... the hour's come ... now me ... another few years. Just let the kids grow up a little, I'm not afraid. Let there be death. Death wish ... the wish for death ... there is such a thing. (*He starts to become weaker, imitating a corpse with the curtain wrapped around him like a shroud*) The movement of death lying frozen in the yellowish light. We've arrived. How could it have happened here? Here's what he was looking at. (*He drops onto the bed*) Is home really important at a moment like that? Death at the proper time. A metaphysical moment. Maybe it's best without all your possessions around to hinder you ... to part quietly from nature, not from people. Sunlight, a strip of sky. (*He sobs, unbuttons his shirt*) Really alone. A person alone a little bit. Let's say   (*He is trembling all over*) Here's this terrible anger bursting at last. What is the reason for it? for this life? Who forced me? Is this all? Why did you burden me with life? The unconscious kisses the conscious. Thousands of years have sunk into history. Thousands of years have sunk into history, only the primeval dust, burning, dry and clean. Just let me mourn a little at my death. (*He makes twisted motions on the bed wrapping himself in the curtain*)

A few seconds before the end of his monologue, Aunt Tilly comes in with a basketful of little oranges. She always wears sunglasses. She moves into the middle of the study and watches his convulsions.

EZRA. (*Whispering to her*) Oh, Aunt Tilly, it's you.
TILLY. Has something happened?
EZRA. No, No, nothing. (*He gets up, shakes himself and puts the curtain under the bed*)
TILLY. What about your fever?
EZRA. I don't think I have it anymore.

TILLY. Where's your mother?

EZRA. She's sleeping.

TILLY. In the middle of the day?

EZRA. We made her, she was so tired.

TILLY. I brought you some oranges. I was shopping. The last blood oranges before spring.

EZRA. Fine. (*He is in an increasingly good mood*)

MOTHER. (*Calling fearfully from her bedroom*) Ezra, who's that?

EZRA. It's Aunt Tilly, she brought you some oranges.

MOTHER. Oranges?

EZRA. Blood oranges. The last till spring.

TILLY. I was in the market at Mahaneh Yehuda, Rochelle. I found some nice oranges.

MOTHER. (*Comes out, her hair unkempt*) What am I going to do with oranges?

EZRA. Eat them. What's the big deal?

MOTHER. I don't want to eat anything! What is this, Tilly? What are you bringing me oranges for? What am I going to do with oranges now? I'm always trying to get things out of this house and now you're bringing new ones in. Get them out of here!

EZRA. They're not things, they're oranges.

MOTHER. I don't care, I don't want them. What happened here? How could I sleep? Why did you let me sleep so long? They forced me to go to sleep and now tonight I won't be able to close my eyes. You'll leave and I'll be left here by myself.

EZRA. You'll sleep. You'll sleep.

MOTHER. Why did you make me go to sleep? (*She sits down, exhausted*) And you? Are you crazy? Why did you bring me oranges? Take them away. (*Tilly stays where she is, petrified*)

EZRA. Leave her alone. It's not polite to make her take them back. (*Eva bursts into the apartment*) Eva? What are you doing here?

EVA. Have you forgotten? I told you yesterday I'd be back in Jerusalem. Where's Shira? She didn't wait for me?

EZRA. She's at the conference.

EVA. But when is she coming back?

EZRA. Soon, but we're heading home. Michal has a music

lesson at seven and there's no one to stay with Ayil.

EVA. I've got to talk with her. I've got to talk with her. I just came from the lawyer's, I'm signing the papers on Monday. I've got to talk with Shira. You'll just have to leave for home a little later.

EZRA. We can't. (*Eva starts to cry*)

TILLY. (*Still in her petrified position*) Why is she crying?

MOTHER. It's nothing. Go home, Tilly. I'll call you later. Just take the oranges.

EVA. He didn't back down on anything. But I don't care, I'm signing.

TILLY. Who didn't?

MOTHER. (*Whispering to Eva*) For God's sake, not now! Not in front of her. She'll tell everyone.

EVA. Everyone already knows. I'm getting divorced, Tilly. (*Crying*) I'm getting divorced.

TILLY. Why, sweetheart?

MOTHER. They had a little fight, nothing terrible. They'll make it up. Not now, Tilly. Take the oranges, I'll come by tomorrow. I've got some things to give you. Thanks very much for thinking about us with the oranges. But I haven't got the strength now for an orange. I can barely eat bread.

TILLY. They're blood oranges. You used to like them when you were little.

MOTHER. When I was little ... when I was little ... now where am I?

EZRA. Leave the oranges here. I'll take them, Eva will take them.

MOTHER. No, you won't. You take them. Make juice out of them.

EZRA. Well, I'll make some juice — right now. I'll make juice. Where's the juicer? (*He gets up animatedly*)

MOTHER. All of a sudden you want to squeeze some juice? You'll mess up the whole place.

EZRA. (*Heading for the kitchen closet with his mother at his heels*) I won't make a mess, don't worry. Come on, I'll make you all some juice. Shira will be here soon.

MOTHER. Now it's juice? (*To Tilly*) You see what you've done here with your oranges? What an idea. Wait a second, put on an apron so you don't get dirty.

EZRA. All right. Get me a big pitcher.

MOTHER. Maybe I should do it.

EZRA. No way. I'm going to do it.

EVA. What's come over you? You're in such a good mood all of a sudden. What have you been doing all day?

EZRA. (*He starts squeezing the oranges with a big juicer, his mother tagging after him worriedly*) I was just here. I didn't leave at all.

EVA. You were here all day with Mama? How could you?

MOTHER. He decided on his own not to go anywhere. I didn't tell him to stay. Put down some newspaper so you don't make a mess. (*Aunt Tilly has been sitting petrified the whole time, not stirring*) Well, Tilly, here are the oranges we took from you. Thank you very much. They'll drink the juice. Give the first glass to Aunt Tilly.

EZRA. For everyone. You too.

MOTHER. Not for me.

EVA. What are you so happy about?

EZRA. Me, happy? Why should I be happy? Do I look happy?

EVA. (*Sobbing bitterly from inside*) I want to talk with Shira so much . . . I've got to.

MOTHER. Now, Eva, do you want to see these white gloves? (*From the box she removes the long white gloves which went with a wedding dress*) Only you could take them for me.

EVA. Please! Not now! Can't you see what kind of shape I'm in?

MOTHER. Don't you shout at me! Not in front of Aunt Tilly. Don't you humiliate me.

EVA. I *will* shout! You don't care what happens to me! All you care about is your crap! Your goddamn possessions!

MOTHER. I'm alone . . . I'm leaving this house in two weeks . . . I've got to finish. You're all going off and I'm alone. You could have waited with this divorce of yours.

EVA. Waited for what? For all this junk of yours?

EZRA. (*Getting angry at her for the first time*) You could have waited, Eva. Why are you in such a hurry? Where are you going? What possessed you, in the middle of all this?

EVA. I couldn't. I've already waited a long time.

EZRA. So wait a little longer. You know I never interfere in anything you do, but it's as if you decided to destroy your home, to get rid of your husband—for whom? For what?

EVA. But you know we fight all the time.

EZRA. But you always fought. Why now?

EVA. He seems so old all of a sudden. Why should I ...? I don't want to go on with him any more.

EZRA. Suddenly he seems old? All of a sudden?

EVA. His hands are already dry. He's got this sort of cough in the morning. A long drawn-out cough.

EZRA. A kind of cough?

EVA. Yes, this sort of cough that drives me out of my mind. It's horrible. Why should I go on with him?

EZRA. God, it's all because of Papa.

EVA. What's because of Papa? It's not because of Papa. You saw him yesterday. He's dried up, he's bent over. I feel like he's threatening me. Horrible! Stiff! And we fight all the time. So why not split up and get it over with? What does it have to do with Papa? Because he died. So what?

EZRA. So we immediately begin to identify with decay and death—not to grieve, but identify. We're dragged after him, that's what we're all doing all the time. Mama, you, me—me, too. We don't know how to grieve, only how to identify. To die a little bit ourselves. Of what? Of guilt? But we're not guilty. What are we guilty of? What are you guilty of? What am I guilty of? What is she guilty of? He didn't want to be at home. He couldn't be at home. He begged me himself. Take me. Like Narayama.

EVA. Narayama?

EZRA. The Japanese—father and mother on their backs to the top of the mountain—they say good-bye and they cry. And you? What are you killing here? Your husband? Yourself? Mourn, don't identify—mourn.

MOTHER. (*She doesn't understand. Eva is stunned. Something has touched deep within her. Ezra has kept on making juice the whole time*) You're making a mess, let me.

EZRA. No, I'll ...

MOTHER. But you're making a mess here.

EZRA. (*Angrily*) I'll clean up if I make a mess! (*Deliberately spills some juice on the floor*)

MOTHER. You spilled that on purpose.

EZRA. Of course I did. But I'll clean it up.

MOTHER. (*Shouting*) Why?

EVA. So a little spilled, Mama. So what? So what? I'll clean it up. It's juice.

MOTHER. Let go of me. (*She runs to get a rag*) This isn't your house. On purpose. And the whole thing in front of Aunt Tilly. She'll tell all her friends.

TILLY. (*She has been sitting petrified the whole time, as if she doesn't feel well, but she is paying attention with the depths of her being*) I won't tell a thing. Who would I tell? (*The doorbell rings*)

EVA. Oh, it's Shira. At last. (*She opens the door and Oded is standing there*) What happened?

ODED. Nothing.

EVA. What are you doing here?

ODED. I'm not allowed to come here?

EVA. But what do you want?

ODED. I came to visit your mother. Is that forbidden? And here's Aunt Tilly, too. Hi, Aunt Tilly.

EVA. Don't be a smartass, since when do you visit her?

ODED. Maybe I'll take something from here.

EVA. Bastard.

MOTHER. Leave him alone.

EVA. Don't you interfere. What are you doing here?

ODED. What are you so upset about? Always upset. I came to visit your mother and maybe to take something.

MOTHER. Let him take something.

EVA. You're a genuine psychopath.

MOTHER. Help me, Oded. They don't want to take anything.

EVA. Mother, stop. He only came here to make fun of you— and us.

MOTHER. How can you say that? He'll take something, there's a lot of nice things here.

EVA. What's he going to take?

EZRA. Oded, really . . .

ODED. How are you? How's that fever of yours?

EZRA. It's okay. It was an emotional thing, something mental.

ODED. I'd still ask a doctor . . . in case it's not mental . . . so afterwards there won't be ...

EZRA. It was mental, it was just mental; I'm sure and Shira says so too. It was just mental.

ODED. As long as Shira's taking the responsibility ... I never knew you were so close to your father. You never gave that impression.

EVA. Not like you. You told jokes at your mother's funeral.

ODED. (*Turning as red as a marble*) I told jokes at my mother's funeral?

EVA. That's right, they heard you.

ODED. You filthy liar.

EZRA. That's enough! Stop this right now!

EVA. You should have seen what he did just now at the lawyer's, the way he was haggling.

ODED. She thinks I'm a money-printing press.

EVA. Go on home. What are you doing here? What gives you the right ...?

ODED. Your mother wants me to help her take some things, so I came to take them.

MOTHER. Maybe this cabinet, Oded. For your office. It's a good cabinet

ODED. Sure. Maybe I'll take this bell. (*Reaches for the little copper bell that's standing there*)

MOTHER. The bell? What do you need that for?

ODED. To call my secretary.

MOTHER. No, not the bell. I happen to want to take that with me, in case I get sick.

ODED. But what do you need it for? You'll have an electric bell right next to the bed.

MOTHER. There's an electric bell?

ODED. Sure, what did you expect?

MOTHER. What if there's a short circuit?

ODED. That's true. (*Puts the bell down*) All right, I won't take it.

EZRA. Please, Oded, that's enough. Come have some juice. You too.

EVA. He's just making fun of us. He did the same thing at the lawyer's.

MOTHER. All of a sudden, that particular bell.

EZRA. He was joking, Mama.

ODED. They don't understand jokes. She never made me laugh, either. Never amused me. No smile, always bitterness. Even your father, when he was sick, managed to make me laugh. You don't remember, when we were with him that evening after his second operation, how delightful he was. "You people ought to try some drugs to get you out of your depression." Remember?

EZRA. Yes ... that was maybe the only day.

EVA. What are you talking about? When did you ever visit him in the hospital?

EZRA. Yes, he did, he was there the evening after the second operation. Father woke up after you left and Oded came.

EVA. What are you talking about? He was not. I was there that day.

ODED. She knows everything.

EZRA. Yes, Eva, Oded came after you left. Papa woke up after you left. They didn't give him a very large dose of the anesthetic, and he was right on the borderline, tranquilized and content, lying on his back smiling and hallucinating all kinds of funny things. And Oded came along. We came very piously into the room and Papa said, "Behold, the princes of the British royal house." And that social worker was there, and he thought she was Benveniste's wife. He insisted on saying it, "Benveniste's wife," and he grabbed her hand with such joy. He always had a weakness for her. And he said to her, "What's with you? Where've you been? How did you find me?" And she got all panicky and confused. It was impossible to get him away from her. Then the doctors came and he said, "Quick, where's my wallet?" He thought they were beggars from the Old City and wanted to give them some charity.

ODED. Yes, he was funny that evening. But you didn't laugh. You were kind of scared.

EZRA. I was terribly scared. I was afraid he was losing his mind. And I thought, now what's going to become of us? But he was so delightful.

EVA. (*Listening all the while with a pained look on her face*) You never told me you were with him that night.

ODED. Why should I have told you?

EVA. Why not? It would have been so natural to come home and tell me.

ODED. (*Perplexed*) I didn't know it was so important to you that I was there.

EVA. Even when you gave something, you didn't want me to know, in case I got pleasure from your giving. What a bastard you are, after all.

EZRA. Stop it, Eva!

ODED. What does she want from me?

EZRA. Stop it, Oded, not now.

ODED. All right, I'm going.

MOTHER. So you don't want to take anything after all.

EVA. Leave him alone, let him go.

ODED. I wanted to, but you wouldn't give it to me.

MOTHER. But there's other things besides the bell.

ODED. (*Coughing a long hacking cough*) I might be moving next week — when are you moving?

MOTHER. In two weeks. There's no time.

EZRA. Would you take Aunt Tilly on your way?

ODED. Glad to.

EZRA. Aunt Tilly, he'll take you home.

MOTHER. Just a minute, I'm giving her a can of oil.

TILLY. No, Rochelle.

MOTHER. Yes, here, take this little can of oil. You must. You won't run out on me. (*Oded takes the can of oil and Aunt Tilly gets up heavily. The two of them exit*)

EZRA. Shira will be here soon and we'll be leaving too. (*Blackout*)

Three quarters of an hour later. The cupboards are empty. New cardboard boxes have been brought in. Ezra's suitcase is at one side of the room, closed. There is a feeling of preparation, as if many more possessions have been moved.

EZRA. What happened to Shira? It's almost four. She's gone crazy.

MOTHER. Here, take these toys, too. They belong to the kids.

EZRA. That goes straight in the trash can.

MOTHER. What difference does it make if you wait and take a look when you get home? Let them decide themselves. Maybe there's something that would interest Ayil. And

here's that little gun of yours, too, that you used to love so
much. You used to carry it around in your pocket all the
time. So it would give you courage.

EZRA. (*Taking it and putting it in his pocket*) What's going on
with Shira? She's crazy. (*Rochelle takes out two big packages of
stained, greenish rolls of toilet paper and gives one to each of them*)

MOTHER. And here's the toilet paper I told you about.

EVA. (*Sitting and smoking*) No.

EZRA. Take it, what do you care? I'm taking one too.

EVA. She's hoarded up so much. You've hoarded up so much.

MOTHER. I kept thinking there might be a long war. After the
siege of Jerusalem I wasn't sure any more. Here, Eva, I'm
giving you this frying pan anyway.

EVA. No way.

EZRA. Take it. It's not so terrible. Throw it out afterwards,
throw it out on your way home. Let's liberate the living
and take leave of the dead and then mourn in peace. Help
her, for my sake — she's collapsing under it, have pity on
her. (*Shira comes in*) Shira? What the hell happened to you?

SHIRA. Eva's here! How are you, Eva? I didn't know you'd be
here today. (*They kiss*)

EVA. I've been waiting for you. Didn't Ezra tell you I'd be
here this afternoon?

SHIRA. You didn't tell me she'd be here.

EVA. Why didn't you tell her? And I need to talk to you so
much.

EZRA. What happened? Why are you late?

SHIRA. It went on longer than expected. Nobody wanted
to stop. All of a sudden there was real enthusiasm —
excitement.

EZRA. We've got to get going.

EVA. Hold on, Ezra. Hold on.

MOTHER. (*Offering Shira a glass of juice*) Have something to
drink. Here, Ezra squeezed this juice.

SHIRA. Oh, lovely! Why is it so red?

EZRA. Aunt Tilly brought some blood oranges.

SHIRA. Oh, this juice is wonderful — it was so hot and stuffy in
the auditorium.

EVA. What was the conference about?

SHIRA. Nietzsche.

EVA. Oh, I want to talk to you. (*Starts to cry*) I've got to tell you what he's doing to me. When can we talk? When can we talk ...?

SHIRA. What happened? Were you at the lawyer's today?

EZRA. Not now, Shira, we've got to get going, Michal's got a lesson at seven and I promised her we'd be back — it's already five. (*Eva is crying soundlessly*)

MOTHER. What makes you cry so easily? Always crying.

EVA. Just a minute, Ezra, I want to talk with her. (*Ezra signals with his head to Shira that it's impossible*)

SHIRA. Why don't you come over on Saturday?

MOTHER. (*Holding the pitcher of juice and filling glasses*) Here's some more juice, finish it up. Don't leave it for me.

EZRA. You have some too, Mama.

MOTHER. Not me.

SHIRA. Why not? It's terrific.

MOTHER. It gives me heartburn.

SHIRA. It won't give you heartburn. Drink up.

EZRA. Drink up.

EVA. Drink up, Mama. (*Rochelle gives in and drinks. Ezra begins to take things out of the house. He goes out and comes back afterwards*)

SHIRA. Did you get some sleep?

MOTHER. Maybe five hours, but it's going to stop me from sleeping tonight.

SHIRA. Come over on Saturday, Eva.

EVA. I'll try. (*Rochelle sticks some more things in Ezra's box*)

EZRA. (*Coming in*) What are you putting in there, Mama?

MOTHER. Nothing, just that little pot. (*Ezra restrains himself from saying anything*) Shira said it was okay. Shira wants it.

EZRA. Shira, we haven't got room for it.

SHIRA. Don't worry, we'll find room.

EZRA. All right, come on. Hey, what's this? (*Takes a framed portrait of Rochelle as a young woman out of the box*)

MOTHER. That's a nice frame with an old picture of me. If you want, you can take out the picture and just use the frame. Have pity on me, I haven't got room.

EZRA. You haven't even got room for your picture ...

MOTHER. I haven't got room. None of you understand. Throw
out the picture and use the frame, what do you care?

EZRA. God Almighty! All right. Hurry up, Shira. Let's get out
of here.

MOTHER. Are you coming next week?

SHIRA. Ezra will come.

MOTHER. There's still a lot of things.

SHIRA. It'll work out okay.

MOTHER. (*To Eva*) You're going too? Stay a while.

EVA. No, I've got to run, too.

MOTHER. Stay with me a while. They forced me to sleep in the
afternoon and now I won't be able to close my eyes all
night.

EZRA, EVA, AND SHIRA. You'll sleep, you'll sleep.

MOTHER. I won't sleep. Everything upsets me.

EZRA. I'll come next week. (*Kisses her good-bye*)

EVA. I'll try to come too.

MOTHER. There's still a lot of things. You can't imagine. We've
just begun. This closet is still full.

EZRA. We'll get rid of everything.

MOTHER. (*As if seeing him now for the first time*) Are you feeling
better? You look better. See a doctor.

EZRA. I'll be okay.

MOTHER. Call me when you get home.

EZRA. Shira, we've got to run. (*He leaves. Shira kisses Rochelle
and Eva*)

EVA. I only came to Jerusalem because of you. When am I
going to see you?

SHIRA. Let's talk tonight. But don't be in a hurry to split up.
(*She leaves*)

EVA. Goodbye, Mama.

MOTHER. Think about me. Come visit.

EVA. Okay, I will.

MOTHER. Call me when you get to Tel Aviv.

EVA. Okay, I will. (*She also takes some things and then leaves. The
light dims. Rochelle bolts the door and begins organizing the things.
After a while, the doorbell rings*)

MOTHER. Who is it?

DANIELLA. It's me, Daniella.

MOTHER. Who?

DANIELLA. For the curtain. (*Mother opens the door*) I came for the other part.

MOTHER. Ah, it's you.

DANIELLA. Are they gone already?

MOTHER. Yes.

DANIELLA. Too bad, I wanted to meet his wife. (*Rochelle nods her head mechanically*) But where's the curtain? You got it down already.

MOTHER. (*Noticing that the curtain is no longer up*) The curtain? Yes. Now where . . . where did it disappear to?

DANIELLA. I don't know.

MOTHER. Didn't he take it down for you? Where could it be?

DANIELLA. I don't know. When I left here we left the other part hanging so it wouldn't wrinkle.

MOTHER. Strange. Where could it have disappeared to? (*She begins searching intensely. Daniella follows her*)

DANIELLA. Did he say anything? I might have insulted him.

MOTHER. (*Not hearing, paying no attention, continuing to search*) Where is it? Where is it? Where could they have hidden it? (*Finds it under the bed in the workroom*) Here's where he hid it. Why on earth? (*Pulls the curtain out from under the bed*)

DANIELLA. I hope it didn't get dirty.

MOTHER. No, the floor's clean here. Come, I'll help you fold it. You're taking it to the laundry?

DANIELLA. Yes. (*They fold it and go back to the living room*)

MOTHER. Wait, before I forget. I wanted to show you something. (*She takes the parasol out of the cupboard and, for the first time, opens it in all its glory*)

DANIELLA. What's that?

MOTHER. A parasol. I thought you might want to buy it.

DANIELLA. I don't know.

MOTHER. Know what? Think about it.

DANIELLA. (*Smiling, sitting down as if distracted*) All right, I'll think about it.

yosef bar-yosef

difficult
people

(a comedy of sorts)

TRANSLATED FROM THE HEBREW BY
BARBARA HARSHAV

characters

RACHEL-LEAH GOLD: called Rachel, a 44-year-old spinster

MEIR-SIMON GOLD: called Simon, her brother, a 47-year-old bachelor

ELIEZER WEINGARTEN: called Layzer, a 41-year-old divorcé from Jerusalem

BENNY ALTER: an elderly bachelor, Rachel's landlord

setting

The action is confined to one room of a house in a large English port city. It continues uninterruptedly during one evening. The time is late fall, 1967.

act 1

Rachel is seated. Simon is pacing up and down behind her.

SIMON. Don't those sirens ever stop?

RACHEL. They're ships. (*Sounds of a shoemaker's hammer on the other side of the wall*)

SIMON. (*Stops pacing*) That handsome landlord of yours, your Benny, pounding away ...

RACHEL. He likes to fix shoes.

SIMON. Onions!

RACHEL. He likes onions.

SIMON. What a life! (*The hammer is heard again*)

RACHEL. (*After a moment*) What happened there?

SIMON. (*Coming to her*) What should happen?

RACHEL. I don't know. You come back, I ask you how it was and you ...

SIMON. I what?

RACHEL. I don't know. You walk around, you look mad. I don't know why. You don't say anything. You were so eager to go. You always tell me so much. But this time, you didn't see anything. You didn't get anything.

SIMON. (*Sits*) I got a slipped disc. (*Turns to her, sighs*) And I got something else—for you. I got you a husband.

RACHEL. I don't get it.

SIMON. I got me a slipped disc. I got you a husband. You'll get it soon enough. (*Three strong hammer blows are heard on the other side of the wall*) He got it. (*Addressing the wall, loud*) That rotten anarchist who dreams of marrying you.

RACHEL. I don't understand. (*A knock at the door, the door opens; Benny enters wearing a shoemaker's apron, holding a shoe*)

SIMON. Good evening, my dear sir. How nice of you to come! To what do we owe this honor? Or, rather, to what does my sister owe this honor? Her landlord, a notorious anti-capitalist, exploits his landlord's rights and bursts into her flat so casually?

BENNY. (*Rages helplessly, speaks in bursts*) You I wouldn't give a flat ... not even at twice the rent ... more! Not even if

you were starving, sick, naked. You I wouldn't let in! You
I'd leave in the street. (*Exits*)

SIMON. Look what you're missing!

RACHEL. I still don't understand.

SIMON. What don't you understand? I got you a husband from
Jerusalem. (*To the wall*) Something better than that. (*After
a moment*) His name is Eliezer Weingarten, they call him
Layzer. Six generations in Jerusalem, a distant relative on
mother's side, divorced, one daughter. No alimony. She
gave in just to get a divorce. (*Pause*) Cafés ... (*Pause*) She
wanted him to take her to cafés, he took her to his relatives.
He doesn't have any friends but he does have lots of
relatives. What do you say to that?

RACHEL. What do you want me to say?

SIMON. Nothing. He's a shlimazel. The kind of guy who's
always changing jobs. Last time he was a clerk. Once he
wanted to be a plumber. But the family was against it.
They're very orthodox. He's not. He was in the army and
he's proud of it. God doesn't interest him but he's crazy
about truth and justice. A professional noodnik. He talks
all the time. To anybody. But only serious things. No
how's the weather. There is no weather. No how are you;
right to the point, down to business right away. Talks
about himself too. And keeps looking for relatives. He'll
look for his relatives here too. Even at Buckingham Palace.
And he'll find some if the Queen gives him enough time.
Say something already. (*In the same breath but in a different
tone*) We talked about it before I left. You didn't say
anything — and silence is consent. Right? You can't say no
now. It's too late. I got him already. They showed me the
Wailing Wall, the Jordan River and ... and I went looking
for a husband for you. Answer me. Say something!

RACHEL. Some more tea?

SIMON. (*Turning to her*) Oh! My aching back!

RACHEL. Maybe you should see Dr. Blau.

SIMON. You're driving me crazy. (*Pause*) And another thing:
he was in a mental hospital. Only three months, a long
time ago. He was cured, but you should know. Now what
do you say?

RACHEL. I'll make you another cup of tea.

SIMON. (*Turns to her sharply, in pain*) Another cup of tea? I haven't finished this one.

RACHEL. Drink it.

SIMON. (*Drinking quickly and angrily*) OK, here. I'll drink it. Now, what did you get out of that? (*Rachel gets up and takes the empty cups from the table to the kitchenette. Simon stands up*) Listen. I didn't put an ad in the paper. I found him and he agreed to the deal. That's all there is to it, make the best of it. There's nobody else around. (*Pause*) He's not so bad. I've made him look worse than he really is. I just don't want you to expect anything. I don't want you to be disappointed again. One more disappointment for you and — I'll go crazy. (*Rachel makes tea. After a moment*) He's ... special. If you want, he has a special kind of charm, if you want it very much. Yes, he has a charm, if you want. With his last little bit of money he took a hotel room. He didn't want to stay at my flat, that would sort of be on me. Coming here from Jerusalem on me — that was all right; it's not his fault you live in England. But now he's here, he wants to pay his own way. (*Looks around for her*) Where are you? (*Sees her, says loudly*) Get married for once, will you!! Sit down for once! Why are you standing up?

RACHEL. I'm making you another cup of tea.

SIMON. Who said I want another cup of tea?

RACHEL. I asked you.

SIMON. But I didn't say I wanted one. What do you want to do, drown the world in tea? It's high time you sat down.

RACHEL. I want to make you another cup of tea.

SIMON. (*After a moment*) I'd really like a cup of tea. Could you please make me one?

RACHEL. Right away.

SIMON. (*Sitting*) Yes, a special charm, if you want. He didn't even want to come here with me, he says I'm from your side. Marriage is a meeting between two armies, he says, and he wanted to come at the head of his own army. Alone in town, with only a few pounds to his name and he's shlepping his whole army around with him. Terrific, isn't it? And his English — he got his first lessons in English from aspirin bottles. His father used to send them aspirins wholesale from America. They get lots of headaches in his family; they take lots of aspirins. They also put potato plasters on their foreheads. His mother was wearing one when I went to see her. (*Rachel pours tea as he speaks*) Stop crying.

RACHEL. I'm pouring tea.

SIMON. Rivers of tears flow in your tea. Stop it! (*Rachel brings the cups to the table. Simon rises and unwittingly blocks her way*) The best thing about him is that he wants a wife in the worst way. That's how a man should want a wife. He's miserable, he's divorced, he's alone and he wants a wife. He's really healthy — a healthy husband with a headache. (*Rachel tries to get to the table*) His headache, you know. That's his ... his ... thing. He's crazy to have children. He told me he'd marry you and show her. Show her!

RACHEL. Enough!

SIMON. What?

RACHEL. Let me put the tea on the table. (*Puts the cup on the table. Sits*)

SIMON. (*Turns to her sharply, in pain*) You, him, this slipped disc, you're all trying to kill me. (*Sits*)

RACHEL. (*Moves the cup to him*) Here.

SIMON. (*Takes the cup, holds it but doesn't drink*) Maybe he's not good enough for us. But who is? We're good enough for us. We're the only ones good enough for us, right? That's our pride and joy — our good taste, our high standards. You deserve something better, of course you do, we always deserve something better. How come? Because we see everybody else's weaknesses? I know. We see our own too. Ha, ha, ha! That's really something. So that's why we have the right to love ourselves. I'm sick and tired of eating myself up.

RACHEL. (*Bows her head*) What do you want from me?

SIMON. (*The cup shakes in his hand*) What?

RACHEL. What do you want from my life?

SIMON. (*Grabs the cup, drinks quickly. The tea goes down the wrong way and he almost chokes*) Live! Live!

RACHEL. Enough, Simon.

SIMON. Enough of Simon. In Jerusalem, I'm not Simon. Meir-Shim'on. Rakhel-Leah. Meir-Shim'on. And what good did you get out of all your free love?

RACHEL. Why must you ...?

SIMON. (*Stands up*) Seven years you kept Steven. Supported him. Free love? You were his slave! Until he got his degree, packed up and left. So you found yourself another first-year medical student so it'd be another seven years till he left you too. They study medicine for seven years. Right? What do they study there all that time? And it's been six years since then.

RACHEL. Why do you have to humiliate me for nothing?

SIMON. (*Not hearing her*) Enough medical students! It's high time you got married in style. (*After a moment, quietly*) Why don't you ever tell me: Go to hell? Go on, say it: Go to hell! What do you want from me? What if you are my brother? Worry about yourself. I can jump off the roof if I want. This is a free country! And who says I've got to have a husband? Have you got a wife? Go on, why don't you tell me to go screw myself? (*A knock at the door. Benny enters holding a pair of women's shoes*) Again? He just knocks and walks in. Why bother knocking?

RACHEL. (*To Benny*) My old shoes. I was looking for them. Thanks a lot, Mr. Alter.

SIMON. I get it. He took them without telling you so he could fix them. The big bad anarchist dispenses secret charity. Wonderful! (*Benny drops the shoes in Simon's lap; exits*) Look. He stopped fixing them right in the middle. He took off the old heels and didn't put on new ones. He ruined your shoes.

RACHEL. It doesn't matter. They were worn out anyway.

SIMON. No! He has to pay you for them. Let him buy you new ones! If you don't tell him, I will.

RACHEL. (*Quietly*) I live here. He's my landlord.

SIMON. So?

RACHEL. I owe him three months rent and he doesn't say a word. He needs the money, he's got even less than I do. I caught a cold. I was sick and he brought me food. (*A stammering horn is heard from the other side of the wall*)

SIMON. (*Quietly*) How nice! The pleasures of the poor. A world of grace. Very touching. You know, when my heartstrings are strummed like this, when I smell this world of grace ... (*Loud, with suppressed rage*) the blood rushes to my head. I'll give you a husband just because you'll take whatever I give you, whatever this world of grace gives you. I'm sick of your bowed head and your good moist eyes. Sick of your nice cups of tea. Sick of your medical journals. Two medical students! Two! Fourteen years of medicine! And you still get those medical journals! Enough! I'm sick of how you walk down the street clinging to the wall. Walk down the middle of the street with your head high. That's how you should walk down the street. Say something!

RACHEL. I did but you didn't hear.

SIMON. What didn't I hear?

RACHEL. Why do you have to humiliate me for nothing?

SIMON. For nothing? Humiliate you?

RACHEL. Let him come. We'll see. I've been trying to tell you all along.

SIMON. What?

RACHEL. Maybe. (*A brief silence*)

SIMON. (*Embarrassed by repressed anger*) All right ... OK. That's good enough. (*Gets up, puts on his coat*) You entertain him. You'll get along fine. I've done the best I can. He should be here any minute. (*Exits*)

At first, Rachel seems to want to stop him, then she takes a mirror and begins fixing herself up. The doorbell rings. She hesitates. Another ring. She opens the door. Simon is standing there.

SIMON. Ah! Splendid! You're fixing yourself up. Good. I forgot the most important thing: he's forty-one and so are you, not a day older. He asked me twice, it sounded too good — such a young bride, only forty-one, on top of a trip here at my expense. He won't ask again. He certainly won't ask you. He suspects everybody's cheating him. He asks once, maybe twice and that's it, no more. He doesn't want to insult anybody. You'll work it out later somehow. As for children, you can do that even when you're fifty, right? What a world! (*Exits. Rachel turns back into the room, slowly.*

The doorbell rings again. Simon enters) One more thing. This flat — it's yours. That's what I told him. And I'm rich, a successful agent. We'll figure that out later too. He's honest, he won't walk out on you. It was his wife who walked out on him. I'll be back soon. (*Exits. Rachel clears the table. The doorbell rings. She opens it. Benny stands there*)

RACHEL. Oh, Mr. Alter. Come in. My brother's not here. I hope you ... you know how he ... really. Come in ... some tea?

BENNY. (*In the doorway, embarrassed, agitated*) I just want to explain ... those shoes ... it's not against you. No! I really want to fix them, even now. But after what I heard I can't ... lying to me. To me! Not your fault ... me ... I'm no good. I'm poison. I, myself. (*Exits*)

After a moment, Rachel opens the door as if to tell Benny something. Layzer stands there. She closes the door in panic. The doorbell rings. She opens it. Layzer stands in the doorway, wet with rain.

LAYZER. (*With exaggerated self-confidence, almost gaily*) Hello.

RACHEL. Hello. Please come in.

LAYZER. First you should know who I am. (*Holds out his hand*) Eliezer Weingarten.

RACHEL. Yes. Rachel. (*Holds out her hand*)

LAYZER. (*Squeezes her hand too hard*) Very nice.

RACHEL. (*In pain*) Likewise. Very nice. (*After a moment*) Please come in. (*Closes the door*) Simon went out for a while. (*Pause*) Please sit down.

LAYZER. First I must take off my coat, no?

RACHEL. Of course. Sorry. You're soaking wet.

LAYZER. The coat that's wet. (*Starts to take off his coat. Stops*) Oh. Sorry. First I have something for you. (*Takes a box of chocolates from under his coat and gives it to her*) A present for you. Women like chocolates.

RACHEL. (*Taking it*) Thank you. (*Puts it on the buffet*)

LAYZER. (*Holding his coat*) Where should I hang up my coat?

RACHEL. Sorry. Give it to me.

LAYZER. It's too heavy for you. A porter's coat. My father brought it from the United States of America, from New

York. He was working there. There, in the summer, they all sweat and there's soot and, in the winter — it's cold and ice.

RACHEL. (*Points to the coatrack*) There.

LAYZER. Thank you. (*Hangs up his coat*) Where should I sit?

RACHEL. Of course. (*Laughs*) Sorry. Here, at the table. Sorry.

LAYZER. (*Sits down*) You say too much I'm sorry.

RACHEL. What? ... I almost said it again. Sorry.

LAYZER. (*Looks at her; suddenly, in a loud voice*) It's not nice that I sit and you stand.

RACHEL. Of course. (*Pause*) I forgot my ... (*Sits*)

LAYZER. (*Pause*) The chocolates?

RACHEL. Pardon?

LAYZER. I brought you chocolates.

RACHEL. Oh, yes. On the buffet.

LAYZER. Please allow me to ask you to bring them to the table. Women like chocolates but they like their figures better. This is my present and I don't want that you should go on a diet with it. Eat now, please. I want to see that they didn't cheat me.

RACHEL. (*Pause*) Fine. (*Gets up and puts the chocolates on the table. Pause*) I'll eat the chocolates but you'll drink a cup of tea. (*Goes to the kitchen and puts on the kettle*)

LAYZER. (*Without looking at her*) It's not an expensive present.

RACHEL. You didn't have to bring an expensive present.

LAYZER. I don't have enough money for an expensive present. (*Pause*) I also believe that there is no need to bring expensive presents. It's hard to give an expensive present with your whole heart. When you give one, you expect something back. And the person who gets it takes it with greed.

RACHEL. I never thought of that.

LAYZER. Think of it now. (*Pause*) I'll give you an example. Leah-Dvora Villman, the cousin of my mother — she's also related to your mother's aunt Malka — gave me a splendid tea service for a wedding present. (*Stops as if waiting for her answer and then goes on*) She's a poor old widow, with eight children and they eat bread cooked in oil the way people used to do in the Old City. Everybody knows about the Wailing Wall and the synagogues there but they don't know about the poverty that was in the Old City. They hardly eat any vegetables or fruit and there are children, they need it. And they pass on shoes from child to child. And she gave me a tea service that cost one hundred and seventy-eight pounds. Israeli pounds, not English ones, but that's still a lot. It's not nice to take back a present but that would be like stealing. So I gave it back to her and she wouldn't take it. So I went to Freund's and gave it back to him — Freund, the son-in-law of Reb Barukh, the one from Cracow — and I sent her a check.

RACHEL. (*Pause*) She could probably do a lot with that money. (*Brings the tea to the table*) You drink it with milk?

LAYZER. Shmuel-Wolf was killed by the Jordanians. The husband. And ever since then, her life is miserable. People who don't know to think might imagine that dying is the hardest part.

RACHEL. (*Impressed by this*) That's so true, what you just said.

LAYZER. And on top of that, she has a mole on the end of her nose. (*Shows where*) Right here. It looks like a big drop that's going to drip off any minute. You just have to laugh at it. (*Rachel tries hard and laughs. She sits down*) It looks like a drop of chocolate. And she had a reason to give me such an expensive wedding present. She wanted me to help Yerukham get a job in the Welfare Department. Her oldest son. (*Puts a lot of sugar in his tea*) But I didn't work anymore in the Welfare Department. She just didn't know that. With all the things she has to worry about, she really doesn't know what goes on in the world. But she does remember all the *yortseits* in the family. She always comes to the cemetery. She has enough reason to come. She cries more than the orphans themselves.

RACHEL. Take as much sugar as you like.

LAYZER. The Hasid rebbe finally got him a job in the bank. Yerukham. In Jerusalem, sometimes, they help people but they laugh at you at the same time. They help you and at the same time they're laughing like crazy about how they're going to tell somebody else about your troubles.

RACHEL. I'll eat your chocolates. You don't have to apologize.

LAYZER. (*After a moment*) For what do I have to apologize?

RACHEL. You don't have to.

LAYZER. For what don't I have to?

RACHEL. For the present, for ... Oh, it doesn't matter. I just said that.

LAYZER. You didn't just say that. People don't just say things.

RACHEL. (*After a moment*) That's so true. Anyway, let's forget it. You know what I meant.

LAYZER. Not really.

RACHEL. Anyway, let's just forget it. Maybe I'm saying the wrong thing. (*After a moment*) I'm a little confused. That's natural, isn't it? (*Opens the chocolates, eats, says gaily*) They're good. They didn't cheat you. Now, drink your tea. We made a deal, didn't we? (*Layzer drinks. She drinks. Short silence. The light dims. Hammering is heard on the other side of the wall; it stops when the conversation suddenly resumes. The two of them begin talking at the same time*)

LAYZER. Do you have something ... RACHEL. What do you think ...

RACHEL. Please ...

LAYZER. No. You ...

RACHEL. You're the guest.

LAYZER. That's no good. You first.

RACHEL. (*After a pause*) I only wanted to ask you what you think of the progress of medicine in our time.

LAYZER. Excuse me?

RACHEL. I think that medicine is the only sphere where the progress of civilization has brought people genuine happiness. Not just comfort or power, but real happiness. Just think—only fifty years ago, half the babies used to die before they learned to talk. (*Layzer coughs lightly. Rachel continues, ill at ease*) Of course, it doesn't make people any better but it does make them suffer less. So they're happier. (*Pause*) Of course, doctors aren't better people either but medicine helps them do good.

LAYZER. Do you like to sit in cafés?

RACHEL. What? No. There aren't any cafés here. They have pubs instead. I don't go to pubs very much. Sometimes. Why do you ask?

LAYZER. I'll tell you in a minute. (*Pause*) Does your plumbing need to be fixed?

RACHEL. Pardon?

LAYZER. If something is wrong with the plumbing — say, the water doesn't go down in the toilet or the faucet leaks — I can fix it.

RACHEL. Thank you, there's no need. Everything's fine.

LAYZER. I wanted to be a plumber. It's a good trade. People always need plumbers. You make a pretty good living being a plumber. I'm sick to death of working in the government. It's like slippery pipes there. Everybody's climbing on top of everybody else just to get to the top. I used to work for Moshe Cohen, the plumber. But I had to stop. My father and mother said it made them ashamed. I felt ashamed too. I didn't want to feel ashamed but they made me. Even when a man's all alone, he's not free to do what's good for him, what he wants to do.

RACHEL. That's so true.

LAYZER. They used to say there's a demon in man.

RACHEL. Oh.

LAYZER. Is your watch all right?

RACHEL. Pardon?

LAYZER. If it's not, I can fix it.

RACHEL. Thanks, but there's no need. It's fine.

LAYZER. After plumbing, I started to learn watchmaking from Yakov, the redhead. But I had to stop. I got such awful headaches — much worse than usual — and Dr. Block said it came from eyestrain. I think it was the ticking. Open clocks on a table look beautiful but even two exact clocks don't tick together. Like they're chasing each other. They don't rest even a minute. They're racing all the time. And they're just clocks.

RACHEL. I see.

LAYZER. They say it's dog eat dog. But a dog doesn't eat a dog, not when he's full and not when he's hungry. (*Pause*) I didn't tell you all these stories I told you just to tell you stories. I want to present myself to you. And I'm also giving you points about the not-so-nice part of my life, my marriage. You didn't notice. I like that. I don't like a woman with a big nose who sticks it into every little thing. So I'll present myself to you in a moment in the right order. (*Pause. A ship's siren is heard*)

RACHEL. What do you think of this town, if you can form an opinion in such a short time? (*She doesn't feel comfortable about her question*) It's a gray town, like tin. Sometimes I just want to pick up a rake and scrape off all the rust. It must be hard for you Israelis to understand why we talk about the sun so much. You have so much light there. Simon goes to Israel every two years. I've been there twice, I toured around a bit and, in the end, there I was in your post office, writing letters home. The English built your post office and it's a lot like the buildings here.

LAYZER. How late do you sleep in the morning?

RACHEL. (*Not surprised this time, smiles*) I get up early, too early. They say that's a sign of guilt. Even when I go to bed late, I get up early. Then I'm tired all day long.

LAYZER. See my coat?

RACHEL. Yes.

LAYZER. You can't see my coat like that, you can see only me.

RACHEL. (*Turning her head*) I see it.

LAYZER. You asked me about this English town. I'll tell you something about the English. Our toilet was in the yard, it's like that in the old neighborhoods in Jerusalem. One day my father had a stomachache and had to go out— excuse me—before dawn. The English put a curfew. They ruled Eretz Israel and they didn't want to leave. What did he do? He got down on his hands and knees and went like that to the toilet at the end of the yard, on his hands and knees, so the soldiers would think he was an animal. On the way he barked twice like a dog so they'd be sure it was a dog. Imagine: a man ... a grown up man ... a man who works hard ... all because of politics.

RACHEL. (*After a moment*) You said you'd tell me about your coat.

LAYZER. My father used to cover me with this coat at dawn. Our house was small, there wasn't room for all the children inside so I had to sleep outside, on a closed little porch outside. They called it a closed porch but the rain dripped from the roof onto the porch and right on my bed. I used to sleep pretty good in that wet bed because I was young and tired. But when he got up to pray *Shakhrit*, he used to cover me with the coat and then I'd be warm and sleep even better. (*A brief silence. It grows almost completely dark. A blinking neon light comes on somewhere in the street*)

RACHEL. Simon carried me on his shoulders for three days. Just when we started to escape from Russia, I got scarlet fever. My father wasn't with us, so Simon was the head of the family. I was red as a beet.

LAYZER. It's good for a woman to have scarlet fever before she gets married.

RACHEL. What? (*Understands*) Oh, yes. Our mother died in Russia, in Siberia. We loved her very much. We remember her well to this day. She died in a snowstorm.

LAYZER. In England they eat lots of chips.

RACHEL. Oh, not as much as they say. But they do. It's cheap.

LAYZER. It takes a lot of oil.

RACHEL. I deep-fry them — that way, the chips come out good and the oil stays pretty clean. Then I put the oil back in a special bottle and use it again.

LAYZER. I was testing you. Maybe a person shouldn't do that but I admit that I was testing you. (*After a moment*) I was married. I'm divorced. I have a little girl. My wife used to make chips and then throw away the oil. She loved to throw away that oil. She liked to throw away everything. We used to fight because of that. Once she told me I should put the toothpaste back in the tube after I brush my teeth.

RACHEL. Oh. (*Laughs*)

LAYZER. Why do you laugh?

RACHEL. (*After a moment*) It's funny.

LAYZER. Who?

RACHEL. Nobody. It's ... it's funny, putting toothpaste back in the tube. You have to laugh at something like that, don't you? (*Repeats*) Don't you?

LAYZER. (*After a pause, stands up; in a loud, angry voice*) I already told you I'm divorced and I have a little girl. I want to tell you things. I have to tell you the truth. She was the one who wanted to divorce. She ran away from me like I was some kind of monster. She didn't even want her dowry back, one thousand eight hundred pounds. I sent it to her after the divorce.

RACHEL. You don't have to ...

LAYZER. She was hiding from me. I found the place and came to her to give some clothes to the little girl and she yelled when she saw me at the door like I came to kill her. I didn't even say a word, just seeing me — like I came to kill her. And before, before I went up there, when I was standing down in the street, I heard her laughing with the child.

RACHEL. You really don't have to ...

LAYZER. I have to tell you the truth. For me, my little girl is dead and all the doctors in the world can't help. I don't know why. For me it's darkness. You can ask all the questions you want and I'll answer you just what it was. Maybe from what I'll tell you you'll be able to figure out something I don't know.

RACHEL. No, I don't have any questions. You don't have to ...

LAYZER. Then I'll tell you something else. I have to tell you the truth. Maybe you could open the light.

RACHEL. Yes, of course, sorry. (*Stands up and turns on the light. The lamp over the table casts a strong light while, all around, it becomes darker*)

LAYZER. Something happened to me after the divorce. I'll tell you about it so you'll know everything. I don't want what happened then to happen again. That there's a husband and wife and they don't know anything about each other. That they have a living child and they hate each other so much the child is like dead. I want us, even before we get married, to be like real family, like brother and sister, without secrets and lies between them. So, I want you to know it was very bad for me after we divorced. I didn't know the world. Everything went black. I couldn't button up my pants.

RACHEL. You don't have to ...

LAYZER. They put me in a crazy house. They cured me, but inside, sometimes, it's still bad.

RACHEL. You're suffering for no reason now. I know all about it. It doesn't bother me.

LAYZER. (*Quietly*) What do you know?

RACHEL. Everything you've told me. It makes you miserable all over again and there's no need to.

LAYZER. Where do you know this from?

RACHEL. (*Begins to be afraid*) Simon . . .

LAYZER. (*Pause*) He told you . . . everything?

RACHEL. (*Pause*) Yes. (*Pause*) Maybe you'd like another cup of tea?

LAYZER. (*Looks hard at her as if he wants to get a better view of her face, which is in shadow on the other side of the table. He thrusts his head forward and his face is lit by the strong light falling on the table. Quietly*) It's not good to say something about somebody behind his back. Especially not secrets. That's two against one. That's . . . that's to laugh at somebody. That's everybody against one.

RACHEL. (*Loudly, nervously*) He is my brother, isn't he? He is my brother. (*Pause*) I'll make you another cup of tea. (*The horn is heard on the other side of the wall*)

LAYZER. (*Restless, with suppressed anger*) What's that?

RACHEL. What?

LAYZER. Somebody's playing. Like from the wall. Like a trumpet but not a trumpet.

RACHEL. (*Glad at the apparently relaxed tension*) Oh, that's my landlord, Benny Alter. He's a bit strange but he's a good person. He's very sensitive. He likes fixing shoes. It's an ideology with him. According to him, we should all learn a simple craft and go back to nature. Nice, isn't it?

LAYZER. He's not fixing shoes now, he's playing.

RACHEL. Yes. He likes playing.

LAYZER. He's rich.

RACHEL. They say his parents were very rich over there, before the War. But he's not. Most of his tenants have more than he does.

LAYZER. (*Getting at what really concerns him*) You'll forgive me if I ask you a question. They say you don't ask women such questions. How old are you? (*The playing stops*)

RACHEL. I beg your pardon?

LAYZER. How old are you?

RACHEL. (*Laughs in embarrassment*) Oh. (*Pause*) Is that so important to you?

LAYZER. I asked you something.

RACHEL. (*Stands up, trying to gain time*) They say a woman doesn't have to tell her real age. They say that, after a certain age, she shouldn't tell her real age. After all, age is ... it's a sort of prejudice, isn't it? It's really important only on passports, isn't it? What really matters is how you feel, what you still want, what you can do. Or how you look. (*Chuckles*) How old do I look?

LAYZER. I want you to tell me how old you are. I want to know what people are telling me. I'm not from here, I don't have any family here.

RACHEL. I was born in 1924.

LAYZER. How old does that make you?

RACHEL. Forty-four.

LAYZER. Forty-three. I just figured it up.

RACHEL. I was born in January. I'm almost forty-four.

LAYZER. You told me the truth now.

RACHEL. I never told you anything else.

LAYZER. Your brother told me something else.

RACHEL. He wanted to help me. He's used to worrying about me. He's the one who saved my life. It's ... (*Pause*) Maybe you'd like another cup of tea.

LAYZER. My head hurts all of a sudden.

RACHEL. Maybe you'd like another cup of tea.

LAYZER. No, thank you, don't bother.

RACHEL. It's no trouble. I like to make tea.

LAYZER. Maybe you could open the light?

RACHEL. I did, it's on.

LAYZER. Yes. (*Pause*) When will your brother return?

RACHEL. Soon, I suppose. (*Pause; in a loud and nervous voice*) You don't have a slipped disc, do you?

LAYZER. Pardon?

RACHEL. You don't have any trouble turning your head. Simon

can't. He brought a slipped disc back with him from
Israel.

LAYZER. Yes. (*He stands up; they stand facing each other*) Maybe
you could tell me where . . . where the lavatory is.

RACHEL. In the hall, the first door on the right. (*Turns to go*)
Excuse me, I have to make the bed. I just can't manage in
the morning. I'm a working woman. (*Exits*)

*Layzer goes to his coat hanging near the door, takes some aspirins
from it and swallows them. The door opens and Benny enters. The
door hides Layzer and Benny does not see him. Benny looks for the
shoes he brought back earlier, finds them, takes them, then sees
Layzer as he turns to go.*

LAYZER. Hello. I'm not from here. She — the lady of the house
will come back right away . . . hello.

BENNY. Don't hello me! There is no hello! Back to Jerusalem
with you! Saints! Prophets! Sure! Not you! The prophets
had something to say about Jerusalem. "Those that add
house to house and join field to field till there is room for
none but you to dwell in the land!" Thieves! Now you're
thieves too — and prophets, hah!

LAYZER. I'm only a guest. Looking for the toilet.

BENNY. Lies! All lies!

LAYZER. No . . . I really have to . . . I don't know . . .

BENNY. I know . . . I heard everything. Turn everything over
and examine it and open it all, just like an object in a
store . . . Peddlers! That's all you know! She's not a piece
of merchandise! (*Turns to go, comes back to Layzer*) Trumpet!
I don't play a trumpet! A horn! That's more than your
whole Jerusalem! Music! I played and now I'll fix for her . . .
(*Waves the shoes*) Now I can . . . without any lies. Take her
as much as you want. To take . . . it's nothing. You'll
throw her away later on . . . I know! So what did you take,
hah? She'll walk on my soles, not in Jerusalem! Not anywhere! On my soles!

LAYZER. I really have to . . . (*Goes out to the corridor. The doorbell
rings. Benny opens the door. Simon enters. Waves a bottle of wine.
Benny waves the shoes and exits. Rachel enters*)

SIMON. (*Looking around*) Where is he?

RACHEL. In the toilet.

SIMON. You're looking down. A bride-to-be should be looking up. In the toilet. Hmmm ... (*Pause*) You don't like him, am I right? The whole business, right? Well, listen: You'll take it. I didn't buy him a ticket here just to buy him a ticket back. I don't have enough money for that and you know it. These trips to Israel are ruining me. Only in Jerusalem can I tell myself and everybody else I'm Marks and Spenser. Understand?

RACHEL. Don't shout. We're not alone.

SIMON. What?!

RACHEL. I didn't say I don't like him.

SIMON. Huh?

RACHEL. Or that I do.

SIMON. Ah, ha. So what did you say?

RACHEL. I didn't say anything. Can I say anything to you?

SIMON. So what did you talk about so much, if I may ask?

RACHEL. I didn't say we talked a lot. But at least he let me answer his questions.

SIMON. Ah, ha. What questions, if I may ask?

RACHEL. If I sit in cafés.

SIMON. Yeah, sure.

RACHEL. I don't.

SIMON. Of course not. What else?

RACHEL. If I sleep late in the morning. If I throw out the oil from the chips. How old I am.

SIMON. How old you are! What did you say?

RACHEL. How old I am.

SIMON. How old? How old are you? You just dare tell me you told him! How old did you tell him?

RACHEL. Forty-one.

SIMON. (*With secret pleasure*) Of course. (*Laughs*) You scared me. A man can't be sure of anything nowadays. (*Suddenly*) Did you say something?

RACHEL. Do I have something to say?

SIMON. What's that supposed to mean?

RACHEL. Do I have to say something?

SIMON. That's better. (*Pause*) That's what's bothering you, right? What's getting you down. That you lied to him, right? Well, we've got a deal here so we'll just clinch it, you hear? We forget the past too fast, right? Later on, when you're his wife nice and proper, later on you can long for the marvelous days of your youth. (*A guitar is heard from the floor above*) Our homo! He plays nice. Not like Benny. A homo who chases women. Goes both ways! He stinks of tar. Where does he get that from? But he does play nice. We have something nice, too. Right? (*The guitar suddenly stops*) Oh! He never finishes. Nerves! I used to think that *Goyim* just don't have nerves. Rivers don't have nerves. But that's not right either. Just look at a river, how it keeps flowing all the time, never in a straight line. Nerves! (*Pause, half-sincerely, half-ironically*) We're in *Golus*, Rachel-Leah, we have to be redeemed. And we have to take what Eretz Israel sends us, even if it's nothing more than the dregs. (*Without a pause*) Why don't you turn on the light.

RACHEL. It's on.

SIMON. I'm cold.

RACHEL. The heat is on.

SIMON. The heat may be on, but I'm cold. (*Pause*) Something's going on here. Something's going on here. I've been standing here for five whole minutes and you haven't offered me a single cup of tea.

act 2

Same room, immediately following. Rachel and Simon are seated. In front of Simon is a cup of tea.

SIMON. Sitting, right?

RACHEL. What?

SIMON. Sitting. Sitting. There, on the seat.

RACHEL. Yes.

SIMON. You know, I like that. He's not sitting there so long 'cause he's constipated or something. No, sir. He's having a meeting. Consulting, he is. Urgent consultation. He's sitting there and thinking: Should I marry her, shouldn't I marry her. He feels at home there. When I'm in Israel, I sit there a lot too. But what a difference. When I sit in the toilet in Israel, nobody's waiting for me. Except maybe somebody else who wants to sit there. As far as Israel's concerned, I could stay in the toilet till I'm a hundred and twenty. But take him — all a man has to do is be a bridegroom, the worst one you can find, and everybody's sitting around waiting for him. The two of us — we're not doing anything, we're paralyzed, just waiting for him to get through. The whole town's waiting, the whole world's listening for him to flush the toilet.

RACHEL. Your tea's getting cold.

SIMON. What do you mean, my tea? Tea is yours.

RACHEL. You wanted a cup of tea.

SIMON. So? I always get what I want?

RACHEL. It's only a cup of tea. Look what you're making of it.

SIMON. What am I making of it? (*Repeats*) What am I making it it?

RACHEL. I don't know. You never could just take something simply.

SIMON. Ah, ha! You learned to talk. What does that mean — to take something simply?

RACHEL. I don't know. You want something very much, you go to a lot of trouble to get it and then you don't want it.

SIMON. I see. But if you want something and you get it too, that's greed. Right?

RACHEL. I'm sorry.

SIMON. For what?

RACHEL. I don't know. Nothing.

SIMON. You're beginning to pity me. Next time, you'll bring me a bride from Jerusalem. (*Layzer enters and stands in the door to the hall. Simon stands up and goes to him*) So? ... Nu? (*Layzer doesn't answer*) Fine! Silence is consent, we agreed on the match, right? All we need now is somebody to make an announcement, to write it down, to make it stick, that is. Once there was a man and a woman, human beings, and now you have a pair of horses, bride — groom! (*He pours liquor into a shotglass*) What are we waiting for! Now! Tomorrow we'll make the wedding! You'll make the wedding, that is.

LAYZER. I want to go back to Jerusalem. (*Rachel's head droops*)

SIMON. What? Oh, I see. But we didn't talk about that. I thought you two would want to stay here, get rich first like us. Besides, I can't go back to Jerusalem right now. And you wouldn't want to leave me all by myself so fast, right?

LAYZER. You didn't understand me.

SIMON. Oh, that's better. You mean someday you'll go to Jerusalem. Like me, after the holidays, like they say, right? That's good.

LAYZER. You didn't understand me.

SIMON. Not yet? Well, I have trouble understanding myself, so how should I understand somebody else, especially . . .

LAYZER. How old is the bride? (*Brief silence*) How old is the bride?

SIMON. (*Very softly*) Again, please.

LAYZER. I asked, how old is the bride?

SIMON. The bride is — twenty-two. The bride is — seventeen, twelve — the bride. You know what? To finish the deal . . . the bride is seven. My last word and I'm losing on that.

LAYZER. You laugh at me.

SIMON. Really? What do you want me to do?

LAYZER. Answer me.

SIMON. Answer me! Answer me! Hah? Didn't you ask me the same question twice already? In Jerusalem, right? You want it again? Fine. She's forty-one. If you don't believe me, just cut her open like a tree and count the rings.

LAYZER. You are not telling me the truth.

SIMON. You hear him?!

RACHEL. (*Quietly, to Layzer*) I told you. You shouldn't have asked again.

SIMON. (*To Rachel*) What "I told you." (*Pause*) What did you tell him?

RACHEL. How old I am. He shouldn't have asked you. (*Simon comes to Rachel. Layzer remains off to the side*)

SIMON. How old are you? What did you tell him?

RACHEL. The truth. How old I am. I'm forty-four. That's the truth.

SIMON. (*Very upset. Takes a snuffbox from his pocket, puts a big pinch in his nostrils; his movements are slow and exaggerated. His eyes water and his breathing is heavy with excitement, but he does not sneeze. He looks at her for a long time and then says quietly*) Why? (*Short pause*) Answer me.

RACHEL. I don't know. He asked.

SIMON. Not him—me. Why didn't you tell me you told him? You told me something else.

RACHEL. You didn't let me. I was scared of you.

SIMON. Of him you're not scared. And they were one flesh, hah? Already?! From the start?! You paid—you gave everything away even before you got the goods?!

LAYZER. I told her the whole truth about me too.

SIMON. He bought you with his truth, right? For him, it's nothing. He's used to giving the truth. That's his stock in trade. And you, you're just like a baby, a fool. You give him back his truth, the whole thing, right?

LAYZER. I want to go back to Jerusalem.

SIMON. Oh, sure. "Return unto Jerusalem, thy city in mercy." Right? Ah hah! (*Offers him the snuffbox*) And a good pinch of snuff you don't want? *A shmek tabak? A gezinten shmek?*

LAYZER. Thank you. I don't like it. Afterward, I sneeze too much.

SIMON. I don't like it either, believe me. (*Puts a pinch of snuff in his nostrils*) But I take it. Always take, so it is said. What the world gives, take, get rich. (*Inhales the snuff strongly and it burns him*) Ah! Good! What a pleasure! What the world gives! Ahhh ... (*Sneezes in Layzer's face*) Sorry.

LAYZER. It's nothing.

SIMON. Why nothing? I sneezed on you. That's nothing, right? To tell the truth, I want to do it again before you go back ... and go back if you want! (*His nose tickles and he almost sneezes*) Ah ... ah ... it won't come out. (*A horn is heard on the other side of the wall*) Listen ... he's happy. He doesn't know how to play but he plays. He's an amateur shoemaker. He sits and fixes shoes and when he gets excited—nervous, maybe?—when all of a sudden things are very good or very bad, he blows his horn like somebody dragging on a cigarette. Nice, right? Touching, even. Your heart goes out to him, right? You don't want to do anything. You just want to feel sorry for yourself and sleep, die, you want, from a kiss, right? (*His nose tickles*) Ahhh ... (*He sneezes on Layzer*) Fools! Dummies! Want honesty? Two honest block-heads! Looking for truth? Cows! (*Pounds on Benny's wall*) Shut up already! (*The playing stops. To Rachel*) You lied to him. You lied to him with your forty-four years. (*The two of them turn to him. Simon laughs*) Look. Look how the two of you turn to me as one. The miracle worker's here. He'll save you, he'll redeem you, right? Without a miracle, they'll have to part forever, the poor souls, all because of the truth. (*His nose tickles*) Ah ... ah ... sneeze already! No, of course not.

RACHEL. Enough, Simon.

SIMON. You told him the truth, right? That you're forty-four. What a great truth! An eternal truth! But in another year, it won't be so, you'll be forty-five. So it's a lie, a lie! (*Struck by pain in his back*) Ow! You want him, right? That's the truth, the whole truth, and nothing but the truth. And when you told him you're forty-four, you ruined it. It's like you told him you didn't want him and that's the biggest lie of all, right?

RACHEL. (*Stands up*) I can't.

SIMON. What can't you?

RACHEL. I can't stand this anymore.

SIMON. You don't have to stand it. Sit down! (*To Layzer*) With a fool like that in the house, you can sit! You. You want truth! Your truth's fooled you good this time, good. You go looking for truth and you fizzle out. You're sucking her blood. But you ... you're missing the chance of your life. The only woman who won't cheat you. You ... it's a real *mitzvah* to cheat you. You're losing the only woman even you could cheat, you poor, dumb asshole!

LAYZER. It's not because of the years.

SIMON. (*Doesn't hear him*) We lied to you. Next to your truth, our lie is ... it's a miserable kid with dreams. Ask the matriarch Sarah, didn't she lie? And Rebecca, she did some lying. Leah and little Rachel, a few lies there. Go ask all of them why they lied. How many lies they have! The whole Jewish people came from those lies, you, her, me. Sometimes, telling a lie is like begging. And accepting a lie like that, without saying anything, is like giving charity in secret. Yes, charity saves us from death, right? You're the one who goes seeking charity and truth, right? You monster! (*His nose tickles*) Ah ... ah ... (*Sneezes into the air*) Dammit! Where are you? I wasted that one. The whole thing. Who am I talking to? Why am I talking? Can somebody tell me?

LAYZER. (*Declaring*) You believe that I played football in front of my father on Rosh Ha-Shanah, which was for him a holy day and for him to play football on Rosh Ha-Shanah was a sin he would have been killed for?

SIMON. What's that supposed to be?

LAYZER. I asked you something — if you believed that I played football on Rosh Ha-Shanah. You can answer me, no?

SIMON. No, we can't.

LAYZER. I'll answer you. I did play. Because of my friends. My friends dragged me. I didn't want to, I told them that my father might pass by the field on his way to *shul* but they dragged me. They said I was a coward, a traitor. They forced me, they made a big circle around me and begged and pleaded and I went with them and played football on Rosh Ha-Shanah.

SIMON. I must be going crazy.

LAYZER. And my father did pass by on his way to *shul* and he did see. But I didn't know that he saw. When a man is playing with his friends, he doesn't see anything. What do you think he said at night when he came back from *shul*? (*Repeats*) What do you think he said at night when he came back?

SIMON. We don't think anything.

LAYZER. He didn't say a thing. He ... (*He takes off his suit coat, rolls up his shirtsleeves and his trouser cuffs and begins playing like a goalkeeper in a football game, pretending to catch balls, jumping to the side with open arms, spread wide, etc.*) He acted like a goalkeeper, he did what I was doing when I played football on his holy day in front of his eyes, that's what he did to me. That! (*Again he jumps up and stretches out his arms*)

SIMON. (*To Rachel*) Make him stop! Where does he think he is?!

RACHEL. (*Stops him*) Leave him alone.

LAYZER. And my mother didn't understand what was happening. All of a sudden, my father, a sixty-year-old man, is acting like a *mishuggana*. She begged him he should stop, she wept, she pulled her hair. The house was broken into pieces. That's what he did to me, that's how he told me. Like that! (*Again, he pretends to catch a ball in his belly, crouches over and groans*) My friends dragged me to the game, they forgot me in a minute — and my father was a broken man.

SIMON. (*Quietly, as if to himself*) You're crazy.

LAYZER. (*After a moment*) I was crazy. Now I'm not.

SIMON. All right, all right, I'm crazy now. Me. What do you mean by this . . . this performance here? What?

LAYZER. (*To Rachel*) I wanted to tell you why I don't want — why I want to go back. I don't want you to think it's because of your years I don't want you. There's another reason. Friends are like alcohol — you drink and you're happy and warm and later you throw up and your head is clear. Friends are like a drum — noise and joy and inside there's nothing. Friends are like a café — you talk nicenice, and under the table they fight with each other, they steal and men put their hands on a woman's leg who isn't their wife and they shed blood. Friends drag you only for their pleasure, smoke you like a cigarette, crush you, put you out, and forget you. Family is another thing. Family is like a candle and a flame.

SIMON. What's this got to do with anything, for God's sake?

LAYZER. You're not family for me. You don't tell me the truth.

SIMON. (*Grabs Rachel*) She, this fool here, she gave you the truth.

LAYZER. That's not enough. I thought about that a lot. (*To Simon*) You didn't tell me the truth, and you're brother and sister. I know what that is, brother and sister. You can't separate them. You're family, I'm outside.

SIMON. You rotten two-bit saint, you! You forced her to tell you the truth about herself and then you come and say that's not enough for you?! (*In his fury, he pushes Rachel into Layzer's arms*)

LAYZER. (*To Rachel*) It wasn't to test you that I asked you. It was to test the truth that I asked you. I'm all alone here, I don't know the streets, I don't have any relatives here, I don't have anybody here to say hello to. I was sick, I was crazy, as your brother said, and I haven't got my strength back yet. And I don't want to be crazy again. That's the one thing in the world I don't want. So I've got to be careful. So I must not stay here with you in this situation. I've got to go back to Jerusalem.

SIMON. Go back! Go! Get married there to ... your papa! Keep it in the family! (*Approaches Layzer, meanwhile unwittingly pushing him toward Rachel*) Go back! Saved from the desert, from boils, from cholera, from frogs. Saved from the biggest fool in the world, from a purebred moron with a pedigree, from ... from a dinosaur! The Messiah's jackass! A man who keeps ... (*To Layzer*) who keeps himself to himself, a piece of candle with a flame! Stay with your damn family! (*Pushing Rachel back*) You want a family? Go make yourself a family. Go on, make one. You won't get it readymade. No. (*His nose tickles*) Ah ... ah ... (*Sneezes*) Enough already! Go back, dammit! Bug off! Get out!

LAYZER. I need money for a ticket. (*Short silence*)

SIMON. What did you say?

LAYZER. I need money for a ticket home.

SIMON. I need? You need?! You dare?!

LAYZER. I didn't come on my own. You brought me here.

SIMON. Oh boy! Dammit! An old spoiled brat! You old *nebbikh*! Your wife runs away from you by the skin of her teeth. I understand her, I would have left you too but I would even have left you my teeth just ...

LAYZER. You don't have to tell me that. I told you myself.

SIMON. So what? A person walks around the street showing everybody his stinking wounds and that makes him pure and clean. Right? You got a free trip to England. On me!

LAYZER. I didn't want England.

SIMON. Lucky for England.

LAYZER. You brought me here with lies, you have to send me back.

SIMON. Listen to me: I'm not going to give you a penny to get back. But that's not all. I'm also going to make you pay me back every penny I paid to bring you here. And that's not all either. I'm also going to make you pay damages for the torment and shame you've caused my sister and me. You're guilty of breach of promise. Tell the judge you've been cheated, a woman didn't tell her real age. "They cheated me."

LAYZER. She told me the truth. You didn't. Here's the cheat. I'm sure there are more lies and that there will be more lies — that's the point.

RACHEL. (*Suddenly, from her corner*) It's true what he says. There are more lies, a lot more lies. So many more lies that he'd be better off getting out of here with the shirt on his back. This apartment, for instance, isn't mine. And you're not a successful agent. And I borrow money from Benny. Some successful agent you are!

SIMON. What! Stop it!

RACHEL. And I'm not a forty-four-year-old virgin. Maybe that's fine for a somebody from Jerusalem. Maybe he'll think I've been keeping myself for him. I haven't. I'm an old maid of forty-four. I'm an old maid full of sin and shame and forty-four.

SIMON. Stop it!

RACHEL. (*Brings a straw laundry basket to the table, folds the laundry*) I've had men and I lived with them without benefit of clergy, as they say. Oh, and I've loved them, loved them a lot. And enjoyed them, enjoyed, yes, enjoyed. They cheated me and left me, all of them, lots of them, two is like a hundred, more than a hundred. And in the rain. It was raining and they left. I didn't get wet, they did — but that's even worse, isn't it?

SIMON. You're going crazy. You caught it from him.

RACHEL. Of course they had good reasons. Men don't just

walk out on a woman who's devoted to them like a dog. Not in the rain. Maybe I've got bad breath, maybe that's why.

SIMON. You're humiliating yourself. Why? Why?

RACHEL. I want him to leave too. He hasn't lived with me yet and hasn't cheated me. So let him at least leave. I haven't enjoyed him yet but he's the last candidate, and the last candidate — even if he's an idiot — is the one who takes your soul. He didn't only take it, he sucked it out of me. There's nothing left, nothing. I gave him everything.

SIMON. Stop! Stop!

RACHEL. That's why he came. To look for lies. That's it. Let him take them and go. I don't have anything left. How many lies can I collect? Even me? There's a limit, isn't there? If I should remember any more lies, I'll send them to him in Jerusalem, I promise. Now let him go. He said he wants to go. (*To Layzer*) Why don't you go? (*Approaches him*) And I do sit in cafés. In three cafés at the same time. And I stay in bed till noon, sometimes even till night. I eat my lunch in bed. And I throw out all the oil from the chips. I fry a little bit of chips in a great big pot full to the brim with oil and then I throw it all away, while the oil's still hot. That makes a sound like this ... ssss! ssss! I love that sound. And I may even smoke a pipe all of a sudden. (*Goes back to the laundry basket*)

SIMON. (*Grabs her hand, tries to calm her*) He's not worth it. Stop this. This is me talking to you, me, Simon.

RACHEL. He won't go, only with money. With me, it works only with money. With the others, I had to pay them to stay. Him I have to pay to go. (*Takes her purse from the cabinet, pours its contents on the table*) That's all I have! My whole salary! If that won't get him to Jerusalem, let him go to Gibraltar! Just let him get out already!

SIMON. (*Puts his hands on the money*) You won't give him a penny!

RACHEL. (*To Layzer*) Take it! Take it! Lies and money, that's all I've got. I give it all to you.

SIMON. As long as I'm here, you won't give him anything.

RACHEL. (*To Simon*) Don't be here! Get out along with him.

(*Takes his hands off the money*)

SIMON. You never talked to me like that before.

RACHEL. Get your hands off my money. You hear?! And get your hands off my soul. You hear?! I work myself to death over my stupid work, as you call it, for this money. Get your hands off it! You come here to see me every single day, every day. Because you've got nothing to do by yourself and then you tell me what to love and what not to love, what to do and what's stupid. I'm sick and tired of you. Don't come here and don't tell me anything. You don't have the right. I enjoyed and you didn't. Oh, how I enjoyed!

SIMON. Never! Never!

RACHEL. (*Folding laundry*) Let them both take the money, let them both do what they want. Let them leave me in peace. I have my own room and I have my own basket full of laundry to iron. I can't go to work not looking tip-top, I just can't.

BENNY. (*Bursts in and gives Rachel a bundle of money*) For his ticket! I heard ... Gibraltar ... not far enough! Jerusalem! (*Exits. Rachel looks at the money in her hand, bursts into quiet, full weeping. She puts the money on the counter, picks up the basket and, unwittingly, turns with it toward Layzer. Also unwittingly, he steps toward her. They stand opposite one another*)

SIMON. We'll give him the money, not you — me, Benny and me, the two of us together. I was wrong. It was crazy. You can't dream dreams, right? We'll give him twice as much, just so he'll go. He's not worth your little finger. Him and all his Jerusalem! Not worth a single tear of yours! (*Turns to them, sees them, falls silent*)

RACHEL. (*To Layzer*) What do you want from me?

LAYZER. If you'll allow me ... you're dragging that basket ... (*Grabs the end of the basket from her hands*)

RACHEL. What don't you like about it?

LAYZER. No. I do like it, very much, the basket. In Jerusalem, they do the laundry in heavy copper basins and, afterward, they drag the dry laundry around in copper basins. They're scared of the smallest little thing that's new, like it's a cross or something. It's nice that you keep the dry laundry in a straw basket.

RACHEL. So?

LAYZER. Nothing bad. The other way around. I already told you, that's good. If you'll allow me, I'll now help you drag that basket wherever you want. I want to give you a hand.

RACHEL. You'll carry the basket for me and meanwhile you'll grope around in the laundry to see if I do it clean enough, as they do in Jerusalem. And then you'll say you don't want me because I don't know how to do the wash. (*Pulls the basket out of his hands*)

LAYZER. (*Grabs the basket and pulls it to him*) No. I won't grope around anymore. I understood a lot of things from what you said and also from what you didn't say and from the opposite of what you said. Now I'm sure you're clean. Your soul is clean.

RACHEL. (*Pulls the basket back to her*) You're torturing me. You take and you throw away and you take again. Even a ball has limits, doesn't it?

LAYZER. (*Pulls the basket back to him. They fight over the basket*) I'm not scared that you had love affairs. And that they cheated you and left you — I'm really not scared of that. The other way around, the disgrace is on their heads. I was only scared of the lies. Now you don't have anything to lie about anymore, you opened up everything. And now I know you're even more alone than I thought. I too am more alone than I think. And I tell you I regret what I said before, that I want to go back. And I ask you to agree that the two of us, you and me, should get married. (*Short silence. She lets go of the basket. The laundry spills out, the basket remains in Layzer's hands*)

RACHEL. I'll make a cup of tea. (*After a moment, repeats*) I'll make a cup of tea. (*Goes to the kitchenette. Layzer gathers up the laundry and puts it in the basket. Simon, stunned and mute, stands opposite Rachel, who brings a tray with two cups of tea to the table. Rachel looks at Simon*) I'll make you a cup of tea, too. (*After a moment*) You didn't ask for one. (*Simon turns aside; Rachel and Layzer sit down. Rachel says, to Layzer*) Drink. It's not hot.

LAYZER. You eat the chocolates.

RACHEL. I don't want any right now.

LAYZER. All right. You don't have to. (*Drinks. Confused, Simon slowly begins pacing around the table. Suddenly, Layzer says to Rachel, in a loud voice*) I'll tell you something nice. In the old neighborhoods of Jerusalem, they dry the laundry on ropes stretched on little wheels between the balconies. On Thursday, you almost can't see the sky because of so much laundry. You mainly see white laundry. There, they wear black and white a lot and they wash the white more.

SIMON. (*Stops across from Layzer and suddenly asks a seemingly idle question*) You like music?

LAYZER. Pardon?

SIMON. Do you like music?

LAYZER. Why do you ask?

SIMON. Why? Just because. I like to know. I'm a modern man, I collect information, in all areas.

LAYZER. Sometimes.

SIMON. Like that? Fine. Which?

LAYZER. Pardon?

SIMON. Which kind of music do you like?

LAYZER. Marches.

SIMON. Marches?

RACHEL. (*To Simon*) Marches.

LAYZER. Yes.

SIMON. How about that! That's interesting, very interesting. That's a special taste. Military ones or funeral ones?

LAYZER. I'm not an expert. Marches. Why do you ask?

SIMON. Why did I ask? You won't believe this, but that's just exactly what she likes. A match made in heaven! I asked just like that, for no good reason, sort of groping blindly and—bingo!—I hit the nail right on the head. You see this cabinet? It's full of records, nothing but marches! She can't listen to any other music, just marches. Amazing! (*Remains standing on the side, a little apart*)

LAYZER. (*To Rachel*) I'll go on with what I started telling you, if you want.

RACHEL. Yes, of course.

LAYZER. You remember Leah-Dvora Villman?

RACHEL. With the wart on the end of her nose.

LAYZER. Everybody remembers that.

RACHEL. (*After a short pause*) What did you want to tell me about her? You started telling me about the laundry on the lines.

LAYZER. It's all connected. When she was young, she used the clotheslines to exchange secret love letters with Nakhman Friedman of Friedman and Sons. And when they proposed important matches to him, he refused them.

SIMON. (*As before, stopping across from Layzer and suddenly asking*) Does she buy journals?

LAYZER. Who?

SIMON. Her ... whatshername? Leah-Hannah, Hannah-Leah, Vissel-Pissel, her ...

LAYZER. Leah-Dvora Villman.

SIMON. Yeah, that's the one, Hannah-Dvora. How could I forget? Does she buy journals?

LAYZER. You're making fun of her. She doesn't have any money, she doesn't have any time and she doesn't have a head for any journals. She doesn't have time to pick up her head and see if there are stars in the sky. She doesn't need all those things. She has children. (*To Rachel*) Do you?

SIMON. Does she what?

LAYZER. You buy journals?

SIMON. Not just journals, medical journals. They're seven times more expensive than plain journals. And the most important thing is she doesn't understand anything in them. But she loves them. And she also buys expensive tickets to concerts. There are cheap ones and there are expensive ones and she buys the expensive ones. She goes without meat and fish but not without that. And one more thing — she looks for stars in the sky. She stands at the window and all of a sudden she says: Look, there are stars! That doesn't cost money but it is a luxury and it's stupid. One star doesn't say to another: Look, there's Rachel!

LAYZER. (*To Rachel*) I asked you.

RACHEL. I always wanted to be a doctor but I didn't make it. I love medicine.

LAYZER. (*Takes a document out of his wallet, spreads it out on the table in front of Rachel*) Read that, please.

SIMON. What is it, if I may ask? (*Reaches for the document*)

LAYZER. I'm talking to her. (*To Rachel*) Please, it's yours.

RACHEL. You tell me what's written there, that's good enough for me.

LAYZER. It authorizes me to collect contributions for the old orphanage in Jerusalem, if I need. (*Stunned, Simon opens his mouth to say something but doesn't; he takes a step back*)

RACHEL. Why do you show me this?

LAYZER. I want you to learn from this that I will work hard to support you. And if I'll succeed and I'll have a lot, you'll also be able to buy things you want, like those journals and I don't know what other things you like. But only from what money we'll have, we won't make debts. Debts are lies.

SIMON. (*Half to Layzer, half to himself*) So you're also an agent for an orphanage?!

LAYZER. (*To Rachel*) I don't mean for that to be my profession. Only for a start. Only for my family. They need donations. They eat from tin plates. And they don't have sheets. They cover themselves with old army blankets. Maybe they're warm and maybe they sleep well and don't feel that those blankets itch. But that's not enough for children and especially not for orphans.

RACHEL. That's right and it's nice that you pay attention to such things.

LAYZER. They'll give me fifty percent.

SIMON. What?!

LAYZER. That's the most you can get. Others give less. But they're poor. It's an old orphanage so they don't have a choice and they have to give more.

SIMON. Did you hear that? Fifty percent of the donations to those orphans with tin blankets ... oh, excuse me — tin plates and army blankets!

LAYZER. It won't come out to very much, fifty percent of donations to orphans. People only give small change for orphans. It's not like a museum. These days nobody wants to work in it. (*Pause*) Should I go on?

RACHEL. What?

LAYZER. With what I started telling you.

RACHEL. Yes, of course.

LAYZER. Well, I told you that Nakhman Friedman exchanged letters with Leah-Dvora Villman and refused all the matches they proposed to him. That's where I got to. Now I'll go on. Until they made him tell why. Until they made him tell that he wanted her. His family made such a fuss. She was a poor girl and wasn't famous for anything special. She couldn't do beautiful embroidery and she didn't have an especially kind heart. There are women who are famous for that. (*Simon approaches and stands opposite him; Layzer stops talking*)

SIMON. Go on, go on. It's a pleasure to listen, a joy to see. The bridegroom is telling the bride tales of the old days. And what tales! What a headache! All of a sudden I have two heads and both of them ache.

LAYZER. I have an aspirin. (*Pulls it out of his pocket*) You can take three at one time.

SIMON. You carry aspirin in your pocket, right? (*To Rachel*) If you've got a husband with aspirin, you don't have anything to worry about anymore. You'll always have aspirin. (*To Layzer*) Three, right? But I only have two heads.

LAYZER. Take two aspirins.

SIMON. Fine. No thanks. I just remembered something much better for headache. Right away ... right away ... you sit there, the two of you, bride and groom sitting at the table, eating golden soup. Don't worry, Rachel, I'll come back. (*Exits to the kitchenette*)

LAYZER. Should I go on?

RACHEL. Yes, of course.

LAYZER. But in the end his parents — of Moshe-Haim Friedman and Sons — they agreed.

RACHEL. But you said her name was Villman, didn't you?

LAYZER. Yes. Because, in the end, nothing came out of it. Because of her. They agreed to the wedding and they were already preparing for it. But then she announced she wouldn't agree to cut her hair before the wedding, like they do there. She had beautiful braids — that's what they say. When she would come down the stairs, her braids would slide along behind her on the steps — that's what they say. All Jerusalem was upset when they heard. But she was stubborn. She was from a poor family and had that wart on the end of her nose. They say he wrote her one last letter and sent it on the clothesline, that she loves her hair more than she loves him.

RACHEL. That's awful.

LAYZER. Nakhman Friedman right away married Rachel Gvirtsman. And her—only Shmuel-Wolf, the deaf-mute, would agree to marry her. He was a mute and he wasn't young either. He didn't ask her to cut off her braids. She herself wanted it.

RACHEL. A woman musn't be stubborn about her long hair because, in the end, she doesn't have hair and she doesn't have anything else, does she? That's what you mean?

LAYZER. No. She really had a good life with Shmuel-Wolf. They had eight children, all of them pretty. When he was killed by shooting from David's Tower, little Ephraim was only two months old. She raised him and all the rest of them healthy and sound on a very small pension, on bread and oil and onions.

SIMON. (*Enters from the kitchenette; slices of potato on his brow held by a wet rag tied around his head; pours himself some tea, says quietly*) What a life! Eight children and so many onions to go with them! (*Rachel bursts out laughing. Layzer doesn't see her laughing, he is looking at Simon. Simon points to the plaster on his head*) A wet rag with potato slices. You know it, right? Potatoes draw out the headache, a Jerusalem remedy, right? No worse than aspirin and cheaper to boot. You make chips with it afterward. It's a poor city, Jerusalem. Mustn't be ashamed of poverty. Oh no—something to be really proud of! A pleasure!

LAYZER. You're making fun of me. You're making fun of the old women of Jerusalem. You're making fun of my mother. You're ... (*Hears and sees Rachel laughing*) You're laughing ... (*Rachel goes on laughing uncontrollably*)

SIMON. (*Only now does he notice Rachel laughing; he too bursts out laughing*) Did you hear how he said: You're laughing? Like: You're dirty, you ... (*To Layzer*) Of course she's laughing, laughing.

LAYZER. (*To Rachel*) You're laughing along with him.

SIMON. (*To Rachel, almost drunk with laughter*) How he said that! Of course. When you told him how they cheated you and left you, when you lowered yourself, you touched his heart. That's how he'd always want you, a hunted creature, just like him. Then your soul would be pure and clean for him. The only luxury he'd let you have — a mole on the end of your nose.

RACHEL. (*Tries to stop laughing*) I can't ... I just can't stop ...

SIMON. Of course you can't. We have to laugh. That's our pleasure. That's our taste. That's our fate. Ten years drop off you when you laugh. Just for that the whole thing was worth it.

LAYZER. (*To Simon*) You don't want me.

SIMON. (*To Layzer*) I don't want you? (*To Rachel, with a little laugh*) He does have a charm if you want, right?

LAYZER. Nothing will help. The two of you really don't want me. The two of you really don't need me. I can never be your family, not me. (*Stands up, takes his coat. Rachel is amazed, stands up too, has stopped laughing. Layzer puts on his coat and hat*) But you did help me decide an important question. Before it was dark and I remembered my little girl. I'm going to start saving for an apartment for my daughter. Her mother won't let me see her and maybe for a long time she won't know I'm alive. But when she'll grow up she'll find somebody proper and she'll want a family, she'll find a house ready that I build for her. She'll need me in the end. Goodbye. (*Exits. Rachel sinks down, weeps silently*)

SIMON. (*With forced joy*) What do you say about that? He throws himself out. Without a ticket. Net profit! All of a sudden the room is full of air. And we learned a lesson. Education is important, right? (*Falls silent; his face is tired and worn. The doorbell rings. Brief silence. Another ring. Rachel stands up and opens the door*)

BENNY. (*Standing in the doorway, gives Rachel the shoes he has fixed*) Your shoes ... I took ... You weren't ... better than new now. All your shoes — I'll always fix them. Be sick as much as you need — I'll bring you everything. You deserve it! (*Sees Simon, looks at the potato plaster on his brow*)

SIMON. (*To Benny*) What are you looking at? (*To Rachel*) He's looking at me! (*Puts his hand to his brow*) Potatoes. Why not? You tell me. You're an anarchist, you fix shoes, you blow the horn — why shouldn't I walk around with pieces of potato on my head, a sort of crown? You're not saying anything against me now. I'm a nothing, but I do have a sister, a treasure. Yes, I do have a little sister and that's why I have pieces of potato on my forehead. Why not? They feel nice on my head. Juicy and soft. They suck up all the poison. They make a nice little noise, suck, suck. (*Into Benny's face*) Suck-suck, suck-suck . . .

BENNY. You're too smart for your own good! You jackass! (*Exits*)

SIMON. (*Calling after him*) Suck-suck! (*A horn is heard, louder and fuller than it was before. Rachel pours tea*) He has charm too, right? If you want. All the charming people, me too, we all come to you. Difficult people, right? (*Short silence*) It's all because of Eretz Israel. They get up in the morning happy there. What have they got to be happy about? That white light of theirs — it's like snow. It drove me crazy, Eretz Israel. When I met him, I decided to bring you a piece of that happy cake, a piece of light. Well, there you are! (*Takes the potato plaster off his forehead, puts it in pieces in front of her*) You remember the snow? Their light . . . sunlight — but snow. (*Short silence and then suddenly, loud and angry*) You deserve more, you hear me?! Nothing will help you! You deserve more! If you don't get it, you don't get it, but I won't let them take from you what you deserve! (*He slumps but remains standing where he is. Rachel stands up and slowly clears the empty cups off the table, takes them into the kitchenette. A horn is heard*)

hillel mitelpunkt

buba

TRANSLATED FROM THE HEBREW
BY MICHAEL TAUB

characters

BUBA: about forty

RACHEL: seventeen

ELIE: about thirty

ROBBY: about fifty

YOZHI: about twenty-five

setting

At stage left is a steakhouse: a short wooden counter with two high stools. At stage right is a storage room in a garage: a bench and a water hose. Center stage is Buba's shack: a bed, another mattress under it, two stools, a small thermos on a wooden box, a tool box. In the yard surrounding the shack: small wooden boxes used as chairs, a motorcycle.

scene 1

Night. Buba's at the steakhouse counter, eating a hamburger and french fries from a paper plate. He's eating the fries with deliberate slow motion. Rachel bursts in. She's wearing a tight, light sweater and a skirt, and has a long run in one of her stockings. She's carrying a big tape player and a large canvas bag on her shoulder. She looks around. No one there but Buba.

RACHEL. A dump. A half hour in the rain and I end up in a dump. Anyone here?

BUBA. In the kitchen. They're closing soon.

RACHEL. Closing already? Worse dump than I thought.

BUBA. A salad, maybe they'll make you a salad.

RACHEL. I'm not about to stuff myself with junk.

BUBA. Want me to ask?

RACHEL. At least it's warm here. (*Silence*) Tell me about salad. It's all junk.

BUBA. This is a good place.

RACHEL. Wouldn't close so early if it was.

BUBA. Cars don't stop here no more at night. People now take the main highway.

RACHEL. This isn't the main highway?

BUBA. What?

RACHEL. (*Goes to the door, looks outside*) Almost froze my ass and it's not even the main highway. The jerk could have dumped me in some orange grove.

BUBA. The driver?

RACHEL. Got fed up with him.

BUBA. He told you this was the main highway?

RACHEL. That's what he said. You think I believe anyone? (*Silence*) How far from here to Ramle?

BUBA. It's not good to travel like this at night. You never know what goes on in the driver's mind.

RACHEL. I know, my sister married one.

BUBA. They ... not all drivers are like that.

RACHEL. This one, he kept going until I grabbed the wheel. A truck to boot. He was carrying chickens! They kept jumping up and down. What salads they serve here?

BUBA. (*Offers her his plate*) You can eat this. I'm not hungry.

RACHEL. Then why did you order?

BUBA. What?

RACHEL. (*Splits the bun and looks inside*) Not even enough for a baby. (*Eats in a crude manner. Silence. He looks at her tape player, examines it closely. She pulls it away from him*)

BUBA. Just wanted to look at it. Radio too?

RACHEL. Yeah ... (*Eating*) Japanese.

BUBA. Some day I'll buy one just like it.

RACHEL. The jerk dumped me a half-hour's walk from here and said it was Ramle.

BUBA. You didn't look out the window? There are no houses.

RACHEL. What window? It was raining. (*Silence*) How should I know they had houses in Ramle? Anyway, I'm better off like this than with him. I saw right away he was a suspicious character. Right away.

BUBA. Maybe they have some pies left.

RACHEL. I'm not starving. Got a cigarette? (*Buba offers her a cigarette; she takes it*)

BUBA. Always buy enough to give my friends at the garage.

RACHEL. I figured you worked in a garage.

BUBA. Where they clean buses. I do almost half my work at night. People want to be with their families, so the boss pays me more. It's a good place.

RACHEL. What pies they have here anyway?

BUBA. I can ask in the kitchen.

RACHEL. Make sure it's not junk.

BUBA. They know me here. (*Goes to the kitchen. Rachel is alone: she removes a shoe, pulls up her stocking, puts on the shoe, notices cigarette packs on the counter, takes a few cigarettes, puts them in her bag. Looks towards the kitchen*)

BUBA. (*Returns*) They want us to leave. They're closing.

RACHEL. They can keep their rotten pies.

BUBA. For lunch it's OK here. Workers from the garage and the factory come here. Sometimes the owners and I, we drink beer together, like friends.

RACHEL. The son of a bitch got me all confused. I don't even know where I am.

BUBA. You have family in Ramle?

RACHEL. I'm going to Ramle for a disco competition. It starts in four days.

BUBA. In Ramle?

RACHEL. Too crowded to practice at home. My parents drive me crazy. People stick their noses into everything. Just gossip all the time. Can't take it no more.

BUBA. You win a cup?

RACHEL. What's that?

BUBA. At the competition.

RACHEL. They give you a free flight. The winner can make an international career from it. Last year it was a guy from Bat-Yam, his picture was in the papers, I think he was a house painter, they sent him straight to an international competition in England. (*Lights up another cigarette*) My hair smells awful. This truck, with chickens in the back, picked me up first. (*Silence*)

BUBA. You have . . . a place to stay in Ramle?

RACHEL. I manage. I meet people. You got a car?

BUBA. Yes. My friend has a car. If I want we meet a certain time and drive to the garage together.

RACHEL. Aha .

BUBA. I don't live far from here.

RACHEL. This friend of yours, he lives with you?

BUBA. What? No. It's a small place. I fixed it up. I got everything I need there.

RACHEL. My dream.

BUBA. I like to live alone.

RACHEL. (*Collecting her things*) How far is it?

BUBA. What?

RACHEL. Your place. I've had it with hitch-hiking at night.

BUBA. A short walk on the highway, then over a hill.

RACHEL. OK (*Puts a cigarette pack in her bag, shouts in the direction of the kitchen*) Your food is junk! (*They leave*)

scene 2

The shack. Dark. Elie lies on the bed. Buba and Rachel are heard outside. He gets up, hides behind the door. Enter Rachel. He jumps on her, knocks her down. She screams. Brief scuffle. Enter Buba. He tries to separate them.

BUBA. Elie, Elie, enough ... (*Rachel frees herself, runs out*) Wait. This is my brother ... don't go ...

RACHEL. You said you live alone.

BUBA. This is my brother, Elie.

ELIE. Who?

BUBA. I thought you were in Haifa.

ELIE. (*Walks to the door. Buba stops him*) Buba, who is this?

BUBA. Elie, sit down. She's a dancer. She came to the steakhouse where I usually eat. I told her not to hitchhike at night.

ELIE. It's Robby, he sent her here.

BUBA. No. She hitchhiked in a truck with chickens. (*Elie smells her hair*)

RACHEL. I'll scratch you ... I'm not afraid!

ELIE. Tell us, did Robby send you here? He knows I'm here?!

RACHEL. What Robby?! Never heard of him! (*To Buba*) You didn't say someone was here.

BUBA. This is my brother Elie.

RACHEL. You said nothing about a brother to me!

BUBA. He was in Haifa. He travels a lot.

RACHEL. You told me something else.

BUBA. This is my shack, really.

RACHEL. Is this it?

BUBA. And the yard.

RACHEL. Ah. (*Silence*) If I knew I wouldn't climb the hill. I saw too many rat holes in my life. (*Suddenly Elie jumps on her, grabs her hair and smells it. She screams, scratches him. He lets go*)

ELIE. She stinks. It's the chickens.

BUBA. I told you, she hitchhiked.

RACHEL. If he's going to be like this, I'm leaving.

BUBA. Elie, come sit down. Sit down. (*Elie goes to the door, looks out*) Elie, sit. I'd notice if someone followed us. (*Elie closes the door, sits down*) I didn't know you'd be here.

ELIE. I looked for you at work first.

BUBA. Robby could have seen you there.

ELIE. I only had enough money for the bus. The little bitch took everything. A week ago I took her to a hotel in Haifa. When I get there, not even a letter for me. Lots of rich Arabs from the West Bank stay there.

BUBA. Must be her husband, because of the kids. (*To Rachel*) She left them with his parents and ran away with Elie. You know, soccer fans call him "Handsome Elie." (*Silence*) I'll make some tea.

RACHEL. I don't see where I can sleep.

ELIE. In a hotel.

RACHEL. Your brother brought me here. (*To Buba*) Is this your place or not? (*Buba pulls out the mattress*) If I knew ...

ELIE. Now you do.

BUBA. Elie, how's your foot! (*Takes off Elie's shoe*) Don't worry, Robby doesn't know. Nobody knows you're here. (*Rubs Elie's foot*)

ELIE. She left me broke. Buba, if I get my hands on her

BUBA. How is it now? Hurts?

ELIE. I tell you, she'll pay for everything.

BUBA. The team, they say anything to you?

ELIE. They got a goalie from the juniors. A kid.

BUBA. But you're the goalie. Elie had a motorcycle accident.

RACHEL. I wouldn't ride one if they paid me.

ELIE. They said: "We looked for you six months." I ask you, where did they look? Hospitals? (*Pause*) The kid, his father is with the team's management.

BUBA. Not fair. Three years ago you helped them make it into the major league.

RACHEL. Nice guys finish last. My father, he worked in a factory eight years. When they kicked him out, they gave him a watch as a present. It broke after a week. He got so mad he threw it away.

ELIE. When are you leaving?

RACHEL. In the morning. Don't worry. This is no place for me.

BUBA. One year Elie was an All-Star. I still have the newspaper somewhere. Four years ago Jaffa made you an offer, right, Elie? They offered Elie a partnership in a milkbar.

ELIE. They said, come next month for a physical checkup. I didn't go for the milkbar offer. So they give me a physical ... I said it's a good thing it's winter or you'd make me take off my shirt and check for needle marks. (*Rachel plays a tape, dances*)

ELIE. Did Robby talk to you?

BUBA. What? Asked about you once. Otherwise when he sees me, says hello, that's all.

ELIE. I have no money for them. The bitch took everything I had. (*Silence*) Robby should find a better location for his games and toys in the amusement park. You'll see, he'll make a lot of money.

BUBA. Now lie down. Keep your foot up. (*Prepares tea*) One day Robby brought his brothers with him — had problems with someone in the garage. I was working that night.

ELIE. All his brothers are in America. (*Silence*) It turns out she's a whore.

BUBA. Elie, maybe she did it for the kids? Who knows?

ELIE. (*To Buba*) Your tape?

BUBA. She needs to practice. For the Disco Competition in Ramle.

ELIE. This is not Ramle.

RACHEL. Last year my friend Sofie wanted to compete but didn't even get there. Her brothers followed her and dragged her home.

ELIE. You go home, too. Anyway, it's fixed.

RACHEL. If it is why are so many people competing? They even get dancers from clubs in Tel Aviv. (*To Buba*) If I were you I'd put a lock on the door. I don't like surprises.

ELIE. (*To Buba*) Tomorrow I'm going to Jaffa. Maybe they'll make me another offer. (*Silence*) My left foot doesn't feel right yet.

BUBA. Doesn't matter. You're still their best goalie.

ELIE. I have a friend there. Maybe I'll stay with him a few days.

BUBA. That's good, very good — also because of Robby.

ELIE. The jerk doesn't scare me. The bitch took everything. A

guy from the main bus station owes me some money. I'll
see if I can find him. (*Buba takes out his wallet, hands him a
few bills*)

ELIE. I'll give it back next week.

RACHEL. (*On the bed, taking off her shoes*) Your friend, what time
does he come in the morning?

BUBA. I wait for him on the main road. Seven o'clock.

RACHEL. Wake me up then.

BUBA. (*Pulls out the mattress, spreads out the folded blanket*) You
know, someone promised to give me the headlight covers
for the bike tomorrow.

ELIE. Great.

BUBA. (*To Elie*) If it's too cold, put my coat over the blanket.

ELIE. I'll be all right.

BUBA. I'm going to do some work on the bike. (*Elie takes off his
clothes and boots, lies down on the mattress and covers up*) See the
flashlight and the canvas cover outside? This way I can
work at night even in winter. The most I need is a month
to finish it. (*Silence*) You want the coat on top?

ELIE. It's all right.

BUBA. Good. (*Leaves. Silence*)

ELIE. (*Lights up*) You always sleep with your clothes on?

RACHEL. I'll buy new ones anyway.

ELIE. In the meantime you'll stink.

RACHEL. Enough your brother worries about me.

ELIE. Sure, he'll sleep on the floor.

RACHEL. Give him the mattress. Got a cigarette?

ELIE. You think they're waiting for you there with a prize?

RACHEL. You didn't see me dance.

ELIE. I did.

RACHEL. Not the same as the show.

ELIE. You have a name?

RACHEL. Rachel.

ELIE. Make sure you don't step on me in the morning. I don't
have to be in Jaffa until noon. (*Puts out the cigarette, goes to
sleep*)

scene 3

Evening. Storage room at the garage. Buba takes off his rubber gloves, puts them on a shelf. Enter Robby and Yozhi.

ROBBY. Yozhi, what'd I tell you? At least one of us works here.

YOZHI. We got a bus for you; someone made a real mess on the back seats. (*Laughing*) You'll need a brush to get it off.

ROBBY. Yozhi, I have a headache since morning, so be quiet. (*Silence*) Is everything OK with you, Buba?

BUBA. What? I'm going to get something to eat. I ... I start again — the night shift.

ROBBY. Hard worker, hard worker. I hear the boss gives you a bonus.

BUBA. Yes?

ROBBY. Yes? He doesn't know they love him here.

YOZHI. They give you a bonus, a cat, so you're not alone. (*Laughs*)

ROBBY. I'm happy for you, for the bonus. That's just what I told Yozhi when we came by earlier.

YOZHI. We came in by accident.

ROBBY. I said to Yozhi, in the end everyone manages somehow. They pay you good?

BUBA. OK.

ROBBY. Yes ...

BUBA. I have friends. They help me.

ROBBY. Yozhi, what'd I tell you?

YOZHI. Buba's all set, he's better off than us. Now he'll have a pussycat too. (*Chuckles, silence*)

BUBA. I have to go. I got to eat.

ROBBY. Suddenly I remembered. Suddenly. Lately, I've been looking for your brother, you know, to talk to him.

YOZHI. The earth swallowed him.

BUBA. Haven't you seen him? I don't see him at all.

ROBBY. (*Sadly*) What'd I tell you, Yozhi? The family today is nothing. You should have been in Romania, Buba. My mother, she lived in Braila, a city on the Danube. On holidays or when she was sick my brothers came all the way from Bucharest to see her.

YOZHI. When it comes to family things, he's a fanatic.

BUBA. In the hospital. I saw him in the hospital.

ROBBY. Let him come and talk to me. Maybe we'll arrange to pay back a little at a time. What do you say, Buba? Maybe I'll give him back his old job. It's bad for a soccer player to break a leg twice in the same place.

YOZHI. You know this isn't even half the truth about Robby. Robby has a big soul. Why, only yesterday he said we should give money to orphans. (*Chuckles*)

ROBBY. Since he went away, I got no one to help me in the amusement park. The kids see the dirt in Yozhi's ears and right away they run to the Ferris wheel. In Romania, when I worked for a circus director, I had students working for me. Students!

YOZHI. Just give them good prizes and they'll come. Why should they spend money shooting at targets when all they get is bad balloons? (*Pulls Buba's rubber gloves out of his pockets*)

BUBA. (*Angry*) Leave my gloves alone!

YOZHI. Think I'll steal them? I can get plenty of presents like this . . .

ROBBY. (*Puts them back gently*) They were like this, right, Buba?

BUBA. Sometimes he takes money from me, too. In the end, though, he always gives it back.

ROBBY. What about his girlfriend? She say anything where he was sleeping?

BUBA. What?

BOBBY. They saw you with her yesterday in the steakhouse.

BUBA. By accident. She was there alone. She started to talk to me. She got a ride. When she saw he was taking her to the orange groves . . . later he dropped her off and told her it was Ramle. She's a dancer.

YOZHI. Dancer, eh? Buba always goes with girls in show business.

ROBBY. What about Elie, Buba? Elie!

BUBA. He travels around.

ROBBY. Where?

BUBA. Looking for work, to play soccer.

ROBBY. Buba, you're lying. Yesterday he came to the garage with you. They saw the two of you there.

BUBA. Not me ... yesterday I went to the movies.

ROBBY. Last night he slept in your place!

BUBA. I don't know. (*Robby shoves a hose into Buba's mouth and turns on the water*)

BUBA. In ... Haifa!

ROBBY. Haifa?!

BUBA. Haifa. He has a woman there ... she left her children and ran away with him ... the girl in Haifa is altogether a different girl ...

ROBBY. Yozhi, let's go ... Haifa ... (*Leaves, Yozhi puts the hose inside Buba's shirt. Buba's all wet. Yozhi laughs, leaves. Buba remains, smiles*)

BUBA. If ... if I see him, I tell you.

scene 4

The shack. Evening. Enter Rachel: bag on her shoulder, tape player and big shopping bag in her hands. Turns on the light, is startled by Elie who's in a corner looking at her.

RACHEL. Didn't think anybody was here.

ELIE. I stand like this sometimes. Because of thieves.

RACHEL. Buba said I could come. Anytime I want. I can come.

ELIE. Buba left.

RACHEL. Yes?

ELIE. He'll be gone for a while. Maybe a week. (*Silence*)

RACHEL. I'll wait for him here.

ELIE. No.

RACHEL. He said I could, anytime. If I want, I can come.

ELIE. He didn't tell me anything about it.

RACHEL. He told me this morning when we were walking to the main road. (*Elie comes closer, looks her over good. Takes her shopping bag, opens the door, and throws it out*) You're crazy.

ELIE. Get out.

RACHEL. I don't want to.

ELIE. Get out of here.

RACHEL. This is Buba's place. (*Silence. He grabs her, drags her to the door. She fights back*)

ELIE. Get out!

RACHEL. No. (*She bites his hand. He screams. He throws her out*)

ELIE. Bitch . . . lousy bitch. (*They each push from their own side of the door*)

RACHEL. Let me in.

ELIE. Shut up!

RACHEL. No I won't! I'll tell them you're here. You think I don't know who you are? If you don't let me in, I'll go and tell them.

ELIE. Shut your mouth!

RACHEL. They'll kill you! (*Silence, waits a minute, opens the door. She sits by the door, shoulder bag and tape player between her knees. Elie leaves the door open, she comes in*) You almost ruined my clothes.

ELIE. One more word from you and I'll kill you. I'll bury you in the yard. Nobody will find out. Not even Buba.

RACHEL. I'll tell them about you. I'll tell them you're here.

ELIE. No, you won't, because if you do, you're dead.

RACHEL. I will

ELIE. Sit there. (*Rachel takes off her shirt, revealing a shiny dancer's top. She looks in the mirror*)

RACHEL. You like it? I bought it for tomorrow's competition. It really shines in the light. I got it in a special store in Tel Aviv.

ELIE. Buba gave you money?

RACHEL. Even if he wanted to I wouldn't take it. Nobody paid for me in my whole life. I saved some money. I worked in a garment factory where they make slips.

ELIE. Slips . . .

RACHEL. That's right, slips. For old women. (*Silence*) Where did he go?

ELIE. He has things to do.

RACHEL. I'm sure he went to see a friend. He said he has lots of friends.

ELIE. Sometimes he lies.

RACHEL. I thought so. He's nice to me, so what do I care?

ELIE. He once had a wife. And a kid.

RACHEL. I don't ask questions. (*Elie smiles*) I'm not sure you're not making this up . . .

ELIE. When they got divorced, her lawyer said . . . something was wrong with his head. They didn't let him see his child. They gave him a soda stand when the main road was busy. A whole week he couldn't find the syrup, so one day he got mad, took the whole thing apart and built this shack.

RACHEL. Retarded people can't fix motorcycles.

ELIE. Yeah, did you see it? He only thinks he's fixing it. Sometimes I see his wife. She's lucky she found another husband.

RACHEL. I could tell he once lived with a woman. I can tell, you know.

ELIE. How?

RACHEL. Signs. I know. You can see on the body.

ELIE. What can you tell about me? (*Silence*)

RACHEL. I knew right away something was wrong with him by his fingers. Somebody told me if the nails were square, something's wrong with the head. He said he worked in a garage. (*Silence*) Is it true what he said, your name was in the papers?

ELIE. Come here.

RACHEL. What?

ELIE. Come here.

RACHEL. I don't want to. (*Silence*) What?

ELIE. This is not a hotel, you know. I could tell you to go and I could tell you to stay.

RACHEL. So what if you can? Buba said I can stay.

ELIE. I'm not Buba. (*Goes to the table, opens the shopping bag, pulls out a jump-suit with shiny reflectors on it. She wants to take it away from him. He pulls her and the suit towards him. She falls on him and kisses him*)

ELIE. (*Breaks away from her*) Don't like it when they stick their tongues in my mouth. (*Gets a towel, throws it at her*) Go, wash up first.

RACHEL. I'm clean. (*Goes to the sink, checks the water*) Can't do it like this. The water's cold.

ELIE. Warm it up on the hotplate.

RACHEL. You wash with water from a pot. I didn't ask if you were dirty, did I? (*Slips into bed with him and covers herself up*)

ELIE. (*Picks up the blanket and looks at her*) A skeleton. What can you do?

RACHEL. Put on some music. It's quiet here, I think it's the end of the world. (*Elie turns on the tape player — disco music. They make love. He stares into the void, she smokes. Enter Buba. He freezes briefly, picks up his tool box*)

BUBA. (*Rushing out*) They know you were here! (*Leaves. Elie breaks away from Rachel, follows Buba to the yard. Buba is working on the motorcycle*)

ELIE. What do you mean? Did they ask you?

BUBA. I thought you were in Jaffa. You told me at noon you're going to Jaffa.

ELIE. My foot is bothering me.

BUBA. Yesterday you said you're going.

ELIE. I know what I said.

BUBA. So?

ELIE. What did you think? I'll come to them with my pains and they'll take me right away! There they want you to play soccer!

BUBA. You could say something about the milk bar ... you said someone owed you some money ...

ELIE. These things don't just happen overnight! (*Silence*) What's wrong Buba?

BUBA. They'll be looking for you here.

ELIE. Only if you told them something.

BUBA. I ... didn't.

ELIE. Then everything's OK.

BUBA. They thought she was your girlfriend. I told them she came because of me, that I spoke to her.

ELIE. (*Laughing*) You sleep with her. I'll take the mattress.

BUBA. I told her she can come whenever she wants. She can eat, sleep, do anything she wants here.

ELIE. She already got what she wanted. (*Silence*)

BUBA. They'll come in the morning, that's what they said. You could get killed.

ELIE. You're throwing me out? (*Silence*) You're such a baby. This little bitch is going to clean you out, to your last penny.

BUBA. It's my money. I worked for it. I didn't steal it.

ELIE. Ten hours a day, in a stinking amusement park, a clown's hat on my head, and you call me a thief? Why do you think children drag their mothers to shoot at my targets? Because they recognize me from the papers, from the sportscast on TV. Until last year, you always felt honored when I came to visit you.

BUBA. You came for yourself, not for me. You brought girls with you. I stood guard outside and afterwards made coffee. I used to bring it to the bed and you'd stay all night, eating my food, and I'd have to sleep somewhere else. Sometimes in the summer I'd sleep in the orange groves — the night guard there knew me. I'd give him cigarettes for a blanket. You never even invited me to the ball games. I only went when my friends from the garage asked me to ride with them. They put me in the back with the children. I bought cheap tickets, could hardly see you on the field. People said if I'm your brother, I shouldn't be sitting in the back but up front with the big shots. Sometimes you came on your bike with a girl for me, too. Always prostitutes. I asked them after you'd leave — always prostitutes.

ELIE. You could have kicked them out. I paid them in advance.

BUBA. I didn't want you to pay. I didn't want them here. This is my home.

ELIE. You have one now. I didn't bring her.

BUBA. I said she could stay here. She came for the dance competition.

ELIE. I'll say. She didn't dance when you were at work! (*Silence*) I know these bitches, always on the road and stinking up everything. They're like machines, they think with their bodies. They look like they're dead. You give them something to eat and drink, and still, they look dead. But just give them music, and they'll move for you like broken robots. Only the body can hear the music. Inside their heads everything is empty. You gave her a bed, money for clothes, right? But when she came back and you were gone, the first thing she said was that you're crazy. (*Silence*) You're really something. I don't care, you're free to do what you want with your life. (*Buba takes out a few bills and gives them to Elie. He takes them*) Buba, she'll eat you up alive. (*Leaves. Buba looks after him, returns to the shack. Rachel's clothes and a towel are strewn on the floor. He picks everything up, puts it neatly folded on a chair. Goes to the bed, pulls out the mattress. Rachel wakes up*)

RACHEL. He lied to me. He said you'd be gone for a week.

BUBA. Say anything you like. I'm not retarded. People talk to me, they don't laugh at me. Nobody calls me names. I fixed the bike. And this rat hole. Say what you want about other places, but this is no rat hole!

RACHEL. It's your brother, he talked about you, not me. (*Silence*) Said you had a wife and a kid, that they took the kid from you. But I didn't believe a word. (*Silence*) If you want me to go, I'll go, don't want no favors; I can manage alone, just say you want to be alone and I'm gone. Say it only once and I'm gone. There are other places too, you know. Yesterday I went to a nightclub that has a glass floor with lights underneath pointing to your face. I wanted to practice for tomorrow. I stayed there a few hours, then thought I'd come home to sleep, I thought you'd be worried, only I completely forgot the name of the road. (*Laughing*) There was this taxi driver outside the club, I thought he must know the way, so I told him a road with orange groves at the end, a stinking steakhouse that closes early, a hill, and over the hill is my friend's house. I said that, so they wouldn't think I was a nobody; you know, with no parents. The driver started to laugh; his friends were laughing, too. I didn't like their looks, so I left. I was already two hours on the road, I was sure that if I kept walking I'd find it, but then it started to rain and my shoes got wet, I was so tired I think I was walking and sleeping. Then I saw this house, it wasn't finished yet. I was sure they'd have a night guard there but even if they did I'd ask him to let me stay for the night. It turns out nobody was there. Under the concrete roof there was a pile of sand — very clean and dry. Then I made myself a bed in the sand; I laughed because suddenly, I was like buried but it was comfortable and warm. You see, in the end I always manage.

BUBA. If I had a child nobody would take him from me.

RACHEL. I said the same thing to your brother too. I didn't believe a word he said. You know, if he wasn't your brother, I'd have called the police and told them he raped me. My friend did it once to her hairdresser, he was her father's best friend. Because of you I didn't say anything. (*Silence*) He lied to me, said you left for a week, and things like that. I felt sorry for him because of the accident. He's lucky you're nice to me. You tell him that when you see him.

BUBA. He's not coming no more. They're looking for him.

RACHEL. I saw right away that he's confused. (*Silence*)

BUBA. I don't bring guests here, but you can stay for now. A few days, if you like.

RACHEL. Don't exactly know my plans.

BUBA. Only if you like.

RACHEL. We'll see tomorrow. I'll think about it. (*Smiling*) Only thing I can say for sure is that I just lived another day of my life!

ENTRE-ACT

VOICE OF M.C. AT DISCO CONTENT. Ladies and Gentlemen, we're waiting to find out who the judges selected as the fourth dancer to advance to the final round of the 1980 Israel Disco Competition held this year at the Miami Beach Nightclub in Ramle. The tension is mounting, Ladies and Gentlemen. Three of the twelve candidates have already been decided. They're guaranteed spots in Thursday's next and final round, when they compete again against twelve other candidates, four winners from each week of competition. All these dancers are guaranteed a spot in the final event, which, for at least one of them, will become the most memorable evening in his or her life. As we await the judges' decision, I can assure you that at this very moment, in their dressing room the nine dancers are holding their breath. (*Pause*) Ladies and Gentlemen, we finally have a decision! The last dancer is number ... 37, Rachel Ben-Harosh! (*Applause. Whistles. Blazing disco music*)

scene 5

Noon. The shack. Buba's sitting, preparing macaroni in a big pot. He's wearing an apron. Rachel is lying on the bed.

BUBA. You didn't say the competition was more than one day.

RACHEL. You think I knew? At the club they said the ad in the papers was only one day.

BUBA. What are you going to do now?

RACHEL. What should I do? It's only a week. Nobody's waiting for me anywhere next week. (*Silence*)

BUBA. Seen the bike? Needs only a touch of paint where it got hit. It's his birthday.

RACHEL. Who?

BUBA. Elie. Next week. I've got to finish it for his birthday.

RACHEL. You've got to?

BUBA. What?

RACHEL. If you've got to, then finish it. (*Holding her stomach*) You know why it hurts? I'm sure I ate junk somewhere. (*Silence*) I need new clothes for Tuesday. It's not good to be seen in the same outfit twice. The judges like to see you trying hard.

BUBA. The main thing when you cook macaroni is to add the tomato juice at the right time, not a moment too soon or too late.

RACHEL. Who taught you?

BUBA. Once I worked in a kitchen, in the army.

RACHEL. Better in the kitchen than cleaning shit from buses. One time I took the bus, sat down, and felt something on the seat. So I reached under and what do you know? A used rubber. Some couple probably entered the bus at night, and left it on the seat after they finished. My friend,

Sofie, it happened to her once, and she complained to the bus company. She's crazy sometimes. I told her she was lucky it was only rubbers. What if they came at night and put a bomb where they keep their suitcases. Hitchhiking is the safest thing.

BUBA. Last week I found an umbrella. Somebody forgot it in the bus. (*Silence*) It's not any better in the kitchen. Doesn't matter what you cook, soldiers always complain.

RACHEL. I can't stand soldiers. I knew this soldier, a stock clerk who used to bring me presents, boxes of halvah. It turns out he stole them from the army, but who knew? One day I told him if he's so smart, let's see him steal a tank for me! (*Laughs*) I only said that to insult him, I knew he wasn't a combat soldier. (*She still laughs. Buba laughs, too. Silence*) Yesterday I thought maybe the tape player was broken. (*She turns it on. Disco music. She dances. Pulls him towards her. At first he hesitates, then gets carried away and starts to dance*)

BUBA. (*Dancing*) Rachel ... Rachel ... (*Enter Yozhi in the yard. They stop dancing*)

YOZHI. Robby come quick, I think we're just in time for the wedding! (*Enter Robby breathing heavily from climbing the hill. Rachel turns off the tape and covers it with her body*)

ROBBY. Buba, you live like you're in Heaven. Yozhi, what'd I tell you? Paradise. You looked in the yard?

YOZHI. He's not there.

ROBBY. Not there. Listen, Buba, you think I'm going to spend all my holidays looking for your brother?

BUBA. I told you he ...

ROBBY. You said he was in Haifa. People say he was here with you.

YOZHI. Careful, no lies. It's a commandment in the Bible: "You shall not lie to your friend" ... (*Notices the pot*) So what's for lunch today? Macaroni?

ROBBY. The Sabbath—how nice. So the family's coming to lunch today, right?

BUBA. Really ... I didn't see him.

ROBBY. You hear that, Yozhi? We're wasting our time, he's not coming.

YOZHI. Robby, look at the view, you can see the road from here. Robby, it's true. If I had this place, I'd bring tourists here. Twenty pounds a head for the view and you'd be set for life, Buba. (*Laughs*) It's my lungs. I had problems as a kid. I don't think I would have made it without my mother. She took me to this doctor, a specialist, Dr. Lucian. He told her: he's almost dead, but don't worry, I'll save your little Robert ... Buba, you ever visit your mother?

BUBA. She ... is dead.

ROBBY. She's dead and you're dancing!

YOZHI. Only dancing? He even got himself a performer. Look, Robby, I can see the roof of the factory!

ROBBY. Buba, where is he?

BUBA. If he was here, I'd tell you.

ROBBY. He was here two days ago.

BUBA. I didn't see him.

ROBBY. Where did he go?

BUBA. I don't know. I didn't see him.

ROBBY. It could be the light. Maybe it blinds you. When you live on a hill, the sun can get pretty strong. (*Robby looks in the pot. Kicks it lightly. Rachel tries to get up*)

YOZHI. (*Whispers to her*) What for? (*She sits down*)

ROBBY. Buba, I had an uncle who couldn't see too good. Only indoors, in the shade. That's how it is with some people, the sun just isn't good for them. (*Robby takes the pot, pours the macaroni on the floor and with one quick motion puts the pot on Buba's head*) How is it now, Buba, you see him now? (*Buba tries to remove the pot but Robby pushes it down*) Take your time, Buba, until you can see ... (*Rachel tries to escape, Yozhi catches her and throws her to the ground*) They say she's good with imitations, Yozhi, ask her to do an imitation for us.

RACHEL. (*Frightened*) He was here two days ago. Him, the brother you're looking for. Don't know him, or Buba. I don't care what you do to him, he's nothing to me, really ... just, after I came here I saw he was retarded. I don't know people like that, I damn sure don't go out with them. They let me sleep here, so I came, I didn't know they were crazy. (*Yozhi slaps her*) Don't hit me! Don't hit

me! I don't care what you do to him for lying, but don't
hit me. (*Sobbing*)

YOZHI. Robby, I think I recognize her, from TV. You're a
singer, right?

RACHEL. (*Frightened*) What?

YOZHI. Sing. A quiet song. Sing! Sing something!

BUBA. Jaffa, She don't know nothing. He said he was going to
Jaffa.

ROBBY. Jaffa?

BUBA. Yes.

ROBBY. Where in Jaffa?

BUBA. In Jaffa ... she don't know nothing. He told me he was
going to Jaffa.

ROBBY. You know, in Jaffa there's a beach, a market, a soccer
stadium — where in Jaffa?

BUBA. The soccer stadium.

ROBBY. Yozhi already looked there.

BUBA. In the market. He said he has friends there!

ROBBY. When you lie it's even worse. You have to pay for
your lies.

BUBA. I told you already I don't know! (*Robby puts the pot on his
head again, shoves him into a corner*)

ROBBY. Yozhi, why doesn't she sing? Must I do everything
myself?!

YOZHI. (*To Rachel*) Sing for me. Sing something!

BUBA. Yes ...

ROBBY. Do you see your brother?

BUBA. Yes.

ROBBY. You see him in the pot?

BUBA. Yes.

ROBBY. Great. Life with you, Buba, is really something. (*Silence*)

RACHEL. (*Sobbing*) Not my face ... don't hit my face ... not
my face ... I'm dancing next week ... not my face ...
not my face ...

scene 6

The shack. Buba's lying on the bed. Enter Rachel.

RACHEL. Buba, I didn't know you were here. I need some money.
BUBA. What? I didn't know where you went, didn't see you for days.
RACHEL. You have money, I know you do.
BUBA. Didn't see you for days.
RACHEL. I went home.
BUBA. Where?
RACHEL. Home. I have a home, you know.
BUBA. Ah. So that's why you didn't come to get your dancing clothes.
RACHEL. My stomach hurts.
BUBA. You were the best there. Everybody saw that . . .
RACHEL. It turns out they're always cheating.
BUBA. I bought a ticket and went in. Saw all the dances. From the beginning. People said you were the champion. (*Silence*) I say this so you know. (*Silence*) You can try again next year. They'll give you the prize for sure.
RACHEL. For me, this whole thing is already in the past.
BUBA. I say this because maybe you'd like to try again next year. (*Silence*) They won't come again.
RACHEL. (*Gets up*) I didn't come here to talk.
BUBA. I'll kill them if they come. They know that. I . . . have plans. There are things I can do if they come.
RACHEL. Put a pot on your head.
BUBA. I'm not afraid, and I'm not what you said about me.
RACHEL. How much money you have on you? (*Silence*)
BUBA. What for? Clothes?
RACHEL. I need more.
BUBA. You always come here when you want, leave when you want, you . . .
RACHEL. The sons of bitches started with me because of you.
BUBA. They won't, they won't anymore.
RACHEL. I need money, Buba. I'm not talking about dancing.

Not about dancing money.

BUBA. You always leave.

RACHEL. You have money. You always have some in your pocket.

BUBA. I need it. I want to put in a hot water heater. (*Silence*) Go ask your family, ask your friends, tell them to give you money. I have no money for your clothes.

RACHEL. Not clothes . . .

BUBA. In the end you always . . .

RACHEL. You think I came here just for clothes? I should have listened to what your brother said about you. (*Buba gets up*) Think you'll get out of this just like that? I'll tell them he's yours.

BUBA. What's mine?

RACHEL. If they find out that you're responsible for the baby, if they think you gave me the baby, they can even operate on you.

BUBA. Baby?!

RACHEL. Just give me the money, and you don't hear from me again.

BUBA. Baby? Here? Me . . . a baby? I'll clean for him, I'll cook for him . . . I'll buy him . . .

RACHEL. Think you'll get out of it just like that? I only have to say I didn't want to, that I screamed, the judge can order them to operate on you.

BUBA. Sit, Rachel, sit. A baby . . . I'll make a small chest for him, for his clothes . . .

RACHEL. I don't want a chest! I don't want a baby!

BUBA. What? (*He grabs her, pushes her against the wall*) No good . . . no good . . . no good . . .

RACHEL. Leave me alone, Buba! They'll operate on you. (*Lets go of her, bangs his head against the wall*)

BUBA. No . . . no . . .

RACHEL. Enough. Stop it. Buba! (*Rachel breaks a bottle and points the sharp edge between her legs. He looks at her*) I'll take it out of me, Buba, right now. I'll get it out! (*Silence. He reaches in his pockets, gives her money. He takes the bottle from her, throws it away. She leaves*)

scene 7

Evening. The shack. Buba and Elie.

ELIE. (*Excited*) I took her for a spin. You have no idea how this bike moves. Like new. Listen, I saw this taxi, a Mercedes; so I get on his tail and step on it! We were going towards the orange grove. I know that part of the road good. At a curve in the road I gave it full gas and passed him. You should have seen the look on the guy's face. Those Mercedes drivers, they don't like it when you pass them on a curve.

BUBA. Only the paint needs a little more work. I couldn't finish it.

ELIE. The paint's not important. I'll take it tomorrow to a friend.

BUBA. I'll finish it by myself.

ELIE. The guy has all the tools.

BUBA. I want to finish it by myself.

ELIE. OK.

BUBA. I always say, when you start something, finish it.

ELIE. Tell me, waiter, how long do I have to wait for my meal? (*Buba gives him bread, a slice of onion. Elie eats*)

BUBA. Eat it. This is the onion's baby.

ELIE. (*Eating*) It's a waste for you to work there. Listen, Buba, I have a friend, he got money from his father-in-law and opened a garage. I'll take you to him tomorrow, what do you say? (*Smiles*) "Buba's Bikes." Let them hire a kid to clean the buses. You've got to move on.

BUBA. A kid can't do it. You think if he could I'd stay there? For this kind of job you need a responsible person. My signature's on every release slip.

ELIE. The bike rides like it was never in an accident.

BUBA. (*Smiles*) Yes. I was hoping to finish the paint job by today. I wanted to finish it for your birthday.

ELIE. Remember my birthday two years ago?

BUBA. You came here with your friend and the two Australian girls.

ELIE. You know, today he owns a brush factory in Australia.

BUBA. One girl, I held her head when she threw up in the yard.

ELIE. If I'd slept with her first, I'd be the owner of the brush factory.

BUBA. It's OK, I have plenty of brushes at work.

ELIE. I still have a few good years left. The last few days, Buba, I've been running the whole stretch on the beach, without stopping once. Haven't felt any pain in my foot.

BUBA. What about the sea?

ELIE. What about it?

BUBA. The sea cuts into the shore, the beach is short there.

ELIE. I tell you I ran enough to know I'm OK. Some things from the accident still need to be taken care of. I'm going to Robby tomorrow and close the case. That comes first. He'll talk. I'll talk. I'll offer him something. I could drag it on another week or so, but I don't want him poking around here because of me. What do you say?

BUBA. It's over, you know, I sent her home. She wanted to stay, to be with me, I think she loves me, but I kicked her out.

ELIE. Fine. Now about Robby, I got to do that first, right?

BUBA. Yes. (*Silence*)

ELIE. I tell you, things would have been bad if she stayed.

BUBA. That's it, I kicked her out.

ELIE. It wouldn't have worked out. When my woman agreed to run away with me, we went to a hotel in Haifa, but I knew things wouldn't work out. Too many problems. Too many things to put in order. She worried too much about her children. It all started to die out right then. Because of all the problems. (*Silence*) In the room, I held her a lot, we spent a lot of time in bed, but I knew it was over. I know this from playing soccer. A few more minutes and the game is over. But even though it's over you keep running on the field just for the sake of playing, even though in your head you see yourself taking off the sweaty shirt, getting into street clothes, having a drink, your legs keep going to the end. (*Silence*) One time I saw this player, he

was a kid, just a kid, maybe that's why he was able to do
it, there were a few minutes left and he was running with
the ball, not even eighteen years old, and already they said
he was a star. Coaches from the major league came to
watch him play. As I said, he was running fast, but suddenly
stopped and looked at us. We all knew that something had
happened. No one went to get the ball from him. Even the
referee stopped and looked at him. It looked like the referee
was waiting for the kid to whistle and we'd all walk off the
field. It was winter. The ground was wet and muddy, we
were soaked and tired, the kid just stood there staring at
us and said: "The game is over. Let's go home." There
were still a few minutes left. "Let's go," he says, "it's
cold." No one spoke a word. He looked at us another
minute or so, and then left. We saw him walk through the
empty bleachers and disappear. Never saw him on the
field again. Some years later I was told the kid went crazy.
One night in the army they told him to sit on a hill and
salute the morning when it arrived. He waited and waited,
then in the morning they heard a shot — he shot himself in
the neck. I don't know what went on in his head. Some
people just can't take it. (*Silence*) You know, I've seen
many places and done many things, but I think now
everything's going to be all right. (*Silence*)

BUBA. Stay here as long as you like. Now that the bike is fixed
you can come and go as you please. You know I'm always
home.

ELIE. I have a friend, he has a store where they sell cots to
sleep on. You can buy them used, really cheap.

BUBA. We could . . . put it here.

ELIE. Under the bed where the mattress is now.

BUBA. Yes. (*Enter Rachel: bag on her shoulder, tape player in one
hand, shopping bag in the other. Silence. She tries to get Buba's
attention while Buba's busy rubbing his hands. Elie bursts out
laughing, stops*)

ELIE. Why don't you go home?

RACHEL. This isn't your home either.

BUBA. Did you do what you wanted to do?

RACHEL. I got you a present. (*Shows him a new shirt*) If it doesn't fit, I can change it. I have a receipt. Here, try it on.

BUBA. A boy . . . a girl?

RACHEL. I don't think they can tell right away.

BUBA. You didn't look to see what they took out?

RACHEL. I didn't go at all. I don't know anything about it. They put you to sleep and stick knives in your body. This girl, my friend's sister, died from it.

ELIE. Buba, she wants you to tell her she can stay so she can drop it here. Ask her if that's what she wants. (*Silence*) You know what this means, don't you, Buba? You saw things like this before, right? She'll make a mess and you'll have to run around cleaning after her. You know how it all ends. You've been through it before. She thinks she can do it here, Buba: stink up the place with rotten food and garbage and you'll have to clean up after her.

BUBA. You're not going to do it if I don't agree.

ELIE. What?

RACHEL. What?

BUBA. You're not going to get up tomorrow morning and tell me you're going to take it out. You're not doing things like this without telling me first.

RACHEL. (*Hands him her wallet*) Take the money. Put in the hot water like you wanted to.

ELIE. She'll sweat and cry on your bed, she'll drive you crazy. You never learn, Buba. (*Silence*)

BUBA. I do. Now, I'll try on this shirt.

scene 8

Steakhouse. Noon. Buba's eating at the counter. Enter Yozhi, looks around, sits next to Buba. Buba continues to eat. Yozhi smiles, suddenly bangs on the counter. Buba doesn't look at him. Yozhi reaches for a bottle of beer, wants to drink from it.

BUBA. It's mine. (*Pulls the bottle back*) This is my beer.

YOZHI. May I have some? (*Pause*) It's only beer. You could

treat me to one, I don't have any money. "No speaking at
the table." (*Laughing*) Good. I can do without beer. I can
do without anything. They went out to buy the balloons.
Before, it was me who bought the stinking balloons. You
think I can't take revenge? I'll pour sand in his bike's gas
tank. (*Buba looks at him*) Your brother says you fixed it.
You fixed it? I say you can't even fix your ass. (*Laughs,
stops*) Buy me a beer. (*Pause*) You and I are like garbage!
They pick it up and throw it away. (*Spits*) Nobody knows
me. Don't know me at all. (*Pause*) I'll tell you why Robby's so
big. I'll tell you why he's so strong. The son of a bitch is a
smart operator. He told you to look for your brother inside
a pot, and made you fix his bike, too. Smart operator.

BUBA. I didn't fix anything for him.

YOZHI. Sure. Fix your brain, first. I'm sure they'll give them
defective balloons.

BUBA. I'd never fix a bike for Robby. He doesn't have a bike.

YOZHI. Now he does. (*Pours beer in a glass*) I'll just have a
drop. (*Silence*)

BUBA. My brother, he gave him the bike?

YOZHI. (*Drinks*) What's this? They piss into the bottles?

BUBA. Gave him the bike?

YOZHI. Your brother, really smart guy. Nobody buys a bike
after an accident. Now they don't owe each other anything.
(*Pause*) Don't worry about me. Since this morning I got
plenty of job offers. People heard I quit the game business
and they're already looking for me. I can't see how your
brother and Robby could work together again. As for me,
I was only looking for an opportunity to get out.

BUBA. He didn't say he was going to give him the bike.

YOZHI. He didn't tell you? (*Laughing*) Your head is empty,
Buba. You're not smart enough for them.

BUBA. I'll speak to him.

YOZHI. They went out to buy trophies. (*Silence*) I think you
owe me some money. (*Buba gets up, Yozhi shoves him back into
his seat*) Everything was fine between me and Robby. You
messed it up by fixing that bike. You owe me money. Did
I ever hurt you? You know, I even like you, but it's not
fair I should go empty.

BUBA. I have to go now.

YOZHI. What's that?

BUBA. I'll take the bike back.

YOZHI. I knew you wouldn't like this business. I told them let's wait until we talk to Buba, see what he says. (*Pause*) Go, Buba, go, but first you've got to pay me what you owe me. You're crying? I never saw you cry.

BUBA. I want my bike back.

YOZHI. Why did you fix it? Even Robby said, this thing with your brother was over already. Finished. People heard him say that. (*Buba gets up*) I'll be nice to you. You're not that guilty, after all.

BUBA. I have nothing to give you.

YOZHI. How do you know? Checked your pockets? (*Buba reaches inside his pocket and pulls out a small screwdriver*) Stealing from the garage, eh, Buba? If I tell they won't love you anymore. How about the other pocket? (*Buba doesn't react*) You really don't know me, Buba. You only know me from my work with Robby.

BUBA. I spent all my money to put in the hot water.

YOZHI. You like having fun in the bathtub? (*Pause*) There's something else you could do to pay me back. I think I'll piss in your mouth. What do you say to that? No use looking around. Forget the kitchen. One time I did it to a girl for hours. They stayed inside, then went home. (*Silence*) Want this as payment? (*Sits on the counter, spreads his legs*) On your knees, Buba. It's not the worst thing that could happen to you. (*Pause*) On your knees! (*Buba looks at Yozhi, his hand swings back and forth. He stabs Yozhi in the stomach with the screwdriver. Yozhi remains seated, his mouth open in pain and fear. There's blood on his stomach*)

YOZHI. You idiot, you bastard ... I was only joking.

BUBA. I told you, I have nothing to give you.

YOZHI. Call someone ... in the kitchen ... I'll die. Tell them ... quickly ... (*Buba looks at the blood, doesn't move*) All right, I'll say we were just fooling around. I'll say we were only joking. Call someone, Buba.

BUBA. I'm not afraid of anyone no more.

scene 9

*A few months later. The shack. Elie's lying on the bed. Rachel's
scrubbing the floor*

RACHEL. I thought when I went to the dress shop you'd be
waiting for Buba at the prison gate.

ELIE. I thought so, too.

RACHEL. (*Embraces him*) I can't figure out why they called you
"Handsome Elie."

ELIE. Your belly's hanging out, soon you won't be able to
bend over. (*She kisses him*) Enough, I can't stand this.
Buba's lucky the screwdriver only wounded the guy. A
good thing he's clean or he'd be in for years.

RACHEL. I don't think you'd be crying too much.

ELIE. Two months from now we won't hear you no more.
You'll be just lying in bed, legs apart and stinking up the
whole place.

RACHEL. I could sell it. Lots of people who don't have kids
want them badly. They pay good money, too,

ELIE. People are punished for making kids like this.

RACHEL. Maybe I'll have twins.

ELIE. You? It looks more like a mouse.

RACHEL. If I get rid of it, in three or four months, I can still
enter next year's disco contest. Next year they'll give me
the prize for sure.

ELIE. You're not even worth a lay. Just sit there and shut up.

RACHEL. One more month. After that no more work for me. I
think you should start looking for a job.

ELIE. Maybe an old age home. I have a friend, his parents
have one. They'll give me a room. If I want the sun, the
nurse will take me out. They take it easy there. No rush.
They really take their time there. At noon the nurse comes
ringing the bell: "Lunchtime, Sir." I'll go to the dining
room, eat three portions. Then rest. In the evening the
nurse comes ringing the bell again and says: "Dinner,
Sir." Then I'll go down the steps to the club. Who knows,
maybe they even have an elevator. Maybe they have movies.

I'll play chess. You can easily spend a few years living like
this. (*Enter Buba carrying a bundle of clothes wrapped in a
newspaper*) Buba! We didn't know what happened to you.
(*Slaps him gently on the cheeks*) We thought maybe we got
confused about the date.

RACHEL. Hello, Buba. You're looking good. (*Silence*)

ELIE. Give it to me. I'll put it away for you. (*Wants to take the
bundle from Buba, but he refuses to let go of it*) You think I
wasn't there this morning? I waited two hours. They
couldn't tell me the exact time you were leaving. Ask her.

BUBA. Why?

ELIE. Why what?

BUBA. I went to the movies.

ELIE. (*Laughing*) So here we are, sitting and worrying about
you ... and you're at the movies.

RACHEL. Of course, they have no movies in prison, right,
Buba?

ELIE. Even if they did, Buba's crazy about movies. (*Buba sits at
the table*)

RACHEL. Maybe you're tired ...

ELIE. Fix him some food. (*Rachel goes to the stove and turns it on*)

BUBA. Turn it off.

RACHEL. (*Turns it off*) I cleaned up so you'd feel good when
you got back. I work now in a dress shop.

BUBA. I don't care if he died.

ELIE. Sure. You only care about the damn bike.

BUBA. I don't care if you don't stay here. I don't want you
here anymore.

ELIE. (*Laughing*) The son of a bitch, my brother, wants us to
beg him to let us stay here. What did you think I was
going to do with the bike? Use it and break my other leg,
too? Crash somewhere on the road so you'll come to visit
me in the hospital, right? He likes it when people owe him
something. Buba likes it when people depend on him, likes
it when people feel guilty towards him because of something.

RACHEL. (*To Elie*) At least you should have known. They did
spit on him because of you.

ELIE. He likes it when they spit on him because of me. This
only complicates my debt to him. Right, Buba? In his

head, he's always scheming. I see the wheels turning every time I try to lie to him about soccer: It's because of this shit in his head that I must lie to him. I can't just come up to him and say: "Buba, I've reached the end of the rope, let me stay here ..."

BUBA. I don't want you here anymore.

ELIE. I wouldn't stay even if you fixed ten bikes for me! Look at the bastard, because you decided not to scrape it out he'll let you stay here. He agrees ... as if he had something better to do. Once, only once you took money from him and thought he was retarded and now you won't be able to leave anymore. Now he says, this is just another place, so you'll say: "It's a home, Buba." You know, you'll end up thinking that this is really a home. You'll stink here with your baby — no escaping, and you'll even be glad you have a home at all. (*Collecting his things*) Tell her about your baby, tell her anything you want. Don't worry, I won't be here to tell her otherwise. (*Turns to leave. Buba gets up, walks up to him*) Stabbing people with screwdrivers. Now you think you're God, Buba. (*Leaves. Silence*)

BUBA. If you want, you can leave, too. I'm not holding anyone by force.

RACHEL. Even if you wanted me to stay I only do what I like.

BUBA. Right.

RACHEL. I'm sure you know this about me by now — you just can't order me around and expect me to shut up. I always do what's good for me.

BUBA. I don't care if you stay or not.

RACHEL. In the meantime, I feel fine here. (*Goes to bed, lies down*)

BUBA. Maybe tomorrow I'll ask you for some money. I went to the garage. They don't want me there anymore.

RACHEL. Next month, though, I stop working at the shop. It's getting too heavy, I can't carry it anymore.

BUBA. Just another week. I'll find work. (*Takes out a big lock from his coat pocket, goes to the door, takes a drill and hammer, starts to work*) I bought it today on Jaffa Street. I didn't go to the movies at all. (*Takes out a pair of eyeglasses from his pocket, puts them on*) My eyes, they bother me. I'll put the lock on the door. It'll be a little safer here. It's not true what he said about the baby. You'll have the baby and I'll take care of it. This is different. (*Silence*) Everything was true. Don't listen to what he says. My wife and I, we had a house, we were going to have a baby. She went for a checkup. The doctor said they must take it out. He said something was wrong with it. I went to the hospital, to the waiting room. They took her to a room, covered her with a sheet. Then, when nobody was around, I went to her room. She was sleeping. All around her, machines and a pot, the size of a bucket, maybe bigger, and in it was my little baby — messy, bloody, covered with dirty bandages. I looked at it and saw why the doctor wanted to do it. It was ... crooked. His face, something was wrong with his face. I wrapped it in a towel and ran out with it to the car. I borrowed a car just for this. I put it in bed, closed the shutters, locked the door, and just sat there by myself. They started to knock. I heard people, but I didn't open. I knew why they wanted me to open the door. (*Silence*) It was after a few days that I opened the door and they took it from me. I shouted at them. "You can't just throw it in the garbage." I don't know what they did with it. (*Silence*) After a few days my wife came to see me. She felt fine. She said to me: "God will punish you, Buba, to the end of your days." (*Silence*) The lock is in place. (*Rachel gets up, spreads a clean sheet on the bed, stops, sits down*)

RACHEL. It's the baby, Buba, I can tell ...

BUBA. What?

RACHEL. It's the baby, it's kicking. (*She extends her arm. He takes it, bends over, and presses his ear against her belly. They wait for the baby's next kick*)

about the authors

NISSIM ALONI

Born: 1926, Tel Aviv.

Background: Liberal arts at the Hebrew University and the Sorbonne. Director of his and other authors' works.

Major Works: *The King Is Most Cruel* (1953), *The King's Clothes* (1961), *The American Princess* (1963), *The Bride and the Butterfly Catcher* (1967), *The Gypsies of Jaffa* (1971), *Eddy King* (1974), *The Deceased Goes Wild* (1980).

Translations: *The American Princess*, by Richard Flantz (Tel Aviv: The Institute for Translation of Hebrew Literature, 1980). *Eddy King*, in French by Michel Eckhard (Tel Aviv: The Institute for Translation of Hebrew Literature, 1985).

YOSEF BAR-YOSEF

Born: Jerusalem, 1933, son of renowned novelist Yehoshua Bar-Yosef.

Background: Hebrew literature and Kabbala studies, Hebrew University. Journalist, author of short stories and a novel.

Major Works: *Tura* (1963), *The Ewe* (1970), *Difficult People* (1973), *The Wedding* (1974), *The Orange Grove* (1985), *Gold* (1989).

Translations: *Difficult People*, by Heinz Bernard, Derek Orlans, and Dennis Silk (Tel Aviv: The Institute for Translation of Hebrew Literature, 1975); by Barbara Harshav (1993).

HANOCH LEVIN

Born: 1944, Tel Aviv.

Background: B.A. Theater Studies, Tel Aviv University.

Major Works: *The Queen of the Bathtub* and *You and I and the next War* (1968), *Heffetz* (1972), *Yaacobi and Leidental* (1972),

Rubber Merchants (1978), *The Sorrows of Job* (1981), *Yakish and Popche* (1986), *The Equivocator* (1991).

Translations: *Yaacobi and Leidental*, by Dennis Silk and Shimon Levi (Tel Aviv: The Institute for Translation of Hebrew Literature, Modern Hebrew Drama Series, 1979); *The Sorrows of Job*, by Barbara Harshav (Tel Aviv: The Hebrew Book Club, 1993).

Foreign Productions: *Heffetz*, Edinburgh Art Festival, 1974; *Rubber Merchants*, Edinburgh, 1983.

HILLEL MITELPUNKT

Born: 1949, Tel Aviv.

Background: Theater Studies, Tel Aviv University.

Major Works: *The Swamp* (1979), *Buba* (1982), *The Store* (1982), *Driver, Painter* (1988), *The Lovers* (1991), *Brothers in Arms* (1992).

Translations: *Buba*, by Michael Taub (Binghamton, NY: *Modern International Drama*, 1987); *Driver, Painter*, by Michael Taub (Binghamton, NY: *Modern International Drama*, Forthcoming).

Foreign Productions: *Driver, Painter* (dramatic reading, Michael Taub translator), John Housmann Theatre, NY, Summer 1990.

JOSHUA SOBOL

Born: 1939, Tel Mond.

Background: Lived in Kibbutz Shamir, Haifa, and Tel Aviv. Studied Philosophy at The Sorbonne; journalist; artistic director of the Haifa Municipal Theatre; theatre instructor.

Major Works: *The Night of the Twentieth* (1976), *Jewish Soul* (1982), *Ghetto* (1984), *The Palestinian* (1985), *Jerusalem Syndrome* (1987), *Adam* (1990), *Underground* (1991), *Solo for Spinoza* (1991), *Eye to Eye* (1992).

Translations: *The Night of the Twentieth*, by Chana Hoffman (Tel Aviv: The Institute for Translation of Hebrew Literature, 1978). A French version is also available. Basis for the film *Dreamers*. *Jewish Soul*, by Betsy Rosenberg and Miriam Schlesinger (Tel Aviv: The Israeli Centre of the International Theatre Institute, 1983); by Michael Taub (Binghamton, NY: *Modern International Drama*, 1989); has also been translated into Danish, Swedish, German, French, and Spanish. *Ghetto*, by Miriam Schlesinger (Tel Aviv: The Institute for Translation of Hebrew Literature, 1985); by Kathleen Komar, adapted for stage by Jack Vertal, in Elinor Fuchs, ed., *Plays of the Holocaust* (New York: Theatre Communications Group, 1987); by David Lan (London: Nick Hern Books, 1989); other translations into twelve European languages.

Foreign Productions (partial): *Jewish Soul*, Edinburgh, 1983, Berlin, 1985. *Ghetto*, Circle in the Square, NY, 1989, London's National Theater, 1989. *Underground*, Yale Repertory Theater, 1991.

MICHAEL TAUB

Born: 1946, Lapus, Romania.

Background: Lived in Israel 1962–70. Studied in France, Germany, and Israel and at American universities. Writes on Yiddish drama, Hebrew drama, Yiddish poetry, and Holocaust literature. Translates plays, poetry, and prose from Romanian, Hebrew, and Yiddish.

Work in Progress: A collection of plays, *Israeli Holocaust Drama*.

A.B. YEHOSHUA

Born: Jerusalem, 1936.

Background: Literature at The Hebrew University and The Sorbonne. World renowned novelist and essayist; Professor of Comparative Literature, University of Haifa.

Major Works: *A Night in May* (1968), *Final Treatments* (1973), *Possessions* (1986).

Translations: *A Night in May*, by Miriam Arad (Tel Aviv: The Institute for Translation of Hebrew Literature, 1974). *Possessions*, by Michael Karasick (in *Formations*, 1989).

(Continuation of the copyright page)

Library of Congress Cataloging-in-Publication Data

Modern Israeli drama in translation/edited and with an introduction
by Michael Taub.
    p.   cm.
   Translations from Hebrew.
   Contents: The sorrows of Job/Hanoch Levin — Jewish soul/
Joshua Sobol — The American princess/Nissim Aloni — Possessions/
A. B. Yehoshua — Difficult people/Yosef Bar-Yosef Duba/
Hillel Mitelpunkt.
   ISBN 0—435—08616 2
   1, Israeli drama — Translations into English. I. Taub. Michael.
II. Levin, Hanoch. Sorrows of Job. 1992.
PJ5059.E5M64 1992   92-16637
892.4'2608 — dc20   CIP

329